W9-CEH-676

Entertaining!

Fast
and
Fancy

Cook Easy & Eat Grand

by Renny Darling

Other Simply Delicious Cookbooks
by Renny Darling

The Joy of Eating
The Love of Eating
The Joy of Entertaining
The Joy of Eating French Food
Great Beginnings & Happy Endings
With Love from Darling's Kitchen
Easiest & Best Coffee Cakes & Quick Breads
Cooking Great! Looking Great! Feeling Great!
The Moderation Diet
The New Joy of Eating

Fifth Printing

Copyright ©   1986 by Renny Darling. All rights reserved.
No part of this book may be reproduced in any
form whatsoever, without permission in writing
from the publisher.
Published by   Royal House Publishing Co., Inc.
P.O. Box 5027
Beverly Hills, CA 90210

Printed in the United States of American
Library of Congress Catalog Card Number: 85-60771
ISBN: 0-930440-22-6

The Introduction

Two of the happiest thoughts to cross my mind are, first, how the trend in cooking and entertaining is becoming more relaxed and carefree. Entertaining is no longer that infrequent formal dinner, but has come into the world of casual informal gatherings with family and friends. The second thought is how Americans are cooking and preparing food with grace and style and imagination as never before. So, while the occasions may be informal, the food that is being served is becoming more and more elegant and exciting. Americans are cooking and serving the most attractive and marvelous dishes for even the most casual gathering.

To add to all this, Americans are also very, very busy. The recipes that are most appealing to their heightened tastes, must also be prepared with minimum effort and in the least amount of time. This cookbook is dedicated to the fine cooks in our nation, today, who want to serve with creativity and imagination as their hallmark, even for the most informal of occasions.

Of course, you know, I have dedicated myself to these notions, for more than 25 years. In fact, the opening lines to my very first cookbook, "The Joy of Eating" were:

> "I must confess that I do not like to chore in the kitchen one bit more than necessary ... However, I do love and adore delicious food, prepared in an exciting and different manner. "The Joy of Eating" originated out of these two notions ... the desire for exquisite tasting dishes, prepared in the minimum amount of time."

This philosophy is just as fresh and alive today as ever before, considering all the quick and easy cookbooks on the market today. And, in a sense, I do feel like a prophet, for when I first started my love affair with food, well over 25 years ago, I predicted the trend that is so prevalent today.

My cookbooks all share this underlying philosophy ... quality food, that is easily prepared and marvelously delicious. All of my recipes are within the capabilities of the most novice cook, and hopefully, exciting to the most discriminating palate.

If you are wondering what I feel makes a recipe elegant or fancy, the answer is simple. Even cauliflower soup can be fancy. Consider Creme DuBarry. It is simply a cauliflower soup, but balanced to gastronomical heights. Elegance, for me, is any dish that is gloriously put together ... that is wonderfully balanced in flavor and texture ... and it must have an extraordinary taste, for therein lies the essence of pleasure and satisfaction. Ingredients, unto themselves, are neither common nor grand.

Balancing a menu is another important consideration. Recipes must represent a good proportion of flavor, texture and color. Dishes must taste good, look good and smell good. And the excitement that is generated must also be balanced. For example, if the main course is a simple Roast of Veal, then the accompaniments should be stellar, such as Royal Crown Noodle & Apple Pudding or Molded Ramekins of Carrots with Cream. If the main course is dynamite, like Braccioli alla Salsa Marinara, accompaniments should be simple and interesting, such as Italian Green Beans with Onions & Cheese.

If every dish is bursting with excitement and splendor, then I am afraid **more will become less.** This is an expression I use often when I teach. Remember, **more is less** when you overdo it. The secret is balance and harmony.

A few words about the recipes in this book ... lots of new and exciting combinations of familiar ingredients. For **starters** or **small entrees (lunch,** too) you will find Calzones, Coulibiac of Crabmeat, Bourekas, Mousselines, Pates, Roulades, all new and special. **Soups** sparkled with chestnuts, pumpkin, leeks, garbanzos, apples, raisins, Creme Fraiche, a fine Mexican Chile Soup served with Garlic Cheese Tortillas ... accompanied with Piroshkis, Crispettes, Croustades, Cajun Date Nut Muffins, Red Hot Chile Bread, Honey Corn Muffins, Greek Flatbread, Italian Foccaccio, Biscuits, Scones ... new ways with our favorite ingredients.

Main Courses, fish, chicken, meats with artichokes, cabbage, apples, chestnuts, sauerkraut, black raspberries, buttermilk, honey, pecans. Dozens of sauces with garlic, lemon, pesto, creme fraiche, yogurt. Accompanied with over sixty vegetable dishes made in casseroles, molded ramekins, timbales, frittatas, mini-souffles, puddings, dumplings, stuffed and glazed ... that will please the most jaded palate. Noodles with red peppers, cheese, chives, apples, cinnamon ... brown rice with cabbage, lentils, mushrooms, onions, cici peas. Orzo with raisins, pine nuts, tomatoes, peas ... fettuccini, linguini, angel hair pasta with vegetable sauces, chili.

And for **desserts,** dozens of fantasy cakes, tortes, roulades, ultimate cheesecakes, charlottes, mousses, Tartufo ... dozens of pies with buttery crusts, 2-minute Souffle au Grand Marnier ... grand for every celebration.

And now, I am happy to declare, the old laborious days in the kitchen are officially over. Dear friends, have a banquet, have a feast ... but most of all make each day a celebration.

As always, enjoy with love.

Renny Darling
Beverly Hills, California
January, 1986

The Contents

Creamed Spinach Soup Potatoes, Leeks & Bacon 96
Holiday Cream of Mushroom & Chestnut Soup 97
Spiced Raisin & Walnut Sherry Bread 98
Potage of Tomatoes & Clams 99
Croustades of Garlic & Cheese 99
Creme of Spinach Soup with Onions & Shallots 100
Cheese Piroshkis 100
Farmhouse Split Pea Soup 101
Sesame Crispettes with Garlic & Cheese 101
Cold Cream of Carrot Soup with Apples, Raisins & Cinnamon 102
Cold Dilled Zucchini Soup with Shallots & Creme Fraiche 103
Peasant Cabbage & Tomato Soup 104
Croustades of Cheese & Chives 104
Cream of Honey Chestnut Soup 105
Spiced Pumpkin Muffins 105
Country Cabbage Soup with Black Pumpernickel 106
Raisin Butter with Honey 106

SALADS & DRESSINGS 107-126

Linguini Verde with Brie, Tomatoes & Basil Dressing 109
Molded Spinach Salad with Lemon Creme Fraiche 110
Pasta Primavera with Basil Vinaigrette with Garlic 111
Fresh Vegetable Platter with Imperial Sauce Verte 112
Herbed Tomato & Onion Salad with Garlic Lemon Dressing 112
Red Peppers Vinaigrette with Mushrooms, Onions & Cheese 113
Green Bean Salad with Yogurt & Lemon Honey Dressing 114
3-Bean Salad with Red Wine & Garlic Vinaigrette 114
Tomato & Green Bean Salad with Pesto Cream Sauce 115
Pineapple Chicken Salad with Cashews & Pineapple Honey Dressing 116
Sesame Popovers with Garlic & Herbs 116
French Potato Salad with Mustard Vinaigrette 117
Potato Salad with Horseradish Dressing 117
Tabouleh-Bulgur Salad with Tomatoes & Lemon Vinaigrette 118
Rice Salad Mold with Tomatoes & Red Wine Vinaigrette 118
Mushroom, Onion & Red Pepper Salad with Lemon Dressing 119
Pasta Salad al Pesto 119
Green Bean Salad with Mustard Vinaigrette 120
Cinnamon Carrot Salad with Raisins & Apples & Walnuts 120
Greek Salad with Lemon Dill Vinaigrette 121
Dilled Tomato Mayonnaise for Fish & Shellfish 122
Garlic & Red Pepper Mayonnaise with Lemon & Herbs 122
Pesto Mayonnaise for Pasta Salads or Potato Salads 123
Green Bean, Mushroom & Onion Salad with Dilled Dressing 124
Mixed Green Salad with Italian Herb Dressing 125
Mushroom, Cucumber Salad with Garlic Anchovy Dressing 125
Green Bean & Onion Salad with Lemon Creme Fraiche 126

FISH & SHELLFISH 127-144

Baked Spanish Mackerel with Tomato, Currants & Pine Nuts 129
Herbed Orzo with Tomatoes & Onions 129
Mousse of Fillet of Sole with Dilled Spinach & Chive Sauce 130

9

Lemon Macaroon Torte with Strawberries & Walnuts 254
Chocolate & Mint Cloud Torte with Chocolate Mint Buttercream 255
Chocolate Mint Decadence with Chocolate Mousse Frosting 256
Macaroon Torte with Bananas, Walnuts & Chocolate Chips 257
Greek Honey Cake 258
Spicy Whole Wheat Apple Cake with Currants & Walnuts 259
Apricot & Almond Butter Cake with Almond Cream Glaze 260
Apricot Coffeecake with Cinnamon & Almond Streusel 261
Chocolate Apricot Cake with Walnuts & Bittersweet Chocolate Frosting 262
Double Chocolate Banana Cake with Chocolate Chips & Walnuts 263
Spiced Banana Cake with Cinnamon & Walnut Streusel Topping 264
Old-Fashioned Carrot Cake with Walnuts & Black Currants 265
Carrot & Apricot Cake with Cinnamon Walnut Topping 266
Thanksgiving Orange Pumpkin Apple Cake 267
Sour Cream Vanilla Cake with Chocolate Buttercream 268
Chocolate Fantasy Cake with Chocolate Buttercream 269
Springtime Lemon Cake with Fluffy Lemon Frosting 270
Bittersweet Chocolate Fudge Cake with Chocolate Cream 271
Mocha Roulade with Chocolate Kahlua Cream 272
Spiced Zucchini & Raisin Cake with Vanilla Cream Glaze 273
Royal Babka with Strawberry Jam & Walnuts 274
Cassata Romana with Chocolate & Raspberries 275

Cheesecakes
Light Lemon Cheesecake with Lemon Butter Cookie Crust 276
White Chocolate Cheesecake with Almond Macaroon Crust 277
No-Bake Chocolate Cheesecake with Chocolate & Almond Crust 278
The Ultimate Chocolate Cheesecake wtih Macaroon Crust 279
The Best Chocolate Ricotta Cheesecake 280
Imperial Chocolate Chestnut Cheesecake with Chestnut Cream 281
Easiest & Best Imperial Velvet Chocolate Cheesecake 282

Charlottes
Charlotte au Apricot with Glazed Brandied Apricots 283
Charlotte au Chocolate with Almonds & Amaretto Cream 284

Cookies
Biscocho di Almendra-Almond Biscuit 285
Velvet Brownies with Walnuts & Chocolate Buttercream 286
World's Best Double Chocolate Brownies 287
Bittersweet Saucepan Brownies with Dark Chocolate Frosting 288
Honey Cinnamon Chewies with Raisins & Pecans 289
Chocolate & Walnut Praline Bars 290
Hungarian Butter Cookies with Apricot Jam & Dark Chocolate 291
Lady Fingers-Biscuits a la Cuiller 292
Chunky Pecan & Raisin Spice Bar Cookies 293
Butter Pecan Cookies with Apricot Jam & Chocolate 294
Honey Butterscotch Oatmeal Chewies with Raisins & Pecans 295
Hungarian Butter Cookies—Pogacsas 296
Giant Granola Cookies with Raisins, Dates & Walnuts 297

Custard
Spiced Pumpkin Custard with Vanilla Caramel Sauce 298

Fruit
Spicy Orange Baked Apples with Pecan Streusel & Creme Vanilla 299
Honey Spiced Apples with Orange & Pecans 300

Hors D'Oeuvres
&
Small Entrees

Hors D'oeuvres & Small Entrees

Royal Coulibiac of Crabmeat with Cheese & Chives 17
Tortellini with Garlic Pesto Cream Sauce 18
Smoked Salmon Pate Cheesecake in Dilled Cracker Crust 19
Carrot, Broccoli & Cauliflower Pate with Light Tomato Sauce 20
Spinach & Cheese Pate with Fresh Tomato & Onion Coulis 21
Cheese & Chive Muffins with Smoked Salmon Pate 22
Calzone with Puff Pastry, Chevre & Artichoke Hearts 23
Gorgonzola Pate with Chives, Parsley & Cream 24
Mousseline of Gorgonzola with Lemon & Chives 25
Hot Brie with Raisins & Walnuts 25
Mousseline of Salmon with Sweet Mustard Dill Sauce 26
Royal Crown Mold of Crabmeat Mousse 27
Hot & Spicy Shrimp Salad with Tomato, Basil & Mozzarella 27
Mushrooms Stuffed with Crabmeat, Cheese & Chives 28
Mushrooms Stuffed with Spinach & Cheese 28
Pork Meatballs with Coconut & Hot Apricot Dipping Sauce 29
Clams with Garlic, Parmesan & Herb Stuffing 30
Crusty Brie with Fresh Basil Tomato Sauce 31
French Brie Quiche Topped with Berries & Toasted Almonds 32
Layered Cheese Torta with Basil, Chives & Herbs 33
Eggplant Frittata with Cheese in Light Tomato Sauce 34
Torta Rustica—Quiche with Spinach & Mushroom Pate 35
Torta di Formaggio—Cheese Tart with Tomatoes & Onions 36
Torta Rusticana with Spinach, Bacon & Chives 37
Stuffed Shells with Shrimp, Garlic & Feta Cheese 38
Creme Mousseline of Crabmeat with Horseradish Lemon Sauce 39
Herbed Clams Florentine with Mushrooms & Cheese 40
Phyllo Roulades with Cheese for Soups & Salads 41
Dilled Mousseline of Caviar with Whipped Creme Fraiche 42
Chicken Ginger Dumplings with Coconut in Apricot Peanut Sauce 43
Sesame Bourekas of Cheese (Greek-Syled Piroshkis) 44
Traditional Greek Bourekas of Spinach & Cheese 45
Herbed Chevre Cheese Dip or Dressing 46
Guacamole Dip or Salad Dressing 46
French Mushroom Onion Quiche 47
Hot & Spicy Cajun Cornmeal Beef Pie 48
Angel Hair Pasta with Sun-Dried Tomatoes & Red Pepper Sauce 49
Sun-Dried Tomatoes 49
Chicken Livers with Mushrooms & Herbed Creme Fraiche 50

Royal Coulibiac of Crabmeat with Cheese and Chives

This is probably one of the most elegant dishes you can prepare. Serve it as a small entree, or as a main course for lunch or light dinner. Add a warm vegetable salad and some spiced peaches as lovely accompaniments. The filling has so much depth and character, it will surely please the most discriminating palate.

    2   tablespoons butter
    2   tablespoons minced shallots
    4   cloves garlic, minced
    1/4 pound mushrooms, thinly sliced

    2   tablespoons flour

    1/2 cup cream stirred with 1/2 cup sour cream
    1   teaspoon Dijon mustard
    1/4 teaspoon poultry seasoning
        dash of cayenne pepper
        salt to taste

    1/2 cup grated Swiss cheese
    2   tablespoons grated Parmesan cheese
    1   teaspoon chopped chives, (freeze-dried)
    1   teaspoon parsley flakes

    1/4 pound cooked crabmeat, flaked
    1/2 pound puff pastry (1/2 package Pepperidge Farms)

Saute first 4 ingredients together until shallots are tender and liquid rendered is evaporated. Add flour and cook and stir for 2 minutes. Add the cream mixture, mustard and seasonings and cook and stir until sauce is thick Stir in the Swiss cheese, Parmesan cheese, chives and parsley. Allow to cool. (Can be prepared in advance to this point and refrigerated.) When ready to assemble, stir in the crabmeat.

Roll out the puff pastry to measure a 12x14-inch rectangle, and cut it in half, lengthwise. Place first half on a 10x15-inch jelly roll pan. Spread filling on top, leaving a 1-inch border. Cover with second half of puff pastry. Seal the edges with the tines of a fork and scallop the edges. Pierce top with the tines of a fork.

Brush top with beaten egg and sprinkle with additional grated Parmesan. Bake in a 350° oven for about 30 minutes or until top is golden brown and pastry is puffed and beautiful.

To serve, cut into slices with a serrated knife. Serves 12 as a small entree, or 6 as a main course.

Hors D'oeuvres

Tortellini with Garlic Pesto Cream Sauce

This can be served as a small entree or in a chafing dish to be speared with long cocktail picks. I have served this often, and each time the 'oohs' and 'aahs' and 'm-m-m-m's' are such fun to listen to. This is an unusual hors d'oeuvre and just lovely served in a chafing dish. Starting as it does, with a few humble ingredients, you can hardly believe how delicious it is. And you can serve it at a moment's notice, if you keep these few simple ingredients at hand. It can also serve as a main dish, so please keep that in mind, too.

> 1 package (12 ounces) frozen tortellini. Cook these in a spaghetti cooker in 2 quarts boiling water with 2 tablespoons oil. Cook until tender, but firm. Drain, but leave the tortellini in the basket. Plunge into boiling water to heat before serving.

Garlic Pesto Cream Sauce:
 1/2 cup butter (1 stick)
   3 cloves garlic, finely minced
   1 pint cream

   2 teaspoons dried sweet basil flakes
   4 tablespoons finely grated walnuts
   1 tablespoon chopped chives
     salt to taste

In a saucepan, melt butter and saute garlic for 2 minutes. Add the cream and simmer mixture, until cream is reduced by about 1/3. Stir in the remaining ingredients and simmer mixture for 2 minutes, stirring, now and again.

Place hot sauce and hot tortellini in chafing dish. Have some 4-inch cocktail picks close by for spearing. Delicious! Serves 4 as a main course, 6 as a small entree and 8 as an hors d'oeuvre.

Note: — This is an incredible sauce to serve over any pasta, linguini, fettuccini, and other flat shaped pastas.

— If you add, at the very end, 2 cans minced clams, drained, (7 ounces, each), to the sauce, you will be making a Pesto Vongole, which is just simply delicious. Again, please serve with flat-shaped pasta. Using spaghetti or spaghettini will taste just fine, but it just misses, for my taste.

— While serving this with grated cheese is not uncommon, I do not recommend it. The sauce is so subtle and sublime, the addition of a sharp cheese, will mask its delicacy. Enjoy!

Smoked Salmon Pate Cheesecake in Dilled Cracker Crust

Truly easy and marvelously delicious is this smoked salmon appetizer, sparkled with chives and dill. It presents in a grand manner, with rosettes of chived cream cheese on top.

- 1/8 pound (2 ounces) smoked salmon, cut into 1-inch pieces
- 1 package (4 ounces) cream cheese with garlic and herbs (Boursin, Rondole or Alouette)
- 4 ounces cream cheese
- 3 tablespoons chopped chives
- 1/2 teaspoon dried dill weed
- 3 eggs
- 3/4 cup cream

Prepare salmon. Beat together the remaining ingredients until nicely blended. Stir in the salmon. Scrape mixture into prepared Dilled Cracker Crust and bake in a 350° oven for 25 minutes or until filling is set about 1-inch off center.

Allow to cool and then refrigerate. Decorate top with rosettes of whipped cream cheese and chives and a sprinkling of dill weed. Garnish platter with cherry tomatoes and lemon slices on a bed of parsley. Serves 8 as a small entree.

Dilled Cracker Crust:
- 1 cup cracker crumbs. (Use a tasty cracker like Potato Sesame or Waverly.)
- 1/2 cup grated Parmesan cheese
- 6 tablespoons melted butter
- 1/2 teaspoon dried dill weed

Combine all the ingredients until blended. Pat mixture on the bottom of a 9-inch springform pan and bake in a 350° oven for 8 minutes. Allow shell to cool a little before filling.

Note: — *To make the Whipped Cream Cheese and Chives, beat a 3 ounce package of Cream Cheese and Chives with 1 tablespoon cream, until mixture is light and fluffy.*

— *Entire dish can be prepared earlier in the day and stored in the refrigerator.*

Hors D'oeuvres

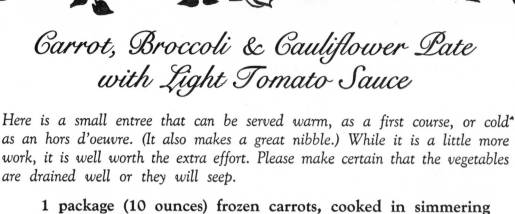

Carrot, Broccoli & Cauliflower Pate
with Light Tomato Sauce

Here is a small entree that can be served warm, as a first course, or cold as an hors d'oeuvre. (It also makes a great nibble.) While it is a little more work, it is well worth the extra effort. Please make certain that the vegetables are drained well or they will seep.

- 1 package (10 ounces) frozen carrots, cooked in simmering water until tender but firm, thoroughly drained and chopped
- 1 package (10 ounces) frozen cauliflower, cooked in simmering water until tender, but firm, thoroughly drained and chopped
- 1 package (10 ounces) frozen chopped broccoli, thawed and drained

- 5 eggs
- 1 cup cream
- 4 ounces cream cheese, softened
- 1/2 cup grated Parmesan cheese
- 1/4 cup chopped chives
- 1/8 teaspoon ground nutmeg
  salt and pepper to taste

Prepare the vegetables separately. Beat together the remaining ingredients until blended.

In a greased 1 1/2-quart souffle dish, spread the carrots evenly and pour 1/3 of the cream mixture. Continue in the same manner with the cauliflower and then the broccoli.

Place the souffle dish in a large pan filled with 2-inches boiling water, and bake in a 350° oven for about 1 1/4 hours, or until custard is set. Remove from water bath and allow to cool in souffle dish. Reheat before serving.

To serve warm, cut into wedges and spoon a little warm tomato sauce on top. To serve cold, cut into thin slices and serve with tomato sauce at room temperature. Serves 8 as a small entree.

Light Tomato Sauce: In a saucepan, simmer together 1 can (1 pound) stewed tomatoes, finely chopped and not drained; 2 shallots, minced; 1 clove garlic, minced; 1 teaspoon chopped parsley; 1/3 teaspoon sweet basil flakes; 1/2 teaspoon sugar; 1 teaspoon oil; and salt and pepper to taste, for about 20 minutes or until shallots are soft and most of the liquid has evaporated.

Spinach & Cheese Pate with Fresh Tomato & Onion Coulis

This delightful pate is quickly assembled and the end result is a very delicious and unusual mold. The garnish of tomatoes and onions, delicately flavored with lemon, is the perfect accompaniment.

    4 eggs
    1 cup cream

    2 packages frozen chopped spinach (10 ounces, each),
        defrosted and thoroughly drained
1/3 cup green onions, minced
2/3 cup grated Parmesan cheese
2/3 cup fresh egg bread crumbs
    1 teaspoon sweet basil flakes
      salt and pepper to taste

Line a 6x10x2-inch baking pan with foil and generously grease the foil. Beat together eggs and cream until blended. Beat in the remaining ingredients until blended. Place mixture into prepared pan. Sprinkle top with an additional 2 tablespoons grated Parmesan cheese (optional).

Place pan into a larger pan with 1-inch boiling water and bake in a 350° oven for about 50 minutes to 1 hour, or until pate is set and top is browned. Allow to cool in pan. When cool, remove from pan and peel off foil lining. Place on a lovely platter, cover and refrigerate until serving time.

To serve, remove from refrigerator about 15 minutes before serving and spread top with Tomato & Onion Coulis. Serve with a bland soda cracker or thin slices of French bread.

Fresh Tomato & Onion Coulis:
    1 medium tomato, peeled, seeded and chopped
    3 tablespoons finely minced green onions (tops only)
    1 tablespoon lemon juice
    1 tablespoon oil

Stir together all the ingredients until blended.

Note: — *Spinach must be drained thoroughly so that the pate will be dense and compact. Place spinach in a strainer and press to remove liquid.*

      — *Pate can be prepared 1 day earlier and stored in the refrigerator. Sauce can be prepared earlier in the day and stored in the refrigerator.*

Cheese & Chive Muffins with Cream Cheese & Smoked Salmon Pate

This is a great hors d'oeuvre and very easy to serve. The pate is prepared 1 day earlier and removed from the refrigerator just before serving. The muffins are baked earlier in the day and warmed a little before serving. Serve with champagne or iced vodka.

      2 eggs, beaten
      1 cup small curd cottage cheese
      2 tablespoons sour cream
      1 tablespoon oil
      1 teaspoon sugar
    1/3 cup grated Parmesan cheese
      2 tablespoons chopped chives
    1/2 cup Bisquick baking mix

Beat together all the ingredients until blended. Grease hors d'oeuvre-size teflon-lined muffin pans and fill 1/2-full with batter. Bake in a 350° oven for about 25 minutes, or until muffins are puffed and lightly browned.

Allow to cool in pans for 2 or 3 minutes, and then remove from pans and continue cooling on a rack. (Can be stored, at this point, in a plastic bag.)

When ready to serve, heat in a 350° oven until warmed through, about 5 minutes. Place pate in a bowl and surround with the muffins. Yields 24 to 30 muffins.

Cream Cheese & Smoked Salmon Pate:
    1/2 pound cream cheese, at room temperature
    1/4 pound smoked salmon, chopped
      2 tablespoons sour cream
      3 tablespoons chopped chives
      2 tablespoons lemon juice

Beat together all the ingredients until blended. Place pate in a lovely shallow glass dish, cover with plastic wrap, and store in the refrigerator until ready to serve. Decorate top with cherry tomatoes, small slices of lemon and a sprinkling of chopped chives.

Note: — The smoked salmon can be substitued with crabmeat or shrimp. A 3-ounce jar of golden caviar is another lovely substitution.

Calzone with Puff Pastry, Chevre & Artichoke Hearts

This is a fabulous hors d'oeuvre or small entree. It is also a nice lunch or light supper. It is a poem of flavor and truly exciting to serve. It is rather unusual from the traditional Calzone, which is basically a double-crusted pizza. If you have any trouble locating the Chevre cheese (made from goat's milk) you can substitute Feta cheese (made from sheep's milk.)

1 package frozen patty shells (6), defrosted

1 package (8 ounces) Chevre cheese, crumbled
1/4 cup chopped chives
1 jar (8 ounces) marinated artichoke hearts, drained and chopped
2 tablespoons sliced olive rings

grated Parmesan or sesame seeds

Stack 3 patty shells together and roll them out to measure 8-inches. Place pastry on a lightly greased cookie sheet. Combine the next 4 ingredients and place in center of pastry, leaving a 1-inch border along the edge.

Roll out the remaining shells in the same fashion and place over the filling. Press and seal the edges with the tines of a fork. Scallop them in a decorative fashion. Pierce top with the tines of a fork, brush top with a little water, and sprinkle with a little grated Parmesan cheese or sesame seeds or both. (Can be held at this point, covered, in the refrigerator.)

Bake in a 400° oven for about 25 minutes or until top is a deep golden brown. Place on a lovely platter and cut into wedges to serve. Serves 6.

Note: — *This can be assembled in advance, but should be baked before serving.*

— **To scallop the edge of the pastry:** *Simply place one index finger on the edge, and with the other finger, push dough toward the center, about 1/2-inch down. Continue around the edge. This will create an attractive; 1/2-inch scalloped border.*

Hors D'oeuvres

Gorgonzola Pate with Chives, Parsley & Cream

What do you do with 8 ounces of Gorgonzola that the children have decided "no way" to taste? Whip it into this very unusual (and very delicious) cheese pate, I say. The end result is a beautiful cheese spread, mildly tempered with the cream cheese and subtly flavored with chives and parsley. This is an outstanding hors d'oeuvre, served with thin slices of crusty bread or crackers for spreading. Of course, a Gougere with a full-bodied wine will herald a party.

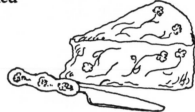

- 1 package (8 ounces) Gorgonzola or other blue-veined cheese
- 1 package (8 ounces) cream cheese, softened
- 3 eggs
- 1/2 cup cream
- 1/4 cup sour cream
- 2 tablespoons chopped chives
- 2 tablespoons chopped parsley
- 1/8 teaspoon garlic powder

Place all the ingredients in a food processor bowl, and blend until mixture is smooth. Pour mixture into a buttered 10-inch glass pie plate and bake at 325° for about 40 minutes or until pate is set. Do not overbake.

Allow to cool and then refrigerate for several hours. Overnight is good, too. To serve, place on a beautiful silver platter and surround with a lovely array of crackers and thin slices of bread. Spread top of pate with a thin layer of sour cream and sprinkle heavily with finely minced chives. Will serve 12 as an hors d'oeuvre.

Note: — This can be prepared 2 days earlier and stored in the refrigerator. Leftover pate can be used for sandwiches or snacks.

— Do not freeze.

— The important point to remember is not to overbake the pate. To test, insert a cake tester in center and it should come out clean. Pate will firm up in refrigerator.

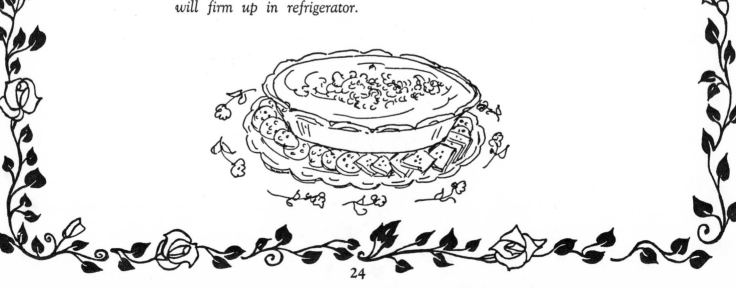

Mousseline of Gorgonzola
with Lemon & Chives

This is an interesting little mold that serves well with sliced, fresh vegetables. Sliced zucchini, cucumbers, celery and jicama are good. Cut carrots into diagonal slices so that you have a larger spreading area. Crackers or thinly sliced Italian bread are also very compatible.

- **1 package (1 tablespoon) unflavored gelatin**
- **1/4 cup cold water**

- **1 cup sour cream**
- **1/2 pound Gorgonzola cheese, crumbled**
- **1/3 cup chopped chives**
- **4 tablespoons lemon juice**
- **1 teaspoon Dijon mustard**

- **1 cup cream, whipped**

Soften gelatin in cold water in a metal measuring cup. Place cup in a skillet with simmering water and stir until gelatin is dissolved.

In a bowl, stir together sour cream, Gorgonzola, chives, lemon juice and mustard. Stir in the whipped cream. Stir in the dissolved gelatin. Pour mixture into a 4-cup ring mold and chill until firm. Unmold onto a lovely footed platter and decorate with green onion frills, lemon slices sprinkled with parsley, and cherry tomatoes.

Note: — Can be prepared one day earlier and stored in the refrigerator.

— Decorate top with additional chopped chives.

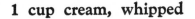

Hot Brie with Raisins & Walnuts

- **1 wheel of brie (8-inch circle) weighing about 2 pounds. Remove the outer rind of mold from the top. Place brie in an 8-inch round quiche dish or porcelain baker.**
- **3/4 cup raisins**
- **3/4 cup coarsely chopped walnuts or pine nuts**

Divide top of brie into 4 wedges. Top alternate wedges with raisins and walnuts. Place brie in a 350° oven and bake for about 20 minutes or until brie is melted. Serve at once with pale soda crackers.

Note: — Some people enjoy eating the outer rind (mold), but I do not.

Mousseline of Salmon with Sweet Mustard Dill Sauce

Poaching Salmon:
- 2 pounds salmon steaks
- 1 cup white wine
- 1 cup water
- 1 small onion, chopped
- 2 thin slices lemon
- salt to taste

Place salmon in one layer in a 9x13-inch pan. Combine the remaining ingredients and pour over the salmon. Cover pan tightly with foil and bake in a 350° oven for about 25 minutes or until fish flakes easily with a fork. Allow salmon to cool in liquid. Remove the bones and skin from salmon and flake fish into small pieces. Set aside. Strain stock and set aside. You will need 1 1/4 cups stock.

Mousseline of Salmon:
- flaked salmon (from above)
- 1/3 cup mayonnaise
- 2/3 cup sour cream
- 4 tablespoons lemon juice
- 1/4 cup chopped chives
- 1/2 teaspoon dried dill weed

- 2 tablespoons gelatin
- 1/2 cup fish stock (from above)
- 3/4 cup fish stock

- 3/4 cup cream, whipped

In a large bowl, stir together first 6 ingredients. Soften gelatin in 1/2 cup fish stock. Bring remaining fish stock to a boil. Add the gelatin mixture and simmer mixture until gelatin is dissolved. Allow to cool a little and then stir gelatin mixture with the salmon. Fold in the whipped cream.

Spoon mousseline into a 6-cup fish mold and refrigerate until firm. Unmold onto a lovely platter and serve with Sweet Mustard Dill Sauce on the side.

Sweet Mustard Dill Sauce:
- 1/2 cup Dijon mustard
- 1/4 cup mayonnaise
- 1/4 cup sugar
- 1 1/2 tablespoons white wine vinegar
- 1/2 teaspoon dried dill weed
- 2 tablespoons oil

Mix first 5 ingredients in a bowl. Slowly beat in oil until it is incorporated. Refrigerate until serving time. Yields 1 1/4 cups.

Royal Crown Mold of Crabmeat Mousse

    1 package (1 tablespoon) unflavored gelatin
1/4 cup cold water

2/3 cup sour cream
1/2 cup mayonnaise
    4 tablespoons lemon juice
    4 tablespoons finely chopped chives
    1 tablespoon finely chopped parsley
    2 teaspoons Dijon mustard
1/2 teaspoon dried dill weed
1/2 pound cooked crabmeat, picked over for bones
    salt to taste

In a metal measuring cup, soften gelatin in cold water. Place it in a pan with simmering water until it is dissolved. In a large bowl, stir the remaining ingredients until blended. Stir in the dissolved gelatin until blended.

Place mixture into a 4-cup ring mold and refrigerate until firm. Unmold onto a lovely footed platter and decorate with green onion frills, cherry tomatoes and lemon slices sprinkled with parsley.

Hot & Spicy Shrimp Salad with Tomato, Basil & Mozzarella

    1 pound cooked medium shrimp, shelled and deveined
1/2 pound Mozzarella cheese, grated
    2 tomatoes, peeled, seeded and chopped
1/4 cup chopped green onions

Hot & Spicy Dressing:
    1/2 cup oil
    2 tablespoons vinegar
    2 tablespoons lemon juice
    1 clove garlic, minced
    1/2 teaspoon sweet basil flakes
    2 tablespoons capers, rinsed and drained
    few drops Tabasco sauce
    pinch of cayenne and dry mustard
    salt and pepper to taste

In a bowl, toss together first 4 ingredients until nicely mixed. In a jar with a tight-fitting lid, shake together the dressing ingredients. Pour dressing to taste over shrimp mixture. Unused dressing can be stored in the refrigerator. Refrigerate salad for several hours to allow flavors to blend. Serves 6 as a small entree.

Hors D'oeuvres

Mushrooms Stuffed with Crabmeat, Cheese & Chives

1 pound medium-sized mushrooms, cleaned and stemmed. Brush mushrooms, inside and out, with melted butter.

1/3 pound crabmeat, picked over for bones
1 package (8 ounces) cream cheese, at room temperature
3 tablespoons chopped chives
1/2 cup grated Swiss cheese
1/2 cup garlic croutons, crushed into fine crumbs

grated Parmesan cheese
paprika

Prepare mushrooms. Stir together the next 5 ingredients until mixture is blended. Mound mixture into mushroom caps. Sprinkle tops generously with grated Parmesan cheese and lightly with paprika.

Place mushrooms on a cookie sheet and bake in a 350° oven until piping hot. Place under the broiler for a few seconds to brown. Serve at once. Yields about 25 to 30 stuffed mushrooms.

Mushrooms Stuffed with Spinach & Cheese

1 pound medium-sized mushrooms, cleaned and stemmed. Brush mushrooms, inside and out, with melted butter.

1 package (10 ounces) frozen spinach, defrosted and thoroughly drained
1/2 cup garlic croutons, crushed into fine crumbs
1/3 cup grated Parmesan cheese
3/4 cup crumbled feta cheese
1/3 cup finely chopped green onions
1/3 cup Ricotta cheese
1 tablespoon lemon juice

grated Parmesan cheese

Prepare mushrooms. Stir together the next 7 ingredients until mixture is blended. Mound mixture into mushroom caps and sprinkle tops lightly with additional grated Parmesan.

Place mushrooms on a cookie sheet and bake in a 350° oven until piping hot. Place under the broiler for a few seconds to brown. Serve at once. Yields about 25 to 30 stuffed mushrooms.

Note: — In both recipes, mushrooms can be assembled earlier in the day and stored in the refrigerator. Bake before serving.

Pork Meatballs with Coconut and Hot Apricot Dipping Sauce

This is a nice hors d'oeurve that everybody loves. Somehow, pork and coconut and hot apricot sauce go so well together.

- 1 **pound very lean ground pork**
- 1 **egg**
- 3 **tablespoons grated onion**
- 1/8 **teaspoon ground ginger**
  salt and pepper to taste
- 1 **green onion, minced**
- 2 **slices egg bread, crusts removed. Soak in water and squeeze dry.**
- 4 **water chestnuts, finely chopped**

Coconut flakes

Combine first 8 ingredients in a bowl and mix until thoroughly blended. Shape mixture into 3/4-inch balls and roll in coconut flakes to coat completely. Place balls on a cookie sheet and bake in a 350° oven, turning now and again, until cooked through, about 10 to 15 minutes.

Serve balls hot with tooth picks and Hot Apricot Dipping Sauce. Yields about 48 meatballs.

Hot Apricot Dipping Sauce:
- 1 **cup apricot jam**
- 4 **tablespoons brown sugar**
- 2 **tablespoons vinegar**
- 3 **tablespoons ketchup**
  dash of cayenne pepper

In a saucepan, combine all the ingredients and simmer sauce, for 5 minutes, stirring. Allow to cool for a few minutes and serve as a dip for pork meatballs. Yields 1 1/2 cups sauce. Any leftover sauce can be used for a glaze on chicken, or stored in the refrigerator for 1 month.

Note: — Meatballs can be prepared earlier in the day and stored in the refrigerator. Tent loosely with foil and heat in a 350° oven until heated through.

— This is a lovely main course if you make the meatballs 1-inch in diameter. Serve with fried rice.

Clams with Garlic, Parmesan & Herb Stuffing

This is a spectacular introduction to dinner in an Italian mood. Highly flavored with garlic and herbs and sparkled with a little Parmesan. Everybody savors every last crumb.

- 1/2 cup (1 stick) butter
- 6 cloves garlic, minced
- 4 tablespoons minced onion

- 1 package (6 ounces) prepared herbed stuffing
- 1 teaspoon Italian Herb Seasoning flakes
- 1 tablespoon chopped parsley
- 6 tablespoons grated Parmesan cheese
  pinch of cayenne pepper
  salt and pepper to taste

- 3 cans minced clams (7 ounces, each) drained.
  Reserve juice.
  grated Parmesan, paprika and oregano flakes for sprinkling on top

In a large skillet, saute garlic and onion in butter until onion is softened. In a large bowl, toss together next 6 ingredients. Add the garlic mixture and the drained clams. Slowly add the reserved clam broth until the stuffing holds together and is moist. (Do not let filling get soggy or stay too dry.) Divide mixture between 12 clam shells. Sprinkle with additional grated Parmesan, paprika and a pinch of oregano flakes. Can be held at this point.

Place clams on a cookie sheet and bake in a 350° oven for about 20 minutes or until piping hot. Serves 12 as a first course.

Note: — *Can be assembled earlier in the day and stored in the refrigerator. Bake before serving, adding 5 minutes to baking time.*

— *Can be frozen. Allow to defrost overnight in the refrigerator.*

Crusty Brie with Fresh Basil Tomato Sauce (Coulis)

If you like Mozzarella Marinara, you'll enjoy this version in a French mood. Use an underripe brie, or it will be too runny. The Fresh Tomato Sauce is served at room temperature, making a nice contrast to the hot brie.

1 package (8 ounces) underripe brie, cut into 4 wedges

flour, seasoned with salt, pepper and garlic powder

1 egg, beaten

dry bread crumbs

Dredge brie in flour, dip in beaten egg, and coat thoroughly in bread crumbs. Make certain that the cheese is completely coated. Can be held at this point in the refrigerator.

Just before serving, deep fry cheese for about 4 minutes, or until coating is golden. Serve at once with Fresh Basil Tomato Sauce on the side. Serves 4 as a small entree.

Fresh Basil Tomato Sauce (Tomato Coulis):
- 1 small onion, minced
- 2 cloves garlic, minced
- 1/2 teaspoon sugar
- 2 teaspoons oil

- 6 Italian plum tomatoes, peeled, seeded and chopped
- 1/2 teaspoon sweet basil flakes
- salt and pepper to taste

Saute together first 4 ingredients until onions are transparent. Add the remaining ingredients and simmer sauce for 5 minutes. Store in the refrigerator until ready to use.

Note: — Sauce can be prepared 1 day earlier.

    — Cheese can be crumbed earlier in the day and dried before serving.

French Brie Quiche Topped with Berries and Toasted Almonds

There is a good deal of commotion lately about bries. A good brie, served "natural" is grand pleasure. Lately, I have been seeing bries made with garlic and herbs, and I must admit, they are delicious. I love bries served with fresh fruit and I thought, pairing them, in this lovely quiche would be something new and delicious.

1 deep-dish frozen pie shell, baked in a 400° oven for about 8 minutes, or until just beginning to take on color.

1/2 pound French Brie. (Remove the outer rind (mold) with a sharp knife.) Cut remaining brie into small dice. Do this when the brie is cold, straight from the refrigerator. Use a slightly underripe brie for this dish.

4 eggs
1 cup cream
   salt to taste

1 package (3 ounces) cream cheese with chives, cut into 1/2-inch dice.
1/3 cup sliced almonds
1 1/2 cups fresh or frozen berries. Can use sliced strawberries, raspberries, blackberries or blueberries.

Prepare pie shell and place brie evenly in shell. Beat eggs with cream and salt until blended and pour over the brie. Place cream cheese pieces into egg mixture, spacing them evenly. Place quiche on a cookie sheet, and bake in a 350° oven for 20 minutes. Sprinkle top with sliced almonds and continue baking for 15 or 20 minutes, or until custard is set and almonds are browned. (Tent lightly with foil if almonds are browning too quickly.)

Remove from the oven and top with berries. Serve at once. Serves 4.

Layered Cheese Torta with Basil, Chives & Herbs

This is an exciting new way to serve cheese as an hors d'oeuvre, and a far cry from the old-fashioned cheese balls. The idea for this hors d'oeuvre was inspired by Torta Marscapone, a very soft, creamy Italian cheese layered with basil and pine nuts. I have deleted the pine nuts, as they become too soggy for my taste. But I thought you should know about it, in the event you might like to try it.

1/2 cup butter (1 stick), softened
2 cups grated Swiss cheese (8 ounces)
2 to 3 tablespoons finely chopped chives

1 package (8 ounces) cream cheese, softened
1/2 teaspoon sweet basil flakes
1/4 teaspoon oregano flakes
1/8 teaspoon garlic powder
2 sprinkles cayenne pepper (just a pinch)
1/4 cup pine nuts (optional, but not recommended)

Beat butter until creamy. Beat in Swiss cheese and chopped chives and beat until thoroughly blended. Set aside.

In another bowl, beat cream cheese until creamy. Beat in the remaining ingredients until blended.

Line a 2-cup mold (without a hole in the center) with plastic wrap. Now layer evenly half the Swiss cheese mixture and half the cream cheese mixture, using a piece of plastic wrap to help you press the mixture into the designs of the mold. Repeat layers.

Cover top with plastic wrap and refrigerate. To unmold, remove plastic cover, invert onto a serving platter and carefully peel off plastic lining. (Sounds like a whole production, but lining the mold with plastic wrap, makes unmolding incredibly simple.) Decorate top with fresh minced chives and surround with lemon slices. Serve with bland soda crackers, or thin slices of crusty Italian bread. Serves 8 as an hors d'oeuvre.

Note: — Gorgonzola may be substituted for the Swiss cheese.

— Can be prepared 2 or 3 days earlier and stored in the refrigerator. Remove from refrigerator 30 minutes before serving.

— Can be served at the end of the meal with fresh fruit . . . just lovely.

Hors D'oeuvres

Eggplant Frittata with Cheese in Light Tomato Sauce

If you are planning an Italian dinner, this is a small entree that everybody loves. It is versatile in that it can be served as a first course, or as a vegetable course. It can be served warm or at room temperature. And many's the time I nibbled on it straight from the refrigerator.

- 1 eggplant (about 1 pound) peeled and sliced
- 1 tablespoon oil

- 2 cups Ricotta cheese
- 1/3 cup grated Parmesan cheese
- 1 cup fresh bread crumbs
- 2 eggs
- salt and pepper to taste

In a 12x16-inch baking pan, layer eggplant slices and drizzle with oil. Cover pan tightly with foil and bake in a 400° oven for 20 to 25 minutes or until eggplant is soft.

In the large bowl of an electric mixer, beat together Ricotta, Parmesan, bread crumbs, eggs and seasonings until blended. Beat in the eggplant. (It will fall apart into small pieces.) Spread mixture evenly into an oiled 9x13-inch pan and bake in a 350° oven for about 50 to 55 minutes or until top is lightly browned. To serve, cut into squares and spoon a little Light Tomato Sauce on top. Serves 8.

Light Tomato Sauce:
- 1 onion, chopped
- 6 cloves garlic, minced
- 2 tablespoons oil

- 1 can (1 pound) stewed tomatoes, chopped. Do not drain.
- 1 can (8 ounces) tomato sauce
- 1 teaspoon sweet basil flakes
- 1/2 teaspoon oregano flakes
- 1 teaspoon sugar
- 1 shake cayenne pepper
- salt and pepper to taste

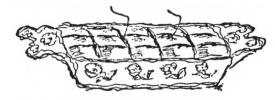

In a Dutch oven casserole, saute onion and garlic in oil until onion is transparent Stir in the remaining ingredients and simmer sauce for 5 minutes.

Torta Rustica — Quiche with Spinach & Mushroom Pate

This delicious quiche-like pie can be served either warm or cold. It is a lovely dish to serve in a rustic setting, like a banquet in the park or a feast in a rolling meadow. It is a dense pie, much like a pate en croute.

- 1/4 pound mushrooms, thinly sliced
- 1 small onion, chopped
- 2 tablespoons butter

- 1/4 pound (4 ounces) cream cheese, at room temperature
- 1/2 cup cottage cheese
- 1/2 cup cream
- 3 eggs
- 1 cup grated Swiss cheese
- 1/2 cup grated Parmesan cheese
- 1/4 cup cracker crumbs (use a savory cracker, like Ritz)
  - salt and pepper to taste
  - pinch of nutmeg

- 2 packages (10 ounces, each) frozen spinach, defrosted and drained

- 1 frozen 9-inch deep dish pie crust, baked in a 350° oven for 7 minutes

In a skillet, saute together mushrooms and onion in butter until onion is transparent.

Meanwhile, beat together the next 9 ingredients until blended. Beat in spinach and mushroom mixture until blended. Spoon mixture into prepared crust and bake in a 350° oven for about 40 minutes or until filling is set and top is lightly browned. (If crust is browning too rapidly, cover top loosely with aluminum foil.) Serve warm or at room temperature. Serves 6.

Note: — *This is a very dense pie and filled with all manner of good things.*

— *Can be prepared earlier in the day and heated at serving time. But it is best served right after baking.*

Torta di Formaggio
(Cheese Tart with Tomatoes & Onions)

This is a dense cheese pie; not quite a quiche, nor a frittatta. It is quite unusual with its cheese and cracker crust. The faint flavor of oregano sparkles the cheese filling.

- 3 eggs
- 1/2 cup cream
- 3 tablespoons grated Parmesan cheese
- 3 ounces Provolone cheese, cut into cubes
- 1/4 pound cream cheese
- 1/2 teaspoon oregano
- 1 green onion, cut into 4 pieces

- 7 very thin tomato slices
- 2 very thin onion slices

In a blender or food processor, place first 7 ingredients and blend for 1 minute, or until mixture is pureed.

Pour mixture into Cheese Cracker Crust and place tomato slices and a few onion rings on top, in a decorative fashion. Bake in a 350° oven for about 25 minutes, or until custard is just set and top is lightly browned. Do not overbake. To serve, cut into wedges. Serve warm or at room temperature. Serves 6.

Cheese Cracker Crust:
- 1 cup Ritz cracker crumbs
- 3/4 cup grated Parmesan cheese
- 5 tablespoons melted butter

Combine all the ingredients until blended. Pat mixture on the bottom and sides of an 8-inch porcelain quiche baker and bake in a 350° oven for 8 minutes. Allow shell to cool a little before filling.

Note: — Torte can be prepared earlier in the day and stored in the refrigerator. Heat before serving.

Torta Rusticana with Spinach, Bacon & Chives

More than an omelet and less than a pate this torta is similar to a frittata. It is filled with all manner of good things. It can be assembled earlier in the day and baked before serving. Can be served for brunch or lunch or as a vegetable accompaniment to dinner.

- 4 eggs
- 1 pound Ricotta cheese
- 1/2 cup cream
- 2 packages (10 ounces, each) frozen chopped spinach, thoroughly drained
- 6 strips bacon, cooked crisp, drained and crumbled
- 1 cup grated Swiss cheese (4 ounces)
- 1/3 cup grated Parmesan cheese
- 1/4 cup chopped chives (finely minced green onions can be substituted
- 1/3 cup fresh bread crumbs
- 1/8 teaspoon nutmeg
  salt and pepper to taste

In a large bowl, stir together all the ingredients until blended. Spread mixture evenly into an oiled 9x13-inch baking pan. (Use about 2 tablespoons oil.) Brush top with a little of the oil that collects on the sides.

Bake in a 350° oven for about 1 hour, or until top is browned and torta is set. Cut into squares or triangles to serve. Serves 6 as a luncheon dish or 8 as an accompaniment to brunch.

Note: — Broccoli may be substituted for the spinach.

— This can be baked earlier in the day and heated before serving, but it's best when freshly baked.

Hors D'oeuvres

Stuffed Shells with Shrimp, Garlic, Lemon, Tomatoes & Feta Cheese

This is a delightful small entree to serve with a dinner in a Greek mood. Served in individual scallop shells or ramekins makes it especially attractive and festive.

- 6 cloves garlic, minced
- 3 shallots, minced
- 6 tablespoons butter

- 2 tablespoons grated lemon
- 4 tablespoons chopped chives
- 2 tomatoes, peeled, seeded and chopped
- 1/4 pound feta cheese, crumbled
- 1 tablespoon chopped black Calamata olives
- 1 cup fresh egg bread crumbs
- 1 pound cooked baby shrimp
  salt and pepper to taste

- 3 tablespoons cracker crumbs
- 3 tablespoons grated Parmesan cheese
  paprika

Saute garlic and shallots in butter until shallots are tender, but not browned. In a large bowl place garlic mixture with the next 8 ingredients, and toss and turn until mixture is well combined. Divide filling between 12 scallop shells and place on a baking pan. Sprinkle tops with a mixture of crumbs and grated Parmesan cheese. Sprinkle a little paprika on the tops for color.

Bake in a 350° oven for about 20 to 25 minutes, or until filling is piping hot. Serve at once. Serves 12.

Note: — Entire dish can be assembled earlier in the day and stored in the refrigerator. Heat before serving.

— The 6 tablespoons of butter is sufficient to moisten fresh bread crumbs. However, if the bread is exceptionally dry, add a little melted butter to moisten the bread.

— Approximately 3 slices of egg bread, crusts removed, will produce 1 cup of crumbs. These can easily be made in a food processor.

Creme Mousseline of Crabmeat
with Horseradish Lemon Sauce

There are few hors d'oeuvres that you can make that are more delicious and elegant than this one. Serve it with small triangle toasted points. Do not use flavored crackers for this one, as it will interfere with the delicate balance of flavors.

        1 package gelatin
     1/3 cup water

     1/2 pound crabmeat, picked over for particles of shells
     3/4 cup sour cream
     3/4 cup cream
        2 tablespoons chopped chives
     1/4 teaspoon dill weed
        3 tablespoons lemon juice

In a metal measuring cup, soften gelatin in water. Place cup in a pan with simmering water, and stir until gelatin is dissolved. Set aside.

In the bowl of a food processor, place the remaining ingredients, and blend until crabmeat is very finely chopped, but not pureed. Beat in the gelatin until blended.

Line a flower mold (about 2-cup capacity and without a hole in the center) with plastic wrap. Press mousseline firmly into the mold, cover with another sheet of plastic wrap and refrigerate until firm.

To serve, remove plastic cover and invert mold on serving dish. Carefully peel off plastic lining. Decorate with scored lemon slices sprinkled with dill and parsley bouquets. Place Horseradish Lemon Sauce on the side, surrounded with toast points. Now, if the party is a very special one, spoon top in a decorative fashion with golden caviar. Just beautiful. Serves 8 as an hors d'oeuvre.

Horseradish Lemon Sauce:
     1/4 cup sour cream
     1/4 cup cream
        1 tablespoon lemon juice
        1 tablespoon prepared horseradish
        1 tablespoon chopped chives
     1/8 teaspoon dried dill weed

Stir together all the ingredients until blended. Refrigerate sauce until serving time.

Herbed Clams Florentine with Mushrooms & Cheese

Exciting and very delicious are these scallop shells filled with spinach and clams and sparkled with mushrooms and cheese. Taste is subtle and delicate and a poem of flavors.

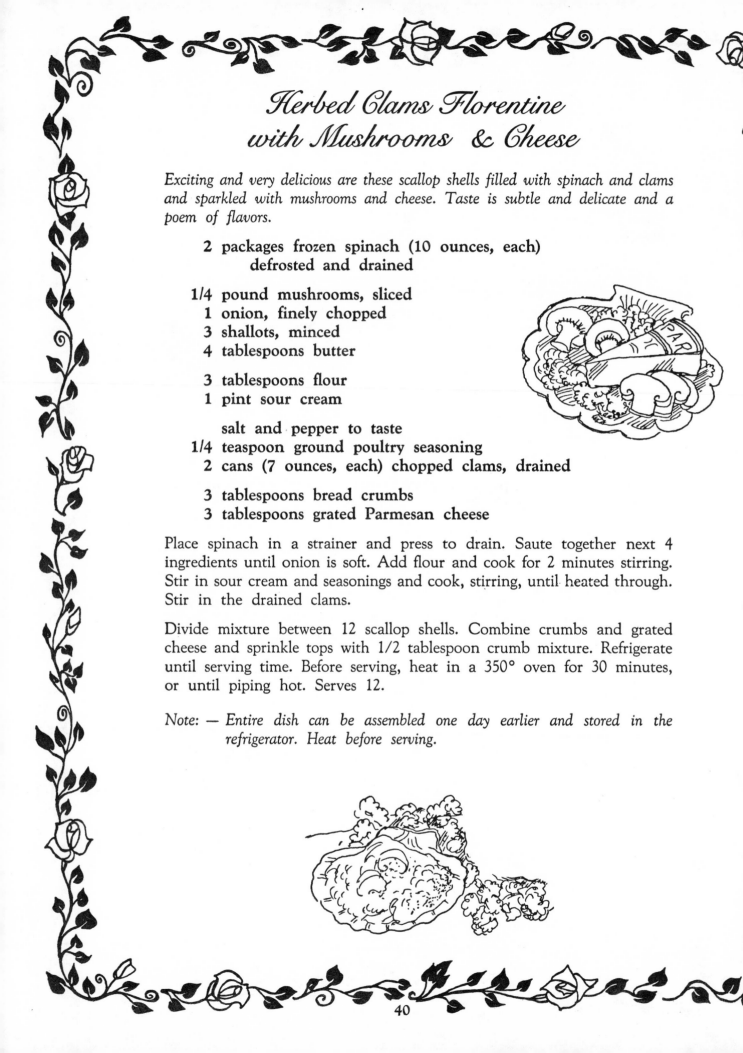

- 2 packages frozen spinach (10 ounces, each) defrosted and drained

- 1/4 pound mushrooms, sliced
- 1 onion, finely chopped
- 3 shallots, minced
- 4 tablespoons butter

- 3 tablespoons flour
- 1 pint sour cream

- salt and pepper to taste
- 1/4 teaspoon ground poultry seasoning
- 2 cans (7 ounces, each) chopped clams, drained

- 3 tablespoons bread crumbs
- 3 tablespoons grated Parmesan cheese

Place spinach in a strainer and press to drain. Saute together next 4 ingredients until onion is soft. Add flour and cook for 2 minutes stirring. Stir in sour cream and seasonings and cook, stirring, until heated through. Stir in the drained clams.

Divide mixture between 12 scallop shells. Combine crumbs and grated cheese and sprinkle tops with 1/2 tablespoon crumb mixture. Refrigerate until serving time. Before serving, heat in a 350° oven for 30 minutes, or until piping hot. Serves 12.

Note: — *Entire dish can be assembled one day earlier and stored in the refrigerator. Heat before serving.*

Phyllo Roulades with Cheese
for Soups & Salads

These heavenly roulades are incredibly delicious and a grand accompaniment to soups or salads. Sliced into bite-sized portions, they are an unforgettable hors d'oeuvre. Phyllo leaves, sometimes known as strudel leaves, have an infinite variety of uses. They can be purchased from Middle European groceries. Many supermarkets carry them in their freezer department. If you buy these frozen, then defrost them overnight in the refrigerator. They are delicate to handle, but hardier than they appear.

To facilitate preparation, it is best to have all the ingredients mixed and ready, butter melted, basting brush handy. Then, assembling is quick and easy. So, have ready

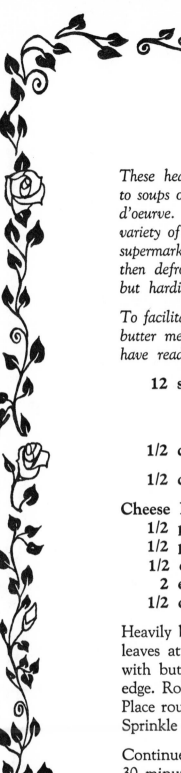

- **12 sheets phyllo pastry leaves (about 11x14-inches). Cover phyllo leaves with wax paper and over all, a damp towel.**

- 1/2 cup butter, melted

- 1/2 cup grated Parmesan cheese

Cheese Filling — Beat until blended
- 1/2 pound cream cheese
- 1/2 pound Ricotta cheese
- 1/2 cup grated Parmesan cheese
- 2 eggs
- 1/2 cup cracker crumbs

Heavily butter a 12x16-inch pan and preheat oven to 350°. Use 2 phyllo leaves at a time, one on top of the other. Baste the top leaf generously with butter. Place about 8 tablespoons Cheese Filling along the 11-inch edge. Roll up 3 times, tuck in the sides and continue rolling to the end. Place roulade in prepared pan and baste top and sides with melted butter. Sprinkle top with 1 tablespoon grated Parmesan cheese.

Continue with remaining phyllo leaves. Bake in a 350° oven for about 30 minutes or until crisp and golden. Cut each roulade into thirds and serve warm. Yields 18 3-inch roulades.

Note: — Can be prepared earlier in the day and stored in the refrigerator. About 1 hour before serving, remove from refrigerator and cut each roulade into thirds. 15 minutes before serving, heat in a 350° oven until heated through and crisped.

Dilled Mousseline of Caviar with Whipped Creme Fraiche

This is a very romantic hors d'oeurve, that is so nice to serve with champagne, for a late evening get-together. Serve it with triangle toasted points, very thinly spread with sweet butter.

- 1 package (1 tablespoon) unflavored gelatin
- 1/3 cup water

- 1 cup cream
- 1 cup sour cream
- 4 tablespoons chopped chives
- 1/4 teaspoon dried dill weed
- 3 tablespoons lemon juice

- 1 jar (3 ounces) golden caviar

In a metal measuring cup, soften gelatin in water. Place cup in a pan with simmering water, and stir until gelatin is dissloved. Set aside.

Beat cream until stiff. Beat in the sour cream, chives, dill weed and lemon juice until blended. Beat in the dissolved gelatin until blended. Very gently, stir in the caviar until blended.

Line a beautiful 2-cup decorative mold (without a hole in the center) with plastic wrap. (A heart mold would be especially nice.) Spread mousseline into prepared mold, pressing lightly to remove any air bubbles. Cover mold with another sheet of plastic wrap and refrigerate until firm.

To serve, remove plastic cover, and invert mold on a serving platter. Carefully peel off the plastic lining. Decorate platter with bouquets of parsley and lemon slices sprinkled with dill weed. Serve with toast points.

To Make Toast Points: Use a good quality, firm-textured, thinly-sliced white bread. Remove the crusts and cut each slice in half, on the diagonal. Toast bread slices in a 350° oven for about 10 minutes, or until the bread is lightly crisped. Spread with a thin layer of butter while still warm. These can be made earlier in the day and stored in a cannister with a tight-fitting lid.

I Love you

Chicken Ginger Dumplings with Coconut in Apricot Peanut Sauce

This is a lovely small entree for a backyard picnic or barbecue with a tropical island theme. If you make the dumplings small, they will serve as a wonderful hors d'oeuvre.

- 1 pound boned chicken breasts (about 2 medium breasts), cubed
- 2 eggs
- 1 shallot
- 1 clove garlic
- 2 tablespoons chopped chives
- 1/2 cup fresh bread crumbs, soaked in
- 1/4 cup cream
- 1/4 teaspoon ground ginger
  salt and pepper to taste

- 1/2 cup coconut flakes

In the bowl of a food processor, combine first 9 ingredients, and blend until chicken is very finely chopped. Shape mixture into 1 1/2-inch dumplings or 1-inch balls. Roll in flaked coconut to coat lightly on all sides.

Place dumplings in a baking pan, in 1 layer, and bake in a 350° oven until cooked through, about 15 minutes, depending on thickness.

Serve with Apricot Peanut Sauce, on the side, for dipping. Yields 2 dozen dumplings or 3 dozen balls.

Apricot Peanut Sauce:

- 1 cup apricot pineapple preserves
- 2 tablespoons brown sugar
- 2 tablespoons lemon juice
- 1/4 cup coarsely ground peanut butter

Combine all the ingredients in a small saucepan and heat until mixture is blended and sugar is dissolved. Serve sauce warm, not hot.

Note: — *Dumplings can be prepared earlier in the day and stored in the refrigerator. Heat just before serving.*

— *Sauce can be prepared 1 day earlier and stored in the refrigerator. Warm before serving, over low heat. Be careful not to scorch the sauce.*

Sesame Bourekas of Cheese
(Greek-Styled Piroshkis with Cheese)

These are incredibly delicious pastries, that serve well as an accompaniment to soups or salads. They will cause a great deal of excitement as an hors d'oeurve. Traditionally, Bourekas are made with an oil-and-water-based dough (which I am sharing for the purists.) However, using the prepared puff pastry is very convenient and it loses nothing in the translation, I promise you.

Cheese Filling:
- 1 cup Ricotta cheese
- 1 cup grated Parmesan cheese
- 1/2 pound finely crumbled Feta cheese
- 2 eggs
- 1/2 cup fresh bread crumbs

Beat together all the ingredients until blended.

Bourekas:
- 1 package frozen puff pastry, (17 1/2 ounces), defrosted (2 sheets)
- 1 egg, beaten
- sesame seeds

On a floured pastry cloth, roll out each sheet until dough is approximately 1/8-inch thick. Cut into rounds with a 2 3/4-inch cookie or biscuit cutter. Collect scraps and roll out to form additional rounds.

Place 1 teaspoon Cheese Filling in center of each round, fold dough over and press edges down with the tines of a fork. Brush tops with beaten egg and sprinkle with sesame seeds. Pierce tops with the tines of a fork.

Place Bourekas on a greased cookie sheet and bake at 400° for about 20 minutes, or until pastry is puffed and top is golden brown. Yields about 4 dozen pastries.

Traditional Greek Bourekas
of Spinach & Cheese

These are the traditional Greek Bourekas that I recall with such nostalgia. Please note that the fillings used in either recipe can be interchanged. The dough is very easily handled and is wonderfully flaky and delicious.

Traditional Greek Dough:
- 1/2 cup oil
- 1/2 cup water
- 1/4 teaspoon salt
- 2 cups flour

Stir together all the ingredients until blended. Add a little more flour, if necessary, to form an easily-handled soft dough. Do not overhandle dough. Divide dough into 16 balls.

Spinach & Cheese Filling:
- 1/2 cup chopped frozen spinach, defrosted and drained
- 3/4 cup Ricotta cheese
- 3/4 cup grated Parmesan cheese
- 1 egg
- 1/4 cup cracker crumbs

Stir together all the ingredients until blended.

To Assemble: Roll each ball out to measure a 5-inch circle. Place 1 heaping tablespoon filling on each round, fold like a turnover, crimp edges and brush top with beaten egg. Sprinkle with grated Parmesan cheese or sesame seeds. Bake in a heavily oiled pan, at 350°, for 25 to 30 minutes, or until tops are golden brown. Yields 16 bourekas.

Note: — These are best served warm. If made earlier in the day, store in the refrigerator and heat before serving.

— To drain spinach, place in a strainer and press to extract juice.

Hors D'oeuvres

Herbed Chevre Cheese Dip or Dressing

Serve this as a dip or salad dressing with dinner in a French mood.

    1 log (10 ounces) Chevre cheese, crumbled
    1/4 cup unflavored yogurt
    2 tablespoons lemon juice
    1 teaspoon Dijon mustard
    1 clove minced garlic
    2 teaspoons minced parsley
    1/4 cup chopped chives
    1/2 teaspoon sweet basil flakes
    salt and pepper to taste

In the bowl of a food processor, place all the ingredients and process for about 10 seconds or until everything is nicely blended. Place dip into a lovely bowl and serve with a large bouquet of sliced fresh vegetables. This is also good with slices of apples and pears. Yields about 1 1/2 cups.

Guacamole Dip or Salad Dressing

This is nice to serve as a dip or salad dressing for dinner in a Mexican or Spanish theme.

    3 large ripe avocados, mashed
    4 tablespoons lemon juice (or more to taste)
    1 medium onion, finely chopped
    2 tomatoes, peeled, seeded and chopped
    1 can (6 or 7 ounces) diced green chiles
    1/2 cup sour cream
    salt to taste

Stir together all the ingredients until blended. Place dip in a bowl and lay plastic wrap directly on top of the avocado mixture, pressing on top gently, to remove any air bubbles. (This will keep the dip from darkening.) Refrigerate until serving time. Serve with sliced fresh vegetables ... jicama, sliced cucumbers, carrot sticks, cherry tomatoes. Corn chips are also nice. This is a lovely dressing to serve over sliced tomatoes and onion rings. It can be prepared earlier in the day and stored in the refrigerator. Yields about 4 cups dip or dressing.

French Mushroom Onion Quiche

Even if you have been quiched to boredom, you will still enjoy these mushroom tarts. The cream cheese imparts little creamy pockets that are simply delicious. This is a good choice for brunch or lunch.

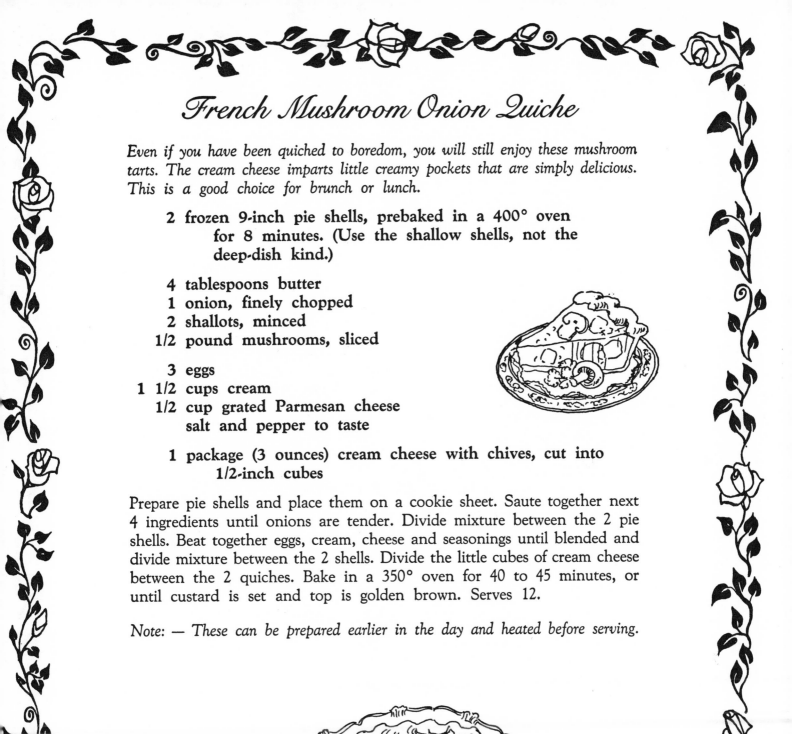

    2 frozen 9-inch pie shells, prebaked in a 400° oven
          for 8 minutes. (Use the shallow shells, not the
          deep-dish kind.)

    4 tablespoons butter
    1 onion, finely chopped
    2 shallots, minced
  1/2 pound mushrooms, sliced

    3 eggs
1 1/2 cups cream
  1/2 cup grated Parmesan cheese
     salt and pepper to taste

    1 package (3 ounces) cream cheese with chives, cut into
          1/2-inch cubes

Prepare pie shells and place them on a cookie sheet. Saute together next 4 ingredients until onions are tender. Divide mixture between the 2 pie shells. Beat together eggs, cream, cheese and seasonings until blended and divide mixture between the 2 shells. Divide the little cubes of cream cheese between the 2 quiches. Bake in a 350° oven for 40 to 45 minutes, or until custard is set and top is golden brown. Serves 12.

Note: — These can be prepared earlier in the day and heated before serving.

Hors D'oeuvres

Hot and Spicy Cajun Cornmeal Beef Pie with Chiles and Cheese

Here is something that is very new and different, and would please those with a love for hot foods. It is an incredibly tasty pie that is spicy and hot. It is very easily assembled and produces a spicy layer of beef and chiles and cheese sandwiched between 2 crusty layers of cornmeal. This can also be served as bread with soup or stews.

- 3/4 pound ground beef
- 1 medium onion, grated
- 4 cloves garlic, minced

- 3 whole green chiles (canned) coarsely chopped (4 ounces)
- 1 cup grated Cheddar cheese
- 1/8 teaspoon cayenne pepper, or more to taste

- 1 cup yellow cornmeal
- 2 eggs
- 1 cup milk
- 1 1/2 teaspoons baking soda
- 1/4 cup melted butter (1/2 stick)
- salt and pepper to taste

In a skillet, saute together beef, onion and garlic until meat is crumbly and loses its pinkness. Drain beef mixture and toss with chiles, cheese, and cayenne pepper. In another bowl, beat together the remaining ingredients until blended.

In a greased 10-inch quiche pan, pour 1/2 the cornmeal batter. Sprinkle meat mixture evenly on top, and pour remaining batter over all. Bake in a 350° oven for about 25 minutes or until top if golden brown and batter is set. Serve warm. Serves 6.

Angel Hair Pasta with Sun-Dried Tomatoes & Red Pepper Sauce

Sun-dried tomatoes add an intense flavor to pasta and is one of the most delicious additions to the culinary scene. However, they tend to be expensive. (I've seen these as high as $25.00 a pound.) With a little experimenting, I have prepared a wonderful alternative, which is every bit as delicious as the imported tomatoes. This is a lovely first course or small entree.

> 1/4 cup olive oil
> 4 cloves garlic, very finely minced
>
> 1/2 cup chopped sun-dried tomatoes
> 1 jar (2 ounces) pimiento strips
> 1/2 teapsoon sweet basil flakes
>   salt and pepper to taste
>
> 1 package (8 ounces) angel hair pasta, cooked firm but
>   tender and drained
> 4 tablespoons grated Parmesan cheese

In a saucepan, saute garlic in olive oil for 1 minute. Add the next 4 ingredients and heat through. In a bowl, toss together sauce, cooked pasta and grated cheese. Serve hot as a small entree, or at room temperature as a salad. Serves 4.

Sun-Dried Tomatoes:
> 2 pounds Italian plum tomatoes, sprinkled with a little salt
> 2 cloves garlic, minced
> 3 to 4 tablespoons champagne vinegar
> 1 teaspoon sweet basil flakes
>   olive oil

Cut tomatoes in half and remove stem and seeds. Place tomatoes, cut side up, on a teflon-lined shallow baker and place in a very low oven at 140°, until tomatoes are shriveled and dehydrated, but not completely dried out, about 6 to 8 hours, depending on the size of the tomato. Tomatoes should not be crisp, but should retain a little moisture.

Place tomatoes in a glass jar with a tight-fitting lid. Toss with garlic, vinegar and basil and cover with olive oil. Can be stored in the refrigerator up to 2 weeks. Use on pasta, in salads and in sauces for extra-tomato flavor.

Chicken Livers with Mushrooms & Herbed Creme Fraiche

While liver is not a favorite among most young people I know (including a few older ones, too), prepared in this manner, it might attract a few new fans.

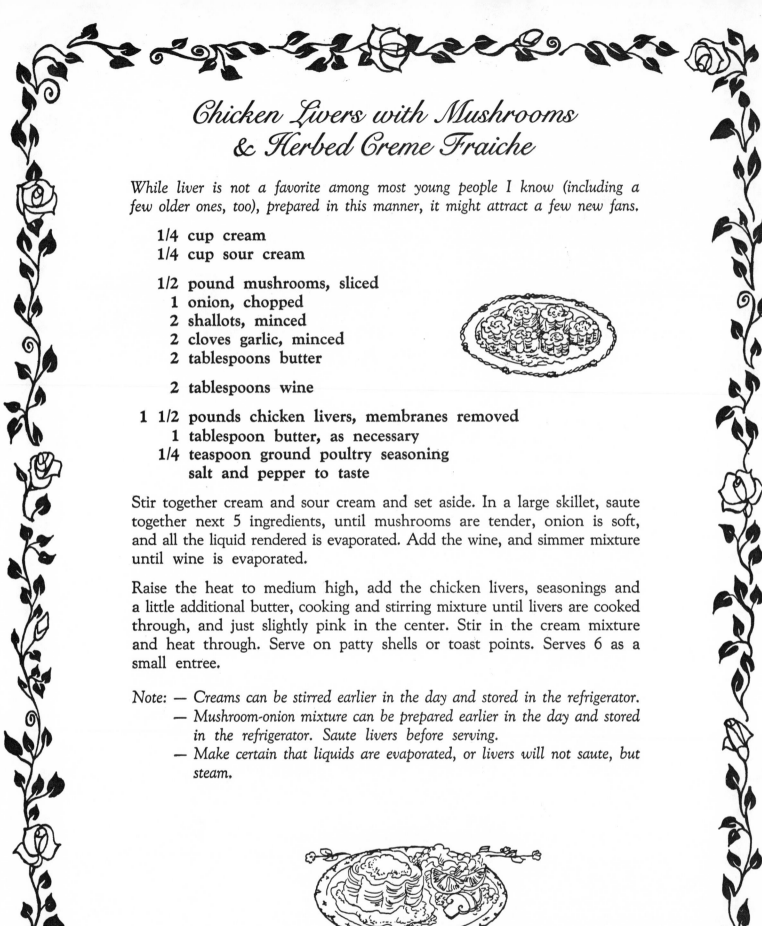

1/4 cup cream
1/4 cup sour cream

1/2 pound mushrooms, sliced
1 onion, chopped
2 shallots, minced
2 cloves garlic, minced
2 tablespoons butter

2 tablespoons wine

1 1/2 pounds chicken livers, membranes removed
1 tablespoon butter, as necessary
1/4 teaspoon ground poultry seasoning
salt and pepper to taste

Stir together cream and sour cream and set aside. In a large skillet, saute together next 5 ingredients, until mushrooms are tender, onion is soft, and all the liquid rendered is evaporated. Add the wine, and simmer mixture until wine is evaporated.

Raise the heat to medium high, add the chicken livers, seasonings and a little additional butter, cooking and stirring mixture until livers are cooked through, and just slightly pink in the center. Stir in the cream mixture and heat through. Serve on patty shells or toast points. Serves 6 as a small entree.

Note: — Creams can be stirred earlier in the day and stored in the refrigerator.
— Mushroom-onion mixture can be prepared earlier in the day and stored in the refrigerator. Saute livers before serving.
— Make certain that liquids are evaporated, or livers will not saute, but steam.

Casseroles

Casseroles

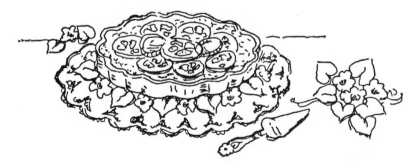

Joey's Favorite Chile Con Carne

This is my son's favorite chili. It is very traditional and does not include beans. When we were young, my mother always served it with beans and pink rice on the side. This might offend purists, but as children we loved it... and I still do.

  3 onions, chopped
  2 teaspoons minced garlic (about 6 cloves)
  2 tablespoons oil

  2 pounds coarsely ground lean beef (chili grind)
  1 pound coarsely ground lean pork (chili grind)

  2 cans (10½ ounces, each) beef broth
  3 tablespoons Masa Harina (finely ground corn meal)

  1 can (1 pound 12 ounces) crushed tomatoes in
      tomato puree
  1 can (7 ounces) diced green chiles
  4 to 6 tablespoons chili powder
  2 teaspoons sugar
  1 teaspoon oregano
  1 teaspoon cumin
      salt to taste

In a Dutch oven casserole, saute onions and garlic in oil, until onions are transparent. Add the beef and pork, and cook until the meat loses its pinkness. Stir beef broth with Masa Harina and add to casserole. Stir in the remaining ingredients and simmer mixture, partially uncovered, for about 45 minutes. Mixture should be very thick. Serve with thick slices of Hot Garlic Cheese Bread. Yields about 2 quarts chili... and will serve from 1 to 8.

Hot Garlic Cheese Bread:
  12 slices thinly sliced French bread (about 1/4-inch thick)
   1 egg, beaten
   6 tablespoons grated Parmesan cheese
1/4 teaspoon garlic powder

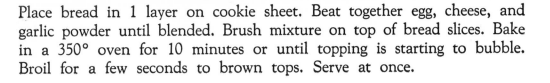

Place bread in 1 layer on cookie sheet. Beat together egg, cheese, and garlic powder until blended. Brush mixture on top of bread slices. Bake in a 350° oven for 10 minutes or until topping is starting to bubble. Broil for a few seconds to brown tops. Serve at once.

Herbed Spinach Frittata with Onions & Cheese

This is a delicious casserole to serve at a luncheon and it's filled with all manner of good things. It will serve 6 as a main course and 12 as an accompaniment. It also is a healthy and delicious nibble.

- 2 packages (10 ounces, each) frozen chopped spinach, defrosted and drained
- 1 pint lo-fat, small curd cottage cheese
- 3 tablespoons grated Parmesan cheese
- 3 eggs, beaten
- 2 slices whole wheat bread, crumbed (2/3 cup crumbs)
- 1/2 cup chopped green onions
- 1/2 teaspoon sweet basil flakes
- 1/2 teaspoon oregano flakes
  salt and pepper to taste

- 1 teaspoon oil

In a large bowl, place first 9 ingredients and stir until mixture is nicely blended. Spread oil on the bottom of a 9x13-inch pan. Place spinach mixture evenly in pan and bake in a 350° oven for about 50 to 55 minutes or until top is browned and casserole is set. Allow to cool in pan.

When cool, cut into 12 parts. Serves 6.

Note: — Casserole can be prepared 1 day earlier and stored in the refrigerator.

Eggplant Lasagna with
Tomatoes, Onion & Ricotta Cheese

6 Japanese eggplants, sliced. (Or 1 medium eggplant, cut
    into quarters and thinly sliced.) Do not peel.
1 can (1 pound) stewed tomatoes. Do not drain.
1 can (8 ounces) tomato sauce
1 onion, chopped
3 cloves garlic, minced
1/2 teaspoon sweet basil flakes
1/2 teaspoon Italian Herb Seasoning
1 teaspoon sugar (optional)
    salt and pepper to taste

1 pint Ricotta cheese
2 eggs
1/3 cup grated Parmesan cheese
1 teaspoon sweet basil flakes

In a Dutch oven casserole, place first 9 ingredients and simmer mixture for about 30 minutes, or until eggplant is soft.

Meanwhile, beat together Ricotta, eggs, Parmesan and sweet basil until blended.

In a 9x13-inch baking pan, spread 1/2 the eggplant mixture. Top with Ricotta cheese mixture and then, remaining eggplant mixture. Sprinkle top with 1 tablespoon grated Parmesan (optional).

Bake in a 350° oven for about 20 minutes or until cheese layer is set. Cut into squares and serve 8.

Note: — Casserole can be baked earlier in the day and heated at serving time.

Red Beans and Pink Rice with Bacon & Onions

     3 tablespoons oil
1 1/2 cups long-grain rice
     3 cups chicken broth
     2 small tomatoes, peeled, seeded and chopped
       salt and pepper to taste

     1 can (1 pound) red kidney beans, rinsed and drained
     6 strips bacon, cooked crisp, drained and crumbled
     3 green onions, chopped. (Use the white and green parts.)

In a saucepan, stir together first 5 ingredients. Cover pan and simmer mixture until rice is tender and liquid is absorbed. Meanwhile, combine beans, bacon and green onions. When rice is cooked, stir in the bean mixture and continue cooking until heated through. Serve as an accompaniment to barbecued chicken. Serves 8.

Honey Baked Beans with Bacon, Onions & Cheese

     3 cans (1 pound, each) baked beans
     6 strips bacon, cooked crisp, drained and crumbled
     1 cup brown sugar
   1/4 cup honey
     2 tablespoons chili powder (or more to taste)
   1/2 cup prepared chili sauce
   1/3 cup finely chopped onions

   3/4 cup sour cream
     1 cup grated cheddar cheese
   1/4 cup chopped green onions

Combine first 7 ingredients in an ovenproof casserole and stir until nicely mixed. Cover casserole and bake in a 350° oven for about 1 1/2 hours or until bean mixture is thickened. Can be held at this point.

Before serving, heat casserole through in a 350° oven. Stir together sour cream, cheddar cheese and green onions until blended. Spread mixture over beans and return casserole to oven, uncovered. Bake another 15 minutes or until cheese is melted. Serve as an accompaniment to hamburgers, barbecued beef or pork. Serves 10.

Demi-Souffle with Mushrooms, Shallots & Swiss Cheese

This very lovely casserole is an excellent choice for brunch or lunch. Mushrooms, sauteed in butter with shallots and sparkled with herbs and cream is a grand combination with the delicate Swiss cheese.

- 1/2 pound mushrooms, thinly sliced
- 6 shallots, minced
- 4 tablespoons butter

- 2 tablespoons flour
- 3/4 cup cream
- 1/8 teaspoon ground poultry seasoning
  salt to taste

- 6 eggs
- 1 package (8 ounces) cream cheese, at room temperature
- 1 cup grated Gruyere cheese (Swiss cheese)
- 1/3 cup grated Parmesan cheese

Saute mushrooms and shallots in butter over moderately high heat until mushrooms are tender and liquid is evaporated. Add flour and cook for 2 minutes, stirring. Add cream and seasonings and continue to cook and stir until sauce is thickened, about 2 minutes.

Beat eggs with cream cheese until mixture is thoroughly blended. Stir in the cheese. Stir in the mushroom mixture until blended. Pour into a buttered 8x11-inch porcelain baking dish and bake in a 375° oven for about 30 minutes or until eggs are set and top is browned. Serve at once. Serves 6.

Note: — *Souffle can be assembled several hours earlier and stored in the refrigerator. Bake before serving.*

    — *Top can be sprinkled with a little grated Parmesan cheese before baking.*

Layered Broccoli Casserole with Cheese & Onions

3 packages frozen chopped broccoli, defrosted and drained,
  (10 ounces, each)
1/2 cup green onion, finely chopped
1 cup grated Swiss cheese

2 eggs
1 cup sour cream
1/2 teaspoon dill weed
2 tablespoons lemon juice

1/4 cup grated Parmesan cheese
1/4 cup cracker crumbs. (Use a savory cracker, like Ritz.)

In an oval au gratin porcelain baker that is lightly greased, evenly spread the chopped broccoli. Scatter onions evenly on top. Scatter cheese evenly over the onions.

Beat together eggs, sour cream, dill weed and lemon juice until blended and pour over the cheese. Combine Parmesan and crumbs and sprinkle over the sour cream mixture.

Bake in a 350° oven for 35 minutes or until casserole is lightly browned. Serve warm with roasted or barbecued chicken. Serves 6 to 8.

Zucchini Frittata with Shallots, Onions & Garlic

2 pounds zucchini, do not peel. Cut into thin slices.
6 shallots, minced
1 onion, chopped
4 cloves garlic, minced
4 tablespoons butter

2 cups cottage cheese
1/3 cup grated Parmesan cheese
3 eggs
1/2 cup cracker crumbs
  salt and pepper to taste

In a large skillet, saute together first 5 ingredients until zucchini are soft, but not browned. In a large bowl, stir together zucchini mixture and the remaining ingredients until blended. Place mixture in a heavily oiled (2 tablespoons) 9x13-inch pan and spread to even. Bake in a 350° oven for about 45 minutes or until frittata is set and top is golden. Cut into squares to serve. Serves 6 to 8.

California Casserole with Potatoes, Tomatoes, Chiles & Cheese

This is a good choice to accompany a dinner with a Mexican theme. It is a delicious casserole and very attractive, too. It is especially nice for buffet serving. Preparing it in a porcelain baker, allows for baking and serving in the same dish.

6 medium potatoes, peeled and cut into 1/4-inch slices.
   (Place sliced potatoes in a bowl of water to prevent
   potatoes from darkening.)
1 can (10 1/2 ounces) chicken broth

3 eggs
2/3 cup half and half or cream

2 tomatoes, peeled, seeded and diced
1 cup grated Swiss cheese
1 can (3 1/2 ounces) diced green chiles (or more to taste)
1/3 cup grated Parmesan cheese
   salt and pepper to taste

Drain potatoes and place in a Dutch oven casserole. Add the broth, cover pan, and simmer potatoes until tender. Allow to cool for 20 minutes.

Beat together eggs and cream until blended. In a large bowl, combine all the ingredients until nicely mixed. Place mixture into a greased 9x13-inch porcelain baker and sprinkle top with an additional 1 tablespoon grated Parmesan (optional, but nice.) Bake in a 350° oven for about 45 to 50 minutes, or until custard is set and top is browned. Serves 8.

Moussaka a la Grecque
(Eggplant Casserole with Meat Sauce & Cheese Topping)

The main difference between the Greek and Turkish versions of Moussaka is the cream layer on top. Baking the eggplant, instead of frying it, saves thousands of calories.

> **2 eggplants (about 1 pound each), peeled and cut into 1/2-inch thick slices.**

Place eggplant in 12x16-inch baking pan, cover pan tightly with foil and cook eggplant in a 400° oven for 20 or 25 minutes or until eggplant is soft.

Sauce:

- 3 onions, chopped
- 3 cloves garlic, minced
- 2 tablespoons oil
- 2 pounds lean ground beef or ground lamb
- 1 can (1 pound) stewed tomatoes, chopped. Do not drain.
- 1 can (8 ounces) tomato sauce
- 4 tablespoons chopped parsley
- salt and pepper to taste

In a large saucepan, saute onion and garlic in oil until onion is soft. Add ground meat and saute until meat loses its pinkness. Add the remaining ingredients and cook sauce for 5 minutes.

Cream Topping:
- 1 pound Ricotta cheese
- 1/2 pound cream cheese
- 3 eggs

Beat together Ricotta, cream cheese and eggs until blended.

Crumb Mixture:
- 3/4 cup bread crumbs
- 3/4 cup grated Parmesan cheese

Combine bread crumbs and Parmesan cheese.

To assemble: In a 9x13-inch porcelain baker, spread a little sauce. Layer 1/2 of the eggplant slices, 1/2 of the sauce and 1/3 of the crumb mixture. Repeat with remaining eggplant, sauce, and 1/3 of the crumb mixture. Spread Cream Topping on top and remaining crumbs over all. Bake in a 350° oven until piping hot and crumbs are lightly browned, about 35 minutes. Serves 8.

Note: — Entire dish can be prepared 1 day earlier and stored in the refrigerator. Heat before serving.

Country-Style Cabbage Rolls in Sweet & Sour Tomato Sauce

1 large head of cabbage (about 1 1/2 pounds). Rinse cabbage and remove the core. Cook it, core-side down, in boiling water for about 12 to 15 minutes. Remove and refresh under cold water. Carefully remove the outer leaves. When the leaves get too small to roll, finely chop them and place them in a large Dutch-oven casserole.

Meat, Onion & Rice Filling:

- 1 pound lean ground beef
- 1 egg
- 1/2 onion, grated, about 6 tablespoons
- 1 1/2 cups cooked rice*
- 1/8 teaspoon garlic powder
- salt and pepper to taste

Stir together all the filling ingredients until nicely blended. Place about 2 tablespoons meat mixture on bottom of cabbage leaf. Tuck in the sides and roll it up. Place rolls, seam-side down, in Dutch oven. Pour Sweet & Sour Tomato Sauce over the rolls, and cook, covered, for about 1 hour over low heat. Yields about 12 rolls.

Sweet & Sour Tomato Sauce

- 1 can (1 pound 12 ounces) crushed tomatoes in puree
- 1 can (10 1/2 ounces) beef broth
- 4 tablespoons lemon juice
- 2 tablespoons brown sugar
- 2 tablespoons sugar
- 1 tablespoon oil
- salt and pepper to taste

Stir together all the ingredients until blended.

Note: — *To Cook Rice: *In a saucepan, place 2/3 cup rice, 1 can (10 1/2 ounces) chicken broth, 2 tablespoons butter, salt and pepper to taste. Cover pan and simmer mixture for about 25 minutes, or until rice is tender and liquid is absorbed. Yields 1 1/2 cups cooked rice.*

— *Any extra cabbage, can be chopped and placed in sauce. Any extra meat, can be shaped into dumplings and cooked along with the rolls.*

Red Pepper Crustless Quiche with Eggplant, Bacon & Cheese

There are few dishes that you can prepare for brunch or lunch that are more exciting and delicious than this one. The eggplant acts as the casing, saving hundreds of calories. The filling is a lovely blend of flavors.

1 small eggplant, (about 1 pound), cut into 1/4-inch thick slices. Place eggplant into a 9x13-inch baking pan, drizzle with 1 tablespoon oil and cover pan tightly with foil. Bake in a 400° oven for 20 minutes or until eggplant is soft, but not mushy.

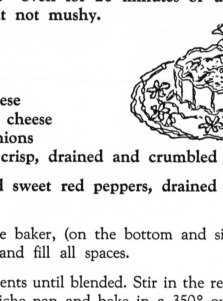

3 eggs
1/2 cup cream
2 cups ricotta cheese
1 cup grated Swiss cheese
1/3 cup grated Parmesan cheese
1/3 cup minced green onions
6 slices bacon, cooked crisp, drained and crumbled

1 jar (8 ounces) roasted sweet red peppers, drained and cut into strips

Line a 10-inch porcelain quiche baker, (on the bottom and sides), with eggplant slices. Overlap slices and fill all spaces.

Beat together the next 7 ingredients until blended. Stir in the red peppers. Place mixture into prepared quiche pan and bake in a 350° oven for 45 minutes or until custard is set and top is browned. Serves 6 for lunch.

Note: — Entire dish can be assembled earlier in the day and baked before serving.

— Entire dish can be baked earlier in the day and heated before serving.

Royal Artichoke & Spinach Casserole with Chives & Cheese

What a lovely, exciting casserole to serve at a buffet, for brunch or lunch. It is also a good choice as an accompaniment to roast chicken or veal. It is very different, but I promise, very, very delicious.

  1 jar (6 ounces) marinated artichoke hearts, drained and cut
    into fourths
  1 package (10 ounces) frozen spinach, defrosted and drained
  1 cup Ricotta cheese, at room temperature
  4 ounces cream cheese, at room temperature
  1 egg
1/4 cup fresh bread crumbs
1/3 cup grated Parmesan cheese
  4 tablespoons chopped chives, finely chopped
    salt and pepper to taste

Prepare artichokes and spinach. Beat together the remaining ingredients until blended. Stir in the artichokes and spinach until blended.

Pour mixture into a buttered 10-inch pie plate (deep dish) and drizzle top with 2 teaspoons oil. Bake in a 350° oven for about 40 to 45 minutes or until top is golden brown. Cut into wedges to serve. Serves 6 to 8.

Note: — *This can be baked in a 9x9-inch pan, and cut into squares at serving time.*

— *Recipe can be doubled. Bake in a 9x13-inch pan and bake for about 50 minutes. Cut into squares to serve.*

— *An oval porcelain baker is just lovely, for baking and serving in the same pan.*

— *Can be baked earlier in the day and heated at serving time.*

Paella Valencia with Chicken, Shrimp & Peas

1 fryer chicken (about 2 1/2 pounds) cut into 10 serving
  pieces. Sprinkle with salt, pepper and garlic powder.

1 large onion, chopped
1 red pepper, chopped
3 cloves garlic, minced
4 tablespoons butter

2 tomatoes, canned or fresh, peeled, seeded and chopped
2 cans (10 1/2 ounces, each) chicken broth
1 can (4 ounces) diced green chiles
1 1/2 cups long-grain rice
1/2 teaspoon turmeric
  salt and pepper to taste

1 pound, medium-sized cooked shrimp
1 package (10 ounces) frozen peas, defrosted

In a 9x13-inch pan, place chicken pieces and bake in a 350° oven for
40 minutes.

Meanwhile, in a Dutch oven, saute onion, pepper and garlic in butter
until onion is soft. Add the next six ingredients, in the order given, and
stir to blend. Place chicken pieces into Dutch oven, cover pan, and simmer
mixture for about 40 minutes or until rice and chicken are tender and
liquid is absorbed. Stir in the shrimp and peas and heat through. Serve
with a White Sangria. Sesame Chive & Cheese Monkey Bread goes well
with this. Serves 8.

*Note: — Entire casserole can be prepared earlier in the day with the exception
of adding the shrimp. Keep the shrimp refrigerated until just before
serving and then add and heat through.*

Vegetable Paella with Zucchini, Artichokes & Onions

Oh what a delicious and spicy casserole that is practically a meal unto itself. It is a grand main course or a hearty accompaniment to dinner. Preparing the rice separately eliminates the problem of its getting gummy with the inclusion of so many vegetables.

1 1/2 cups rice
   3 cups chicken broth
     salt and pepper to taste
   1 teaspoon turmeric
1/8 teaspoon cumin

   1 onion, chopped
   2 cloves garlic, minced
   2 zucchini, unpeeled and sliced
1/4 pound mushrooms, sliced
   3 tablespoons butter

   1 jar (6 ounces) marinated artichoke hearts, drained
   2 tomatoes, peeled, seeded and chopped (fresh or canned)
   1 package (10 ounces) frozen peas
   1 teaspoon turmeric

In a covered saucepan, simmer together first 5 ingredients, until rice is tender and liquid is absorbed. Meanwhile, saute together next 5 ingredients until onions are tender. Now, in a large bowl, mix together all the ingredients and place in a greased 9x13-inch baking pan. Cover pan with foil and bake in a 350° oven until heated through. Serves 6 as a main course or 12 as an accompaniment to dinner.

Note: — Entire casserole can be assembled earlier in the day, covered with foil, and heated before serving. Sprinkle casserole with 2 tablespoons water before reheating, to prevent rice from sticking to the bottom of the pan.

     — A 12-inch porcelain paella baking pan is especially nice for serving this dish. It is a wonderful investment, for it can be used to serve any number of casseroles.

Casseroles

Brunch Casserole of Crabmeat
in Wine with Scrambled Eggs

This is a delicious and unusual dish to serve for brunch. The divine sauce can be prepared 1 day earlier and stored in the refrigerator. Just before serving, heat the sauce with the crabmeat and scrambled eggs.

- 2 tablespoons butter
- 2 tablespoons flour

- 3/4 cup half and half
- 1 tablespoon chopped parsley
- 4 tablespoons chopped chives
- 6 tablespoons grated Parmesan cheese
- 2 tablespoons dry white wine

- 1 pound cooked crabmeat, picked over for bones
- 12 cooked scrambled eggs
  salt to taste

Cook together butter and flour for 2 minutes, stirring. Stir in the next 5 ingredients and cook and stir until sauce is thickened. (Can be held at this point, in the refrigerator.) Just before serving, heat the sauce, add the crabmeat and scrambled eggs and heat through. Transfer to a heated chafing dish. Serves 12.

To make Scrambled Eggs: Whisk together 12 eggs, 3/4 cup half and half, and salt to taste until blended. Cook eggs in a hot 12-inch skillet with 2 tablespoons melted butter, stirring, until eggs are set. If you do not own a 12-inch skillet, then scramble eggs, in batches, in a smaller pan.

Cannelloni Filled with Gorgonzola in Fresh Tomato Sauce

If you are looking for a delicious dish for a luncheon, or a small entree for dinner, this is a good dish to consider. It can be prepared in advance and heated before serving time. The Fresh Tomato Sauce is light and lovely.

16 crepes (7 to 8 inches) (recipe follows)

Gorgonzola Filling:
- 1 1/2 cups (12 ounces) Ricotta cheese
- 1/4 pound Gorgonzola cheese, crumbled
- 2 eggs
- 1/2 cup fresh bread crumbs
- 3/4 cup grated Parmesan cheese
- 1 teaspoon sweet basil flakes
- salt and pepper to taste

Stir together all the ingredients until blended.

Fresh Tomato Sauce:
- 2 tablespoons butter
- 3 shallots, minced
- 1 clove garlic, minced

- 4 large tomatoes, peeled, seeded and chopped
- 1/2 teaspoon sweet basil flakes
- pinch sugar
- salt and pepper to taste

Saute shallots and garlic in butter until shallots are softened. Add the remaining ingredients and simmer sauce, uncovered, until most of the liquid rendered is absorbed.

To Assemble: Divide the filling between the crepes, (about 2 heaping tablespoons on each.) Roll and place filled crepes, seam side down, and in one layer, in a 12x16-inch pan. (You can also arrange 2 filled crepes in 8 individual au gratin dishes.) Brush tops with melted butter and sprinkle with a little grated Parmesan cheese. Spoon a little sauce over all. Bake in a 350° oven until heated through.

Basic Crepes

While crepes are not as popular today as they were several years ago, they are still lovely and versatile. They can be filled with an infinite number of fillings and can be served for lunch, dinner or dessert.

>   1 **cup flour**
>   1 **cup milk**
> 1/4 **cup water**
>   3 **eggs**
>   2 **tablespoons oil (or melted butter)**

In a large bowl, combine all the ingredients and with a whisk or hand beater, beat until mixture is blended and smooth.

Heat a small omelet-type pan with rounded sides, (7 to 8-inches) and butter bottom with a paper napkin or paper towel. When pan is very hot, but butter is not browned, pour about 1/8 cup batter into the pan. Tilt and turn pan immediately to evenly coat the bottom with a thin layer of batter.

Cook on one side for about 45 seconds or until bottom is lightly browned and top is dry. Turn and cook other side for about 15 seconds. Makes about 16 to 18 crepes.

Herbed Crepes: To the above add 2 tablespoons chopped chives, 1 tablespoon chopped parsley and 1/2 teaspoon sweet basil flakes.

Parmesan Crepes: To the above add 2 tablespoons chopped chives and 2 tablespoons grated Parmesan cheese. Crepes can be filled simply with chopped tomatoes, Mozzarella cheese and chopped green onions, to taste.

Dessert Crepes: To the above add 2 tablespoons sugar, 1 tablespoon Grand Marnier liqueur and 1 tablespoon grated orange. Crepes can be filled with orange marmalade that is sparkled with lemon juice and chopped walnuts. Place in a greased porcelain baker and heat through.

Note: — Crepes can be lightened with the addition of water. In the above recipe, water can be increased to 3/4 cup and milk can be reduced to 1/2 cup.

Breads
&
Muffins

Breads & Muffins

Spiced Banana Bread with Raisins & Walnuts 71
Whole Wheat Orange Pumpkin Bread 72
Sour Cream Apricot Bread with Streusel Topping 73
Chewy Date Nut Muffin Cakes 74
Easiest & Best Crusty Cornbread 74
Honey Gingerbread Muffins with Raisins 75
Cajun Honey Corn Muffins with Currants 75
Blueberry Oat Bran Muffins with Honey & Walnuts 76
Cajun Date Nut Muffins with Orange & Walnuts 77
Fig & Walnut Whole Wheat Bran Muffins 78
Orange Marmalade Butter 78
New Orleans Red Hot Chile & Cheese Bread 79
Green Onion Bread with Carrots & Parsley 80
Sesame Chive & Cheese Monkey Bread 80
Green Buttermilk Flatbread with Lemon, Green Onions & Feta 81
Sauerkraut Rye Bread with Yogurt, Onions & Bacon 82
Focaccio Italian Flatbread with Tomatoes & Cheese 83
Fluffy Cheddar Biscuits & Chives 84
Buttery Raisin Scones with Walnuts 85
Breakfast Biscuits with Currants & Oats 86
Lemon Devonshire-Type Cream 86

Spiced Banana Bread with Raisins & Walnuts

This is an excellent bread to serve for a brunch buffet or mid-morning coffee. It cuts into the thinnest slices so a little goes a long way. It is very moist and wholesome. Note that it is moistened with water, producing a less caloric loaf.

1 cup sugar
2 eggs
1/2 cup oil
1 cup water

2 1/2 cups flour
2 teaspoons baking powder
1 teaspoon baking soda
1 teaspoon cinnamon
1/4 teaspoon ground nutmeg
1/4 teaspoon ground cloves

2 bananas, coarsely mashed
1 cup yellow raisins

1/4 cup chopped walnuts

Beat together first 4 ingredients until blended. Stir together the next 6 ingredients and add, all at once, beating until blended. Stir in bananas and raisins.

Divide batter between 2 greased 4×8-inch loaf pans and sprinkle each with 2 tablespoons of the walnuts. Press the nuts gently into the batter. Bake in a 325° oven for about 45 to 50 minutes, or until a cake tester, inserted in center comes out clean. Allow to cool in pans for 10 minutes, and then remove from pans and continue cooling on a rack. Yields 2 breads.

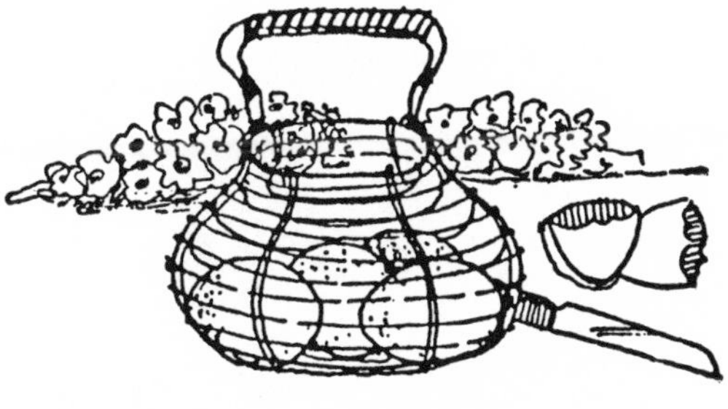

Breads & Muffins

Whole Wheat Orange Pumpkin Bread
with Walnuts & Raisins

This is a grand bread, fragrant and delicious and slices beautifully. It is filled with good things... orange, raisins, walnuts and lots of spice.

   2 eggs
1/2 orange, grated. Use fruit, juice and peel.
1/2 cup orange juice
1 1/8 cups sugar
   1 cup canned pumpkin puree
1/3 cup butter, softened

   1 cup whole wheat flour
   1 cup flour
   2 teaspoons baking powder
   1 teaspoon baking soda
   1 teaspoon cinnamon
   2 teaspoons pumpkin pie spice
   1 cup yellow raisins
   1 cup chopped walnuts

Beat together first 6 ingredients until blended. Combine and add the remaining ingredients and stir until dry ingredients are just moistened. Do not overmix.

Divide batter between 4 greased baby loaf foil pans, 6x3x2-inches, place pans on a cookie sheet and bake in a 350° oven for 40 to 45 minutes, or until a cake tester, inserted in center, comes out clean. Allow to cool in pans for 15 minutes and then remove pans and continue cooling on a rack. Serve "Natural" or with a lovely Orange Glaze. Yields 4 mini-loaves.

Orange Glaze:
   2 tablespoons orange juice
   2 tablespoons grated orange
   1 cup sifted powdered sugar

Stir together all the ingredients until blended.

Sour Cream Apricot Bread
with Streusel Topping

This is a nice bread to consider as a gift from your kitchen. The Streusel Topping is a dressy cover-up and optional. The bread stands alone quite well.

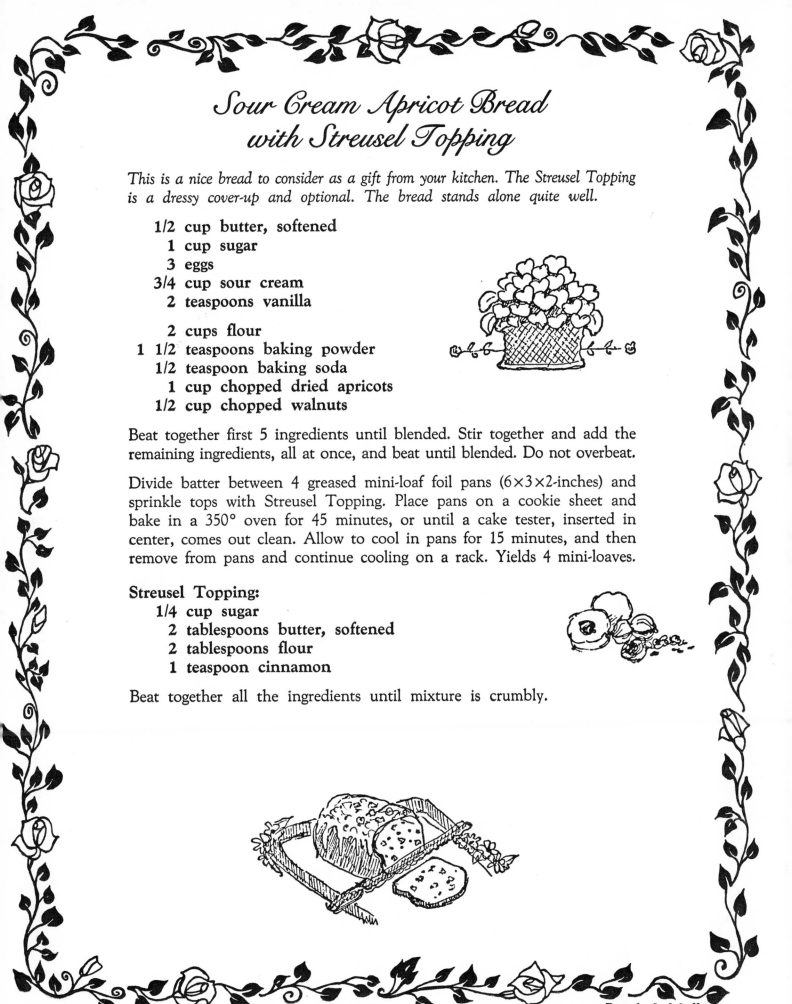

    1/2 cup butter, softened
      1 cup sugar
      3 eggs
    3/4 cup sour cream
      2 teaspoons vanilla

      2 cups flour
1 1/2 teaspoons baking powder
    1/2 teaspoon baking soda
      1 cup chopped dried apricots
    1/2 cup chopped walnuts

Beat together first 5 ingredients until blended. Stir together and add the remaining ingredients, all at once, and beat until blended. Do not overbeat.

Divide batter between 4 greased mini-loaf foil pans (6×3×2-inches) and sprinkle tops with Streusel Topping. Place pans on a cookie sheet and bake in a 350° oven for 45 minutes, or until a cake tester, inserted in center, comes out clean. Allow to cool in pans for 15 minutes, and then remove from pans and continue cooling on a rack. Yields 4 mini-loaves.

Streusel Topping:
    1/4 cup sugar
      2 tablespoons butter, softened
      2 tablespoons flour
      1 teaspoon cinnamon

Beat together all the ingredients until mixture is crumbly.

Chewy Date Nut Muffin Cakes

These are not quite muffins, not quite cakes, but a truly delicious accompaniment to brunch or lunch. These are small, so that they could easily accompany a hefty lunch.

    4 eggs, beaten
1 1/2 cups sugar
    1 teaspoon vanilla

1 1/2 cups flour
    1 teaspoon baking powder
      pinch of salt

    1 cup chopped walnuts
    1 cup chopped dates

Beat eggs, sugar and vanilla for 1 minute until light. Add flour, baking powder and salt and stir until dry ingredients are just moistened. Do not overmix. Stir in walnuts and dates. Spoon batter evenly into 24 paper-lined muffin cups and bake at 400° for 20 to 25 minutes or until a cake tester, inserted in center, comes out clean. Yields 24 muffins.

Easiest & Best Crusty Cornbread

This is a basic cornbread, just right for serving with Chili, chili soups or chili stews. It is deliciously crusty and very flavorful.

    1 cup yellow cornmeal
    1 cup flour
1/2 cup sugar
    1 tablespoon baking powder
1/4 teaspoon salt
1/2 cup butter (1 stick), cut into 8 pieces

1/2 cup sour cream
1/2 cup milk
    1 egg

In the large bowl of an electric mixer, beat together first 6 ingredients, until the mixture resembles coarse meal. Beat together the sour cream, milk and egg until blended. Pour this mixture into mixer bowl and beat until dry ingredients are moistened and mixture is blended, about 30 seconds to 1 minute. Do not overbeat.

Spread batter evenly into a greased 8-inch square baking pan, and bake at 375° for about 30 minutes, or until the top is golden, and a cake tester, inserted in center, comes out clean. Allow to cool in pan. When cool, cut into squares to serve. Serves 8.

Honey Gingerbread Muffins with Raisins

These muffins are dark and chewy and quite spicy. They are a good choice to serve with a hot and spicy soup or stew.

- 1/2 cup butter
- 1/2 cup sugar
- 1 egg
- 3/4 cup honey
- 1 cup sour milk (made with 1 cup milk and 1 teaspoon vinegar)

- 2 1/2 cups flour
- 1 1/2 teaspoons baking soda
- 1 teaspoon cinnamon
- 1 teaspoon ground ginger
- 1/4 teaspoon nutmeg
- 1 cup raisins
- 1/2 cup chopped walnuts

Beat together first 5 ingredients until blended. Stir together the remaining ingredients and add, all at once, beating until blended. Do not overbeat. Divide batter between 18 paper-lined muffin cups and bake in a 350° oven for about 25 minutes, or until a cake tester, inserted in center, comes out clean. Allow to cool for 10 minutes, and then remove from pans and continue cooling on rack. Yields 18 muffins.

Cajun Honey Corn Muffins with Currants

- 1 cup yellow cornmeal
- 1 cup milk
- 1/4 cup sour cream
- 1 egg
- 1/4 cup honey
- 1/3 cup butter, melted
- 1/3 cup sugar

- 1 1/4 cups flour
- 1 tablespoon baking powder
- 1 cup dried currants

Beat together first 7 ingredients until blended. Stir together next 3 ingredients and add, all at once, stirring until blended. Do not overmix. Divide batter between 12 paper-lined muffin cups and bake in a 400° oven for 22 minutes, or until a cake tester, inserted in center comes out clean. Allow to cool for 10 minutes, and then remove from pan and continue cooling on a rack. Yields 12 muffins.

Blueberry Oat Bran Muffins
with Honey & Walnuts

These plump muffins are filled with all manner of good things, including oat bran, honey and blueberries. These are on the dense side because of the high content of oat bran. An excellent choice for breakfast.

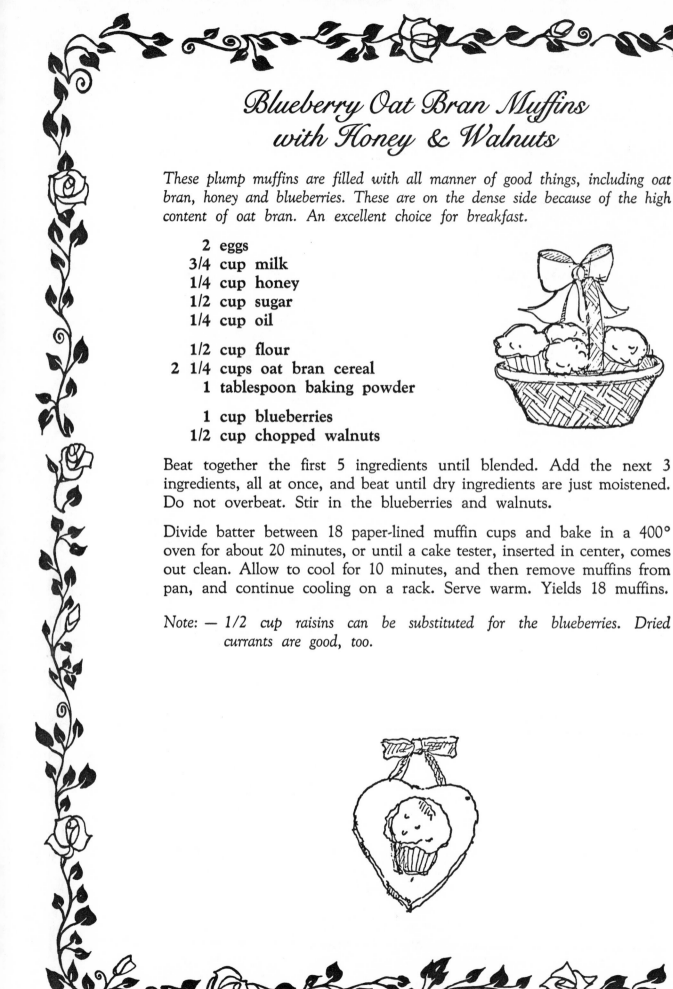

        2 eggs
    3/4 cup milk
    1/4 cup honey
    1/2 cup sugar
    1/4 cup oil

    1/2 cup flour
  2 1/4 cups oat bran cereal
      1 tablespoon baking powder

      1 cup blueberries
    1/2 cup chopped walnuts

Beat together the first 5 ingredients until blended. Add the next 3 ingredients, all at once, and beat until dry ingredients are just moistened. Do not overbeat. Stir in the blueberries and walnuts.

Divide batter between 18 paper-lined muffin cups and bake in a 400° oven for about 20 minutes, or until a cake tester, inserted in center, comes out clean. Allow to cool for 10 minutes, and then remove muffins from pan, and continue cooling on a rack. Serve warm. Yields 18 muffins.

Note: — 1/2 cup raisins can be substituted for the blueberries. Dried currants are good, too.

Cajun Date Nut Muffins
with Orange & Walnuts

When you serve one of the hot peppery Cajun dishes, this is a nice accompaniment to consider. It is a perfect taste balance. It is deeply flavored with orange and sparkled with raisins, dates and walnuts.

   1 egg
   1 cup buttermilk
1/3 cup melted butter
3/4 cup sugar
   1 medium orange, grated (about 6 tablespoons)

1 1/4 cups flour
   1 cup whole wheat flour
   2 teaspoons baking powder
   1 teaspoon baking soda
   1 teaspoon cinnamon
   1 cup chopped, pitted dates
1/2 cup yellow raisins
3/4 cup chopped walnuts

In a large bowl, beat together first 5 ingredients until blended. Combine the remaining ingredients and add them, all at once. Stir until dry ingredients are just moistened. Do not overmix.

Divide batter between 12 paper-lined muffin cups and bake in a 400° oven for 22 to 25 minutes, or until muffins are lightly browned and a cake tester, inserted in center, comes out clean. Allow to cool for 10 minutes, and then remove muffins from pan and continue cooling on a rack. Serve these warm with whipped, creamy butter Yields 12 generous muffins.

Fig & Walnut Whole Wheat Bran Muffins

This is a very tasty muffin that is filled with all manner of good things ... whole wheat, bran, figs. The recipe is a good basic one and can also be prepared with dates or apricots or raisins, instead of figs.

1 1/2 cups 100% all-bran cereal (not bran flakes)
1 1/2 cups milk

1 egg
1/3 cup oil
1 cup brown sugar
1 teaspoon vanilla

1/2 cup whole wheat flour
1/2 cup flour
1 tablespoon baking powder
1 teaspoon cinnamon
1 cup chopped dried figs
1/2 cup chopped walnuts
2 tablespoons grated orange peel

In a bowl, soak bran in milk for 15 minutes. Beat together egg, oil, sugar and vanilla until blended. Beat in bran mixture. Stir together the remaining ingredients, and add, all at once, stirring until blended. Do not overmix.

Divide batter between 12 paper-lined muffin cups and bake in a 375° oven for about 25 minutes, or until a cake tester, inserted in center, comes out clean. Serve warm with Orange Marmalade Butter. Yields 12 muffins.

Orange Marmalade Butter:
1/2 cup butter (1 stick), softened
1/3 cup orange marmalade
1/3 cup yellow raisins
1 tablespoon cinnamon sugar

In a food processor, blend all the ingredients until raisins are finely chopped. Place in bowl or crock and store in the refrigerator. Remove from refrigerator about 10 minutes before serving. Yields 1 cup.

New Orleans Red Hot Chile & Cheese Bread

This is a nice bread to serve with hot and spicy New Orleans dishes, soups or stews. It has quite a bite, for me. But red pepper (cayenne) can be increased to taste.

1/2 cup butter, cut into 8 pieces
2 cups flour
2 teaspoons baking powder

1 cup grated Swiss cheese
2 tablespoons grated Parmesan cheese
1 can (4 ounces) diced green chiles
1/4 teaspoon cayenne pepper

2 eggs
1/2 cup sour cream

1 tablespoon oil (for bottom)
1 tablespoon oil (for top)
2 tablespoons grated Parmesan cheese
2 tablespoons sesame seeds

In the large bowl of an electric mixer, beat together butter, flour and baking powder until butter particles are like coarse meal. Stir in the next 4 ingredients until nicely combined.

Beat eggs with sour cream and add to flour mixture, beating until a soft dough forms. Spread 1 tablespoon oil in a 12-inch round baking pan. Scrape batter into pan and spread to even. Drizzle top with 1 tablespoon oil. Sprinkle with grated Parmesan and sesame seeds.

Bake in a 350° oven for 35 to 40 minutes or until top is golden brown. Allow to cool in pan. Can be served at room temperature or warmed before serving. Cut into wedges or squares to serve. Serves 10.

Note: — Can be prepared earlier in the day and heated before serving.

Green Onion Bread with Carrots & Parsley

  2 carrots, sliced
  2 green onions, cut into 1-inch lengths. Use the whole
       onions.
  4 sprigs parsley
  2 tablespoons oil
  2 tablespoons sugar
  1 egg

  1 package dry yeast
1/4 cup water
  2 teaspoons sugar

1/2 cup water
3 1/2 cups flour

Place first 6 ingredients in the bowl of a food processor and blend until mixture is finely chopped. Scrape into the large bowl of an electric mixer. Soften yeast in 1/4 cup water and sugar until yeast starts to foam, about 10 minutes. Add to mixer bowl. Beat in the additional 1/2 cup water and flour and beat mixture for 5 minutes, using the paddle beater. Scrape batter into a 12-inch round, oiled baking pan and leave in a warm place to rise, until doubled in bulk. (Cover lightly with plastic wrap.)

Bake in a 350° oven for about 40 minutes, or until bread is lightly browned. Delicious!

Sesame Chive & Cheese Monkey Bread

  2 packages (10 count, each) flaky biscuits
  4 tablespoons butter, melted
  1 tablespoon sesame seeds
  1 tablespoon chopped chives
1/4 cup grated Parmesan cheese

Separate biscuits and brush with melted butter. Combine the remaining ingredients in a flat plate and sprinkle biscuits with this mixture. Space 5 biscuits evenly on the bottom of a 10-inch tube pan. Stagger the remaining biscuits on the top and sides of these. Bake in a 400° oven for about 15 minutes or until golden brown. Ease biscuit ring out of the pan and allow your guests to pull off a roll at a time.

Greek Buttermilk Flatbread with Lemon, Green Onions & Feta Cheese

A marvelous bread to serve with dinner in a Greek mood, very different and very interesting. It is an excellent accompaniment to soup or salad, and will create a great deal of excitement at the table.

- 1/4 cup oil
- 1 egg
- 1 1/2 cups buttermilk
- 3 tablespoons sugar
- 1/2 cup chopped green onions
- 1 tablespoon grated lemon. Use fruit, juice and peel.
- 3 cups flour
- 4 teaspoons baking powder

- 1/4 pound (4 ounces) feta cheese, crumbled

- 2 tablespoons oil
- 2 tablespoons sesame seeds
- 2 tablespoons grated Parmesan cheese

Beat together first 8 ingredients until blended, about 45 seconds. Do not overbeat. Stir in the feta cheese. Place 2 tablespoons oil in a 12-inch round baker and spread batter evenly in pan. (Brush top with a little oil that collects on the sides.) Sprinkle top with sesame seeds and grated cheese.

Bake in a 350° oven for 45 minutes or until top is golden brown. Allow to cool in pan. Serve warm or at room temperature. Serves 10.

Note: — *Cut into wedges to serve or serve whole and allow friends to tear off a piece or two.*

— *Bread can be prepared earlier in the day, or 1 day earlier, and stored in the refrigerator, properly wrapped in foil. Heat before serving.*

Sauerkraut Rye Bread with Yogurt, Onions & Bacon

This rather unusual bread is a fine accompaniment to hefty soups or stews. The flavor of rye is strong, the flavor of sauerkraut is nil. It first appeared in my bread book, but its versatility and speed of preparation merit its inclusion.

- 1 **cup dark rye (stone ground) flour. (Can be purchased in most supermarkets and all health food stores.)**
- 1 **cup flour**
- 4 **teaspoons baking powder**
- 1 **tablespoon dried onion flakes**

- 2 **eggs**
- 2 **tablespoons sugar**
- 1/3 **cup oil**
- 3/4 **cup prepared sauerkraut. Do not drain.**
- 1/2 **cup unflavored yogurt**
- 6 **strips bacon, cooked crisp, drained and crumbled**

In the large bowl of an electric mixer, stir together first 4 ingredients until nicely mixed. Add the remaining ingredients and beat until mixture is blended. Do not overbeat.

Heavily oil (2 tablespoons) a 12-inch round baking pan and spread batter evenly in pan. Brush top with a little oil that collects on the sides. Bake in a 350° oven for about 45 minutes, or until top is golden brown, and a cake tester, inserted in center, comes out clean. Allow to cool in pan.

To serve, cut into wedges. Or serve it whole (very attractive) and let everyone tear off a piece or two. Serves 8.

Note: — This is a moist bread and a little harder to test. Make certain that top is browned and bread starts to pull away from the sides of the pan.

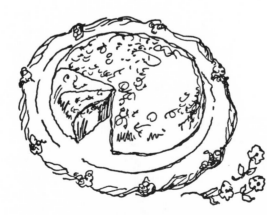

Focaccio-Italian Flatbread
with Tomatoes, Garlic & Cheese

When you serve this bread with Cioppino, the excitement will truly amaze you. This is truly a delicious bread and a wonderful blend of flavors. I do hope you love it as much as our friends did.

   2 medium tomatoes, chopped and seeded, fresh or canned
1/4 cup chopped green onions
   2 cloves garlic, minced
3/4 cup grated Swiss cheese
1/4 cup grated Parmesan cheese
   2 eggs
1/3 cup oil
   2 tablespoons sugar
1/2 cup buttermilk

   2 cups flour
3 1/2 teaspoons baking powder
   1 teaspoon Italian Herb Seasoning
   1 teaspoon sweet basil flakes

Beat together first group of ingredients until blended. Beat in the remaining ingredients until blended, about 1 minute.

Spread batter into a heavily oiled 12-inch round baking pan and brush top with a little oil that collects on the sides. Bake in a 350° oven for about 40 minutes or until top is browned. Serve warm, or at room temperature, and cut into wedges to serve. Serves 6.

Note: — *Bread can be prepared earlier in the day, or 1 day earlier, securely wrapped in foil and stored in the refrigerator. Heat bread in a 350° oven for 10 minutes before serving.*

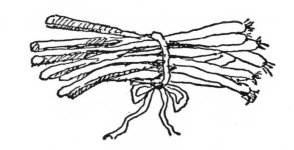

Fluffy Cheddar Biscuits with Chives

Serve these incredibly delicious biscuits with sweet, creamy butter and get ready for applause and cries of "bravo." These are light and flavorful and great for brunch or teatime. And, to add to their virtues, they can be prepared in minutes.

- 1/2 cup butter, cut into 8 pieces
- 1 1/2 cups flour
- 2 teaspoons baking powder
- 1/4 teaspoon salt
- 3/4 cup grated Cheddar cheese
- 2 tablespoons chopped chives

- 1/4 cup milk
- 1/2 teaspoon lemon juice

Place first 6 ingredients in the bowl of a food processor and process with on/off impulses until mixture resembles coarse meal. Stir together milk and lemon juice and add, all at once, and process with on/off impulses, until dough clumps together. Remove dough (it will be thick) and knead it, 2 or 3 times, to hold it together. (Do not overhandle.)

Pat dough out or roll it to 3/4-inch thickness and cut it into 2-inch rounds with a biscuit cutter. Collect the scraps and cut into additional rounds. Place on an ungreased baking sheet and bake in a 400° oven for about 20 to 25 minutes or until biscuits are golden brown. Remove from pan and allow to cool on a rack. Yields 15 biscuits.

Note: — Cheese can be grated in food processor, before preparing biscuits.

— The whole process should take less than 1 minute. The first operation should take about 10 on/off impulses (about 10 seconds) and the second operation should take about 5 on/off impulses (about 5 seconds). Do not overprocess.

Buttery Raisin Scones with Walnuts

This is one of the tastiest scones, so good with cream cheese and jam, or a few fresh sliced strawberries and chopped walnuts. It is not prepared with the traditional ingredients (eggs and sour cream), but the end result is truly marvelous.

    2   cups flour
    2   teaspoons baking powder
    2/3 cup sugar
    1/3 cup butter

    1/2 cup raisins
    1/4 cup chopped walnuts

    2   eggs
    1/2 cup sour cream
    1   teaspoon vanilla

Beat together first 4 ingredients until mixture resembles coarse meal. Beat in raisins and walnuts. Beat together eggs, sour cream and vanilla until blended and add, all at once, to flour mixture. Beat until blended. Do not overbeat.

Spread batter (it will be very thick) into a greased 10-inch springform pan and sprinkle top with 1 teaspoon sugar (optional, but nice). Bake in a 350° oven for 25 to 30 minutes, or until top is browned and a cake tester, inserted in center, comes out clean. Allow to cool in pan. When cool, remove from pan and cut into wedges to serve. Serves 8.

Note: — *Dried currants can be substituted for the raisins. Walnuts can be omitted, but are a nice addition.*

Breads & Muffins

Breakfast Biscuits with Currants & Oats

These are nice to serve at breakfast, with sweet butter and jam. Preparing them in a food processor is totally foolproof... although they can be prepared in a mixer, using a paddle beater. Do not overbeat. This is not a fluffy biscuit, so don't think anything went wrong.

- 1/2 cup butter, cut into 8 pieces
- 2 cups flour
- 1/2 cup quick-cooking oats
- 1/4 cup sugar
- 2 teaspoons baking powder

- 1/3 cup milk
- 1 egg
- 1/2 cup dried black currants

Place first 5 ingredients in the bowl of a food processor and process for 10 on/off impulses, or until mixture resembles coarse meal. Beat together milk and egg, and add, all at once, with the dried currants. Process for another 5 on/off impulses, or until dough clumps together around the center.

Place dough on a floured pastry cloth and pat into a 3/4-inch thick circle. Cut into 2-inch rounds with a biscuit cutter, and place on an ungreased cookie sheet. Collect the scraps and cut into additional rounds. Bake in a 400° oven for about 15 minutes, or until biscuits are puffed and golden. Yields 20 biscuits.

Note: — At teatime, these are nice to serve with Lemon Devonshire-Type Cream, and topped with a few chopped, toasted pecans and sliced strawberries.

Lemon Devonshire-Type Cream: Beat together 1 package (8 ounces) cream cheese, softened; 2 tablespoons cream; 1 tablespoon sour cream; 2 tablespoons sifted powdered sugar; and 1 tablespoon lemon juice until blended. Refrigerate for several hours or overnight.

Soups
&
Garnitures

Soups & Garnitures

Thanksgiving Honey Cream Apple & Pumpkin Soup 89
Leek & Tomato Soup with Garbanzos 90
Mexican Chicken Chile Soup with Orzo 91
Garlic Cheese Tortilla 91
Country Lentil Soup 92
Raisin Bread with Sesame Butter & Honey 92
Honey Spiced Pumpkin Soup 93
Cinnamon Orange Crispettes 93
Spinach & Rice Lemon Soup 94
Crispettes of Butter & Herbs 94
Country Leek & Ham Soup 95
Croustades of Cheese 95
Creamed Spinach Soup Potatoes, Leeks & Bacon 96
Holiday Cream of Mushroom & Chestnut Soup 97
Spiced Raisin & Walnut Sherry Bread 98
Potage of Tomatoes & Clams 99
Croustades of Garlic & Cheese 99
Creme of Spinach Soup with Onions & Shallots 100
Cheese Piroshkis 100
Farmhouse Split Pea Soup 101
Sesame Crispettes with Garlic & Cheese 101
Cold Cream of Carrot Soup with Apples, Raisins & Cinnamon 102
Cold Dilled Zucchini Soup with Shallots & Creme Fraiche 103
Peasant Cabbage & Tomato Soup 104
Croustades of Cheese & Chives 104
Cream of Honey Chestnut Soup 105
Spiced Pumpkin Muffins 105
Country Cabbage Soup with Black Pumpernickel 106
Raisin Butter with Honey 106

Thanksgiving Honey Cream Apple & Pumpkin Soup

This delicious soup is a good choice for Thanksgiving dinner or any frosty night, when the weather is raging outside. It is deeply flavored with spices and should be served with a sweetened quick bread or muffins.

- 2 tablespoons butter
- 2 medium onions, very finely chopped
- 2 large apples, peeled, cored and grated
- 2 tablespoons honey

- 2 cups canned pumpkin puree
- 2 cups chicken broth
- 1 cup apple juice
- 1/4 teaspoon cinnamon, or to taste
  - pinch of nutmeg, or to taste
  - salt to taste
- 1 cup cream

In a Dutch oven casserole, saute together first 4 ingredients until onions are soft. Add the next 6 ingredients and simmer soup for 10 minutes. Add the cream and simmer soup for another 10 minutes. Serve with Sherry Raisin Muffins. Serves 6.

Sherry Raisin Muffins:
- 1/2 cup butter, at room temperature
- 1 cup sour cream
- 1 egg
- 2 tablespoons golden sherry
- 1 cup sugar

- 2 cups flour
- 2 teaspoons baking powder
- 1/2 teaspoon baking soda
- 1 teaspoon cinnamon
- 1/8 teaspoon nutmeg
- 1/2 cup yellow raisins
- 1/2 cup dried currants

Beat together first 5 ingredients until blended. Stir together the remaining ingredients and add, all at once, stirring until blended. Do not overmix. Divide batter between 12 paper-lined muffin cups and bake at 400° for about 20 to 22 minutes, or until a cake tester, inserted in center, comes out clean. Allow to cool for 10 minutes, and then remove from pan and continue cooling on a rack. Yields 12 muffins.

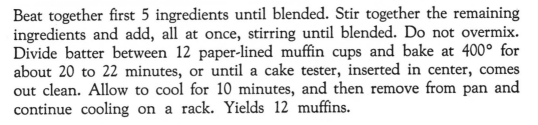

Soups & Garnitures

Leek & Tomato Soup with Garbanzos & Carrots

This is a rather unusual soup, with lots of heart and solid character. It is a grand choice for these frosty nights when the weather is raging. Sip it by a roaring fire with a few good friends close by ... and don't forget some thin slices of French bread covered with butter and honey.

- **2 onions, chopped**
- **2 leeks, chopped (use the white parts only)**
- **3 carrots, chopped**
- **6 cloves garlic, thinly sliced**
- **4 tablespoons butter**

- **1 can (1 pound) stewed tomatoes, finely chopped and not drained**
- **1 can (1 pound) garbanzo beans, drained. (Also known as chick peas or cici peas.)**
- **3 cans (10 1/2 ounces, each) chicken broth**
- **1 tablespoon chopped parsley**
- **1 teaspoon sweet basil flakes**
- **salt and pepper to taste**
- **3 strips bacon, cooked crisp, drained and crumbled**

In a large skillet, saute together first 5 ingredients until vegetables are soft, but not browned. (Do this over a low flame.) Place the vegetables in a blender or food processor and blend until coarsely chopped. Transfer vegetables to a Dutch oven casserole.

Add the remaining ingredients and simmer soup for 20 to 30 minutes, with the cover slightly ajar.

To serve, ladle soup in mugs and sprinkle a little Parmesan cheese on top. Delicious! Serves 6.

Note: — *Soup can be prepared earlier in the day and stored in the refrigerator. Reheat before serving.*

    — *Soup can be prepared 1 day earlier and stored in the refrigerator.*

Mexican Chicken Chile Soup with Orzo and Beans & Garlic Cheese Tortilla

This is a delicious soup, very new and very different. It is a medley of Mexican tastes and flavors. It is also very hearty, and will serve well as a complete meal. My Easiest & Best Cornbread is another lovely accompaniment.

        2 large onions, chopped
        8 cloves garlic, chopped
        1 can (1 pound) stewed tomatoes, chopped and drained
        1 can (8 ounces) tomato sauce
        3 cans (10 1/2 ounces each) chicken broth
        1 can (7 ounces) diced green chiles
        1 tablespoon Chili con Carne Seasoning (Spice Islands)
        1 teaspoon Turmeric seasoning
     1/4 teaspoon ground cumin
           salt and pepper to taste

        1 can (1 pound) red kidney beans, rinsed and drained
     1/2 cup orzo (rice-shaped noodles)
        1 chicken (about 3 pounds), cut into serving pieces

In a Dutch oven casserole, place first group of ingredients and bring mixture to a boil. Add the remaining ingredients and simmer soup, with cover slightly ajar, for about 1 hour and 15 minutes or until chicken is tender. Serve with Garlic Cheese Tortilla Chips or Easiest & Best Cornbread. Serves 6 very lucky people.

Note: — Soup can be prepared earlier in the day or 1 day earlier and stored in the refrigerator. Heat before serving.

Garlic Cheese Tortilla Chips:
        6 corn tortillas. Cut each tortilla into 6 wedges.
             (These will be reassembled.)
        3 tablespoons melted butter
           garlic powder
        6 tablespoons each, grated Jack Cheese, chopped tomatoes
             and diced green chiles

In a 12x16-inch baking pan, reassemble tortillas. Brush tops with melted butter and sprinkle with garlic powder, cheese, tomatoes and chiles. Bake in a 350° oven for 15 minutes, or until cheese is melted. Brown under the broiler for a few seconds. Serves 6.

Country Lentil Soup with Raisin Bread with Sesame Butter & Honey

*What a nice soup to enjoy on nights when family and friends get together.
It is thick and satisfying and the Raisin Bread is the perfect accompaniment.*

- 2 large onions, chopped
- 3 carrots, grated
- 2 shallots, minced
- 3 cloves garlic, minced
- 3 tablespoons butter

- 1/4 cup dry white wine

- 1 can (1 pound) stewed tomatoes, finely chopped. Do not drain.
- 2 cans (10 1/2 ounces, each) chicken broth
- 1 can (10 1/2 ounces) beef broth
- 6 slices bacon, cooked crisp, drained and crumbled
- 1 package (1 pound) lentils, rinsed in a strainer and drained
- salt and pepper to taste.

In a Dutch oven casserole, saute together first 5 ingredients, until onions
are transparent. Add the wine and simmer mixture, until liquid is reduced
by half. Add the remaining ingredients and simmer soup, with lid slightly
ajar, for about 1 hour 15 minutes, or until lentils are very tender. (Add
a little broth if soup is too thick.)

Serve with Raisin Bread with Sesame Butter and Honey. Serves 6.

Raisin Bread with Sesame Butter & Honey

- 6 slices raisin bread
- 6 teaspoons butter
- 6 teaspoons honey
- 3 teaspoons sesame seeds

Spread 1 teaspoon butter on each slice of bread. Spread 1 teaspoon honey
over the butter. Sprinkle tops with 1/2 teaspoon sesame seeds. Place bread
on a cookie sheet and broil for 1 minute, or until sesame seeds just begin
to take on color. (Watch carefully or seeds will burn.) Serves 6.

Note: — Soup can be prepared earlier in the day and heated at serving time.

*— Bread can be assembled earlier in the day, placed on a cookie sheet
and covered carefully with plastic wrap. Remove wrap and broil before
serving.*

Honey Spiced Pumpkin Soup
with Cinnamon Orange Crispettes

1 large onion, finely chopped
2 shallots, finely chopped
2 tablespoons butter

3 cans (10 1/2 ounces, each) chicken broth
1 can (1 pound) pumpkin puree
1/4 cup honey
1 cup half and half
1 apple, peeled, cored and grated
3/4 teaspoon pumpkin pie spice
   salt to taste

1/4 cup cream
1/4 cup sour cream

Saute onion and shallots in butter until onions are soft, but not browned. Add the next 7 ingredients and simmer soup for 10 minutes. Stir together the cream and sour cream until blended and add it to the soup. Heat soup through. Serve with a dollup of sour cream on top and a faint sprinkling of cinnamon. Crispettes flavored with Cinnamon & Orange are a lovely accompaniment. Serves 6.

Cinnamon Orange Crispettes

3 pita breads, split in halves
6 teaspoons butter
6 teaspoons orange marmalade

cinnamon

Spread 1 teaspoon of butter and 1 teaspoon of marmalade on each half of pita bread. Sprinkle top lightly with a dash of cinnamon.

Place bread on a cookie sheet and bake in a 350° oven until lightly browned and crisped. Serves 6.

Note: — Soup can be prepared earlier in the day and heated at time of serving. Bread can be prepared earlier in the day and stored in a covered plastic container, at room temperature.

Soups & Garnitures

Spinach & Rice Lemon Soup with Crispettes of Butter & Herbs

Whenever I make this soup, it summons "remembrance of things past." This soup was one of Mom's staples, and she made it often. It is delicately flavored with lemon and the cream is optional; although I prefer it with cream.

- 1 onion, chopped
- 6 cloves garlic, minced
- 4 shallots, minced
- 2 tablespoons butter

- 3 cans (10 1/2 ounces, each) chicken broth
- 2 packages (10 ounces, each) frozen chopped spinach
- 4 tablespoons lemon juice
- 1 cup cooked rice
- 1/2 cup cream (optional)
- salt to taste

In a Dutch oven casserole, saute together first 4 ingredients, until onions are soft, but not browned. Stir in the chicken broth, and bring soup to a simmer. Add the spinach, lemon juice and rice and simmer soup for 5 minutes. Add cream (optional) and salt to taste. Heat through.

Serve with Crispettes of Butter and Herbs as a lovely accompaniment. Serves 6.

Crispettes of Butter and Herbs:
- 6 slices fresh egg bread, crusts removed
- 3 tablespoons melted butter
- 1 tablespoon minced parsley
- 1 tablespoon minced chives
- 1/3 teaspoon oregano flakes*

With a rolling pin, roll each slice of bread flat. Combine butter and herbs. Brush bread with butter mixture and place on a cookie sheet. Bake in a 350° oven, basting bread and turning until bread is crisp on both sides. Cut bread into triangles or other decorative shapes. Serves 6.

*Note: — *Use an herb that is complimentary with your meal. Oregano is good with an Italian dinner, thyme with French, etc. Dill is a fine choice for many themes.*

Country Leek & Ham Soup with Croustades of Cheese

This is a grand soup to serve on a shivery night, and close to a warm and cozy fire. The Croustades of Cheese are hefty accompaniments, but in the perfect spirit.

> 1 pound leeks (about 4 medium leeks), thinly sliced. (Use the white part with about 1-inch of the soft green tops.)
> 2 medium onions, chopped
> 4 shallots, finely chopped
> 6 cloves garlic, minced
> 4 tablespoons butter
>
> 1/2 cup dry white wine
>
> 3 cans (10 1/2 ounces, each) chicken broth
> 1 slice ham (about 1/4 pound) cut into 1/4-inch dice
> 1/2 cup cream
> salt and white pepper to taste

In a large skillet, saute together first 5 ingredients over low heat until onions are soft, but not browned. Add the wine and simmer mixture until wine is almost evaporated. Scrape mixture into a food processor bowl and blend until pureed.

Place vegetables in a Dutch oven casserole with the broth and ham and simmer mixture for 10 minutes. Stir in the cream and seasonings and bring to a simmer. Serve with Croustades of Cheese. Serves 6.

Croustades of Cheese:
> 3/4 cup grated Swiss cheese
> 2 tablespoons chopped chives
> 1 clove garlic, mashed
>
> 6 teaspoons butter, at room temperature
> 6 slices (3/4-inch thick) French bread

Stir together first 3 ingredients until nicely mixed. Spread each slice of bread with about 1 teaspoon butter, and sprinkle cheese mixture evenly on top.

Place bread on a cookie sheet and broil (watching carefully) until cheese is melted and just beginning to take on color.

Note: — Soup can be prepared earlier in the day and heated at serving time.

— Bread can be assembled earlier in the day and broiled at serving time.

Creamed Spinach Soup with Potatoes, Leeks & Bacon & Green Onion Bread

This is a rich and zesty soup, a bit on the peasant side, and a good choice for an informal dinner. Please be certain to wash the leeks thoroughly and remove every trace of sand.

4 leeks, thinly sliced. Use the white bulbs and about 2 inches of the tender green leaves.
2 tablespoons butter

3 cans (10 1/2 ounces, each) chicken broth
2 packages (10 ounces, each) frozen chopped spinach
2 potatoes, peeled and cut into 1/2-inch cubes
4 slices bacon, cooked crisp, drained and crumbled
pinch of nutmeg or to taste
salt and pepper to taste

1/2 cup cream

In a saucepan, saute leeks in butter until leeks are soft. Add the next 6 ingredients and simmer soup, with cover slightly ajar, for about 30 minutes, or until potatoes are tender. Stir in the cream and heat through. Serve with Green Onion Bread with Carrots and Parsley as a lovely accompaniment. Serves 6.

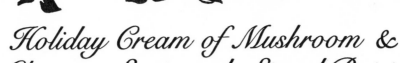

Holiday Cream of Mushroom & Chestnut Soup with Spiced Raisin & Walnut Sherry Bread

What a wonderful soup to serve for a festive holiday dinner. The flavor is superb ... rich and deep. This soup is just a bit more work, as some of it is pureed and the mushrooms are left sliced, but it is worth every bit of the extra effort.

2 onions, finely chopped
4 shallots, minced
4 cloves garlic, minced
1/2 teaspoon dried thyme flakes
1/4 teaspoon ground poultry seasoning
4 tablespoons butter

1/2 cup dry white wine
2 tablespoons flour
3 cans (10 1/2 ounces, each) chicken broth
1 can (15 1/2 ounces) chestnuts, packed in water (not in syrup) and drained

1 pound mushrooms, thinly sliced and tossed with 2 tablespoons lemon juice
2 tablespoons butter

1 cup cream
salt to taste

In a Dutch oven casserole, saute together first 6 ingredients, over low heat, until onions are soft and liquid rendered is evaporated. Add the wine and continue cooking, over medium heat, until wine is evaporated. Stir in the flour and cook for 2 minutes, stirring. Add the broth and chestnuts and simmer soup for 15 minutes. Puree soup in blender or food processor and return to Dutch oven.

Meanwhile, saute mushrooms in butter, over low heat, until mushrooms are tender and liquid rendered is evaporated. Add mushrooms to soup and simmer for 5 minutes. Add the cream, adjust seasoning, and simmer soup for another 5 minutes. Serve with a faint sprinkle of chopped chives, no more. Yields 6 generous portions.

Note: — The Spiced Raisin Bread is a great accompaniment.

— Soup can be prepared earlier in the day and heated carefully before serving.

Spiced Raisin & Walnut Sherry Bread with Raisin Cream Glaze

This is a spicy bread that is nice to serve around the winter holidays. It is a fine accompaniment to soup or salad (unglazed). If you are serving this with coffee or hot cider, the glaze is a lovely addition.

- 1/2 cup butter, softened
- 1 cup sugar
- 1 egg
- 3 tablespoons grated orange (about 1/2 medium orange)
- 1/2 cup golden cream sherry

- 2 cups flour
- 3 teaspoons baking powder
- 2 teaspoons cinnamon
- 1/4 teaspoon ground nutmeg
- 1/4 teaspoon ground cloves
- 1/2 cup chopped yellow raisins
- 1/2 cup chopped walnuts

Beat together first 5 ingredients until blended. Combine the remaining ingredients, and add, all at once, beating until blended. Divide batter between 3 greased mini-foil pans (6x3x2-inches), place pans on a cookie sheet, and bake in a 325° oven for about 45 minutes, or until a cake tester, inserted in center, comes out clean. Allow to cool in pans. When cool, drizzle tops with Raisin Cream Glaze. Yields 3 mini-loaves.

Raisin Cream Glaze:
- 4 tablespoons yellow raisins
- 3/4 cup sifted powdered sugar
- 2 tablespoons cream
- 1/4 teaspoon vanilla

In a food processor, chop raisins with powdered sugar, until raisins are very finely chopped. Place mixture in a bowl and stir in cream and vanilla until blended. Add a little cream or powdered sugar to make glaze a drizzling consistency.

Note: — To chop raisins in the food processor, you must add some of the sugar in the recipe to prevent the raisins from gumming up.

Potage of Tomatoes & Clams with Croustades of Garlic & Cheese

Soup Base:
- 1 can (1 pound) stewed tomatoes, finely chopped. Do not drain.
- 1 can (8 ounces) tomato sauce
- 1 cup tomato juice
- 1 cup clam juice
- 1 onion, finely chopped
- 2 carrots, grated
- 2 cloves garlic, minced
- 2 tablespoons oil
- 1 teaspoon sugar
- 1/2 teaspoon, each, thyme flakes, sweet basil flakes, turmeric
- 2 tablespoons chopped parsley
- salt and pepper to taste

Combine all the ingredients in a Dutch oven casserole and simmer mixture for 30 minutes, with the cover slightly ajar. Now, add and heat through.

- **2 cans (7 ounces, each) chopped clams, undrained**
- **1 cup half and half**

To serve, float 1 teaspoon of sour cream on top with a generous sprinkle of chopped chives. Serve with Croustades of Garlic & Cheese or a crusty French bread with sweet butter. Serves 6.

Note: — Soup base can be prepared one day earlier and stored in the refrigerator. To serve, heat soup, add the clams and cream and continue heating until soup is piping hot.

Croustades of Garlic & Cheese:
- 6 slices (cut 1/2-inch thick) French bread
- 4 tablespoons mayonnaise
- 6 tablespoons grated Swiss cheese
- 1 tablespoon grated Parmesan cheese
- 1 tablespoon lemon juice
- 1 clove garlic, mashed

Place bread on a cookie sheet. Stir together the remaining ingredients and spread mixture evenly on the bread slices. (Can be held at this point, covered with plastic wrap in the refrigerator.) When ready to serve, broil bread for a few seconds or until tops are lightly browned and bubbly. (Watch carefully so as not to burn the cheese.) Serves 6.

Cream of Spinach Soup with Onions & Shallots & Cheese Piroshkis

This is a glamorous soup, just filled with delicate flavor and goodness. The Cheese Piroshkis are the perfect accompaniment. Everybody loves them. This is a substantial first course, as everyone has a tendency to eat an extra piroshki or two (mostly two.)

- 2 onions, chopped
- 3 shallots, minced
- 3 cloves garlic, minced
- 3 tablespoons butter

- 3 tablespoons flour
- 2 packages (10 ounces, each) frozen chopped spinach, defrosted
- 3 cans (10 1/2 ounces, each) chicken broth
  salt and pepper to taste
- 1/4 teaspoon dried dill weed, or more to taste

- 1 cup cream

Saute onions, shallots and garlic in butter until onions are soft. (Do this over low heat as you do not want onions to brown.) Add the flour and cook and stir for 3 minutes. Add the spinach and stir to blend. Place mixture in a food processor and process until pureed. (Add a little broth to facilitate blending.)

Transfer spinach mixture to a Dutch oven casserole and add the broth and seasonings. Simmer mixture for 5 minutes. Add the cream and heat through. Serves 6 to 8.

Cheese Piroshkis: (This recipe can be doubled.)
- 8 strudel filo leaves (sometimes spelled "phyllo")
- 1/3 cup butter, melted

- 1 package (8 ounces) cream cheese
- 1 cup small-curd cottage cheese
- 1 egg, beaten
- 3/4 cup grated Parmesan cheese

Cover filo leaves with damp towel. Have melted butter ready. Beat together the remaining ingredients until blended. Place 2 filo leaves on work surface and brush top leaf with butter. Arrange 1/4 the filling along the bottom edge, leaving 1-inch on each side without filling. Roll 3 times, fold in the sides and continue rolling to end. Brush top with melted butter and sprinkle with additional grated Parmesan cheese. Place on a buttered 12x16-inch pan. Continue with remaining leaves in the same manner. Bake in a 350° oven for about 30 minutes or until tops are browned. To serve, cut into fourths and serve hot. Yields 16 piroshkis.

Farmhouse Split Pea Soup with Sesame Crispettes of Garlic & Cheese

This is another one of my favorite soups. As you probably have guessed by now, I like soups that are thick and hearty and just bursting with flavor and goodness. Consommes are lovely, and do have their place, but when the weather is storming, there is nothing like a bowl of thick soup, filled with all manner of good things.

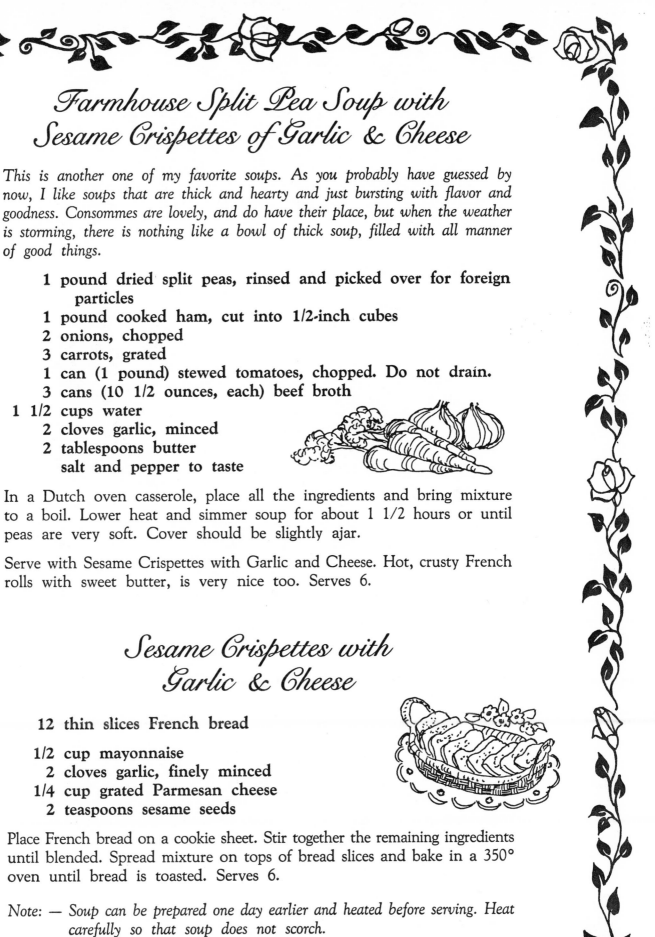

- 1 **pound dried split peas, rinsed and picked over for foreign particles**
- 1 **pound cooked ham, cut into 1/2-inch cubes**
- 2 **onions, chopped**
- 3 **carrots, grated**
- 1 **can (1 pound) stewed tomatoes, chopped. Do not drain.**
- 3 **cans (10 1/2 ounces, each) beef broth**
- 1 1/2 **cups water**
- 2 **cloves garlic, minced**
- 2 **tablespoons butter**
  salt and pepper to taste

In a Dutch oven casserole, place all the ingredients and bring mixture to a boil. Lower heat and simmer soup for about 1 1/2 hours or until peas are very soft. Cover should be slightly ajar.

Serve with Sesame Crispettes with Garlic and Cheese. Hot, crusty French rolls with sweet butter, is very nice too. Serves 6.

Sesame Crispettes with Garlic & Cheese

- 12 **thin slices French bread**

- 1/2 **cup mayonnaise**
- 2 **cloves garlic, finely minced**
- 1/4 **cup grated Parmesan cheese**
- 2 **teaspoons sesame seeds**

Place French bread on a cookie sheet. Stir together the remaining ingredients until blended. Spread mixture on tops of bread slices and bake in a 350° oven until bread is toasted. Serves 6.

Note: — Soup can be prepared one day earlier and heated before serving. Heat carefully so that soup does not scorch.

Cold Cream of Carrot Soup with Apples, Raisins & Cinnamon

On a warm night this elegant soup will brighten the most wilted palate. Carrots flavored with apples and raisins and a sprinkling of cinnamon, is a grand start for Honey Glazed Chicken or Veal.

1 pound carrots, peeled and sliced
2 apples, peeled, cored and sliced
1 onion, chopped
3 shallots, chopped
2 cloves garlic, chopped
2 cups apple juice
2 cups chicken broth
1 tablespoon honey
salt and pepper to taste

1 cup cream, half and half, or buttermilk
1/2 cup sour cream
1/3 cup chopped yellow raisins

cinnamon

In a Dutch oven casserole, place first 9 ingredients and simmer mixture for 30 to 40 minutes or until vegetables are very soft. Transfer vegetables to a processor or blender and blend until mixture is pureed.

Return vegetables to the pot with the broth. Stir together choice of cream and sour cream. Add to the soup with the yellow raisins. Heat mixture through, but do not allow to boil. Remove from heat and allow to cool. Refrigerate until cold.

To serve, spoon top with a dollup of sour cream and a sprinkling of cinnamon. Serves 6 to 8.

Note: — Soup can be prepared 1 day earlier and stored in the refrigerator.

— This delicious soup can be served hot, as well as cold. When reheating, take especial care not to allow the soup to boil or it will curdle.

— To avoid the possibility of curdling, then use cream and sour cream, mixed together and allowed to stand for several hours. This will produce a Creme Fraiche that holds together when heated.

— Enjoy.

Cold Dilled Zucchini Soup with Shallots, Garlic & Creme Fraiche

There is probably no soup you can make that is more elegant and delicious than this one. It is gloriously thick and flavorful and can be served for the most special of all occasions. However, its simplicity makes it a good choice for anytime.

- 6 medium zucchini, sliced. Do not peel
- 6 shallots, finely chopped
- 2 large onions, finely chopped
- 6 cloves garlic, thinly sliced
- 3 cans (10 1/2 ounces, each) chicken broth
  salt to taste

- 1/2 cup cream
- 1/2 cup sour cream
- 1/2 teaspoon dried dill weed

In a Dutch oven casserole, simmer together first 6 ingredients until vegetables are soft, about 40 minutes. Meanwhile, stir together cream and sour cream and allow to stand at room temperature.

When vegetables are soft, remove them with a slotted spoon to a processor or blender and blend them until they are pureed. (If necessary, add a little broth to the blender to facilitate the process.) Return the pureed vegetables to the pan and stir with the broth until blended.

Stir in the cream mixture and the dill weed until blended. Heat the soup through and then transfer it to a porcelain tureen. Refrigerate it until well chilled.

Serve it with Phyllo Roulades with Cheese and keep a sharp eye for any who may faint from ecstacy. Serves 6 to 8.

Note: — *Soup can be prepared 1 day earlier and stored in the refrigerator. Allow to stand at room temperature for about 10 minutes, stir and then serve.*

 — *This soup is just as delicious served warm. Simply heat through before serving.*

Peasant Cabbage & Tomato Soup with Croustades of Cheese & Chives

This is a nice homey soup to serve on a Sunday night when the family joins together for dinner. The Croustades are especially delicious, and a few extras would be in order.

- 2 onions, chopped
- 2 shallots, minced
- 6 cloves garlic, minced
- 2 tablespoons butter

- 1 small cabbage (about 1 pound) coarsely chopped
- 1 can (1 pound) stewed tomatoes, chopped. Do not drain.
- 3 cans (10 1/2 ounces, each) chicken broth
- 1 tablespoon lemon juice
- 1 teaspoon sugar
- 1 teaspoon sweet basil flakes
- 1/2 teaspoon oregano flakes
  salt and pepper to taste
- 1 or 2 shakes of cayenne pepper

In a Dutch oven casserole, place first 4 ingredients and saute mixture until onions are transparent. Add the remaining ingredients and simmer soup, with lid slightly ajar, for about 1 hour, or until cabbage is soft. Serve in deep bowls with Croustades of Cheese & Chives. Serves 6.

Croustades of Cheese & Chives:
- 6 slices Italian Bread
- 6 teaspoons butter
- 6 teaspoons chopped chives
- 6 tablespoons grated Provolone cheese
- 6 very light sprinkles of cayenne pepper

Spread each slice of bread with 1 teaspoon butter. Sprinkle top with chives, cheese and pepper. Broil bread for about 1 minute, or until cheese is melted. Serves 6.

Note: — Onions, shallots, garlic, cabbage, tomatoes can be chopped, in batches, in a food processor, using the steel blade.

— Soup can be made earlier in the day and heated before serving.

Cream of Honey Chestnut Soup with Spiced Pumpkin Muffins

What a nice soup to serve around the holidays, when families get together. This is an unusual soup and a nice change from the more usual pumpkin soup.

- 1 apple, peeled, cored and grated
- 1 small onion, chopped
- 2 tablespoons butter

- 1 can (1 pound) chestnuts, drained
- 2 cans (10 1/2 ounces, each) chicken broth
- 3 tablespoons honey
- 1/2 teaspoon pumpkin pie spice
  - salt to taste
- 1 pint half and half

In a Dutch oven casserole, saute together apple and onion in butter until onion is soft. Puree apple mixture and chestnuts in a food processor, using some of the broth to help you. Return mixture to Dutch oven and stir in all the ingredients. Simmer soup for 15 minutes. Adjust taste, adding a little more spice or honey. Serve with a dollup of sour cream and the faintest sprinkle of Cinnamon Brown Sugar. Memorable. Serves 6.

Cinnamon Brown Sugar: Sift together 1/2 cup brown sugar and 2 teaspoons cinnamon. Stir and sift again. Store in a jar with a tight-fitting lid.

Spiced Pumpkin Muffins:
- 1 egg, beaten
- 1/3 cup oil
- 1 cup sour cream
- 3 tablespoons grated orange (1/2 medium orange)
- 1 cup canned pumpkin puree
- 2 cups flour
- 1 tablespoon baking powder
- 2 teaspoons pumpkin pie spice
- 2/3 cup sugar

Beat together all the ingredients until blended. Do not overbeat. Divide batter between 12 paper-lined muffin cups and bake in a 400° oven for 20 minutes. Yields 12 muffins.

Soups & Garnitures

Country Cabbage Soup with Black Pumpernickel & Raisin Butter

Not quite a soup and not quite a stew, this thick meaty potage is practically a meal unto itself. It is very hearty and satisfying and just right for sipping by the fire.

- 2 pounds lean flanken ribs or boneless chuck, cut into 1/2-inch cubes
- 3 cloves garlic, minced
- 2 onions, finely chopped
- 3 carrots, grated
- 1 can (1 pound) stewed tomatoes, chopped
- 1 cup sauerkraut, with juice
- 1 head cabbage (about 1 1/2 pounds), shredded or coarsely chopped
- 3 tablespoons sugar
- 3 tablespoons lemon juice
- 3 cans (10 1/2 ounces, each) beef broth
- salt and pepper to taste

In a Dutch oven casserole, combine all the ingredients and bring mixture to boil. Lower heat and simmer mixture, with cover slightly ajar, for about 2 hours, or until meat is tender. Remove any trace of fat.

Serve with a dollup of sour cream and some black crusty bread with sweet butter and raisins. Serves 6 to 8, depending on size portions being served.

Raisin Butter with Honey:
- 1/2 cup butter (1 stick)
- 3 tablespoons honey
- 2 tablespoons chopped raisins

Beat together all the ingredients until blended. Place in a pretty bowl or crock and spread on slices of black pumpernickel. Black pumpernickel with raisins is also very nice.

Note: — Soup can be prepared one day before serving and stored in the refrigerator. Skimming off the fat will be easier done when soup is cold. Soup gets even better the next day.

Salads
&
Dressings

Salads & Dressings

Linguini Verde with Brie, Tomatoes & Basil Dressing 109
Molded Spinach Salad with Lemon Creme Fraiche 110
Pasta Primavera with Basil Vinaigrette with Garlic 111
Fresh Vegetable Platter with Imperial Sauce Verte 112
Herbed Tomato & Onion Salad with Garlic Lemon Dressing 112
Red Peppers Vinaigrette with Mushrooms, Onions & Cheese 113
Green Bean Salad with Yogurt & Lemon Honey Dressing 114
3-Bean Salad with Red Wine & Garlic Vinaigrette 114
Tomato & Green Bean Salad with Pesto Cream Sauce 115
Pineapple Chicken Salad with Cashews & Pineapple Honey Dressing 116
Sesame Popovers with Garlic & Herbs 116
French Potato Salad with Mustard Vinaigrette 117
Potato Salad with Horseradish Dressing 117
Tabouleh-Bulgur Salad with Tomatoes & Lemon Vinaigrette 118
Rice Salad Mold with Tomatoes & Red Wine Vinaigrette 118
Mushroom, Onion & Red Pepper Salad with Lemon Dressing 119
Pasta Salad al Pesto 119
Green Bean Salad with Mustard Vinaigrette 120
Cinnamon Carrot Salad with Raisins & Apples & Walnuts 120
Greek Salad with Lemon Dill Vinaigrette 121
Dilled Tomato Mayonnaise for Fish & Shellfish 122
Garlic & Red Pepper Mayonnaise with Lemon & Herbs 122
Pesto Mayonnaise for Pasta Salads or Potato Salads 123
Green Bean, Mushroom & Onion Salad with Dilled Dressing 124
Mixed Green Salad with Italian Herb Dressing 125
Mushroom, Cucumber Salad with Garlic Anchovy Dressing 125
Green Bean & Onion Salad with Lemon Creme Fraiche 126

Linguini Verde with Brie, Tomatoes & Basil Dressing

Pasta salads are so popular nowadays. Pasta shops are springing up all over and the combinations are exciting and creative. It is a far cry from the macaroni salads I had as a child. This is an exceptionally attractive salad, bright red and green.

1 pound semi-ripe brie. Remove rind and cut into small pieces while brie is chilled.

4 tomatoes, peeled, seeded and chopped

3 cloves garlic, minced

1/4 cup chopped green onions

1/2 cup oil (can use part olive oil)

1/4 cup red wine vinegar

2 teaspoons dried sweet basil flakes

1/2 cup grated Parmesan cheese
salt and freshly ground pepper to taste

1 pound linguini verde, broken into 2-inch pieces, cooked firm but tender and drained

In a large bowl, place first 9 ingredients and toss to blend. Cook linguini in a spaghetti cooker and plunge basket in cold water until linguini is chilled. Drain thoroughly.

Toss linguini in bowl with brie mixture until nicely mixed. Refrigerate until serving time. Serves 6.

Note: — *Can be prepared 4 to 6 hours before serving and stored in the refrigerator.*

— *Linguini should be broken into small pieces so that tomato and brie can better combine.*

— *Ziti or rotini or similar pasta can be substituted.*

Salads & Dressings

Molded Spinach Salad with Lemon Creme Fraiche Sauce

This is simply lovely as an hors d'oeuvre or salad course. It definitely is not pedestrian or commonplace. But it is delicate and delicious, and it presents beautifully.

        2 packages unflavored gelatin
    1/3 cup water

        4 green onions, (use the green parts also)
    1/4 cup chopped parsley
  1 1/2 cups sour cream
        1 cup mayonnaise
        4 tablespoons lemon juice (or more to taste)

        2 packages (10 ounces, each) frozen chopped spinach,
            defrosted and drained

In a metal cup, soften gelatin in water. Place in a pan of simmering water and stir until gelatin is liquefied. Set aside.

In a food processor or blender, place onions, parsley, sour cream, mayonnaise and lemon juice and blend until mixture is smooth. Stir in the spinach and gelatin until blended. Place mixture into a 4-cup ring mold and refrigerate until firm.

To serve, unmold on a lovely platter, and decorate with cucumber, zucchini, carrots, all decoratively sliced. Mask the top with a drizzle of Lemon Creme Fraiche. This can also be served with a pale, bland soda cracker. Delicious!

Lemon Creme Fraiche:
    1/3 cup cream
    1/3 cup sour cream
      2 tablespoons lemon juice
      2 tablespoons chopped chives

Stir together all the ingredients until blended. Allow mixture to stand at room temperature for several hours, until thickened. Refrigerate until serving time.

Note: — *Entire dish can be prepared 1 day earlier and stored in the refrigerator until serving time.*

— *For a formal party, I would recommend substituting chopped chives (1/3 cup) for the green onions, to produce a more delicate flavor.*

Pasta Primavera with Basil Vinaigrette with Garlic

3/4 pound spiral pasta, cooked tender but firm (al dente)
1 bag (1 pound) Del Sol vegetables, defrosted. (Del Sol is a combination of broccoli, cauliflower and carrots. Many food companies make this combination.) Cook the vegetables according to the directions on the package until tender.

In a large bowl, toss together pasta and vegetables until nicely mixed. Now, pour Basil Vinaigrette with Garlic over all and toss until pasta and vegetables are evenly coated. Refrigerate for several hours. Overnight is good, too.

To serve, decorate top with an additional sprinkling of grated cheese and minced green onion. Serves 6 as a small entree.

Basil Vinaigrette with Garlic:
    1/4 cup grated Parmesan cheese
    1/2 cup oil (use part olive oil)
    1/4 cup red wine vinegar
    2 tablespoons lemon juice
    1 tablespoon Dijon mustard
    1 shallot, minced
    2 cloves garlic, minced
    2 green onions, minced
    1 teaspoon sweet basil flakes
    salt and pepper to taste

Place all the ingredients in a jar with a tight fitting lid and shake until blended. Refrigerate for several hours. Yields about 1 cup dressing.

Note: — *Pasta is bland and absorbs dressing like a sponge. Dressing may need a bit more vinegar. Taste after tossing.*

    — *Dressing can be prepared 1 day earlier and stored in the refrigerator. But, please know that the shallots intensify in flavor if allowed to sit in the dressing for too long.*

Salads & Dressings

Fresh Vegetable Platter with Imperial Dilled Sauce Verte

Arrange a large platter of sliced carrots, celery, cucumbers, zucchini, mushrooms, cherry tomatoes, jicama, etc. in any combination you desire. Slice the vegetables straight, on the diagonal, into circles, sticks, curls, etc. Dip the ends of butter lettuce leaves in paprika for a pretty effect. Arrange vegetables on a lush bed of butter lettuce (or other soft lettuce). Place the Sauce Verte in the center and enjoy.

Imperial Dilled Sauce Verte:
- 3/4 cup mayonnaise
- 3/4 cup sour cream
- 2 small green onions (use the green tops and white bulbs)
- 4 sprigs parsley (remove stems and use only the leaves)
- 2 tablespoons lemon juice
- 1/2 teaspoon dried dill weed
  - salt to taste

- 1/2 cup frozen chopped spinach, defrosted and drained

Place first 7 ingredients in container of food processor and blend at high speed until vegetables are pureed. Place mixture into a bowl and stir in the spinach. Cover bowl and refrigerate until ready to use. Yields 2 cups sauce.

Herbed Tomato & Onion Salad with Garlic Lemon Dressing

- 6 medium tomatoes, peeled, seeded and thinly sliced
- 1 medium onion, sliced into the thinnest rings

- 4 tablespoons olive oil
- 4 tablespoons lemon juice
- 4 tablespoons grated Parmesan cheese
- 1 clove garlic, minced
- 1 tablespoon chopped parsley
- 1 teaspoon sweet basil flakes
  - salt and pepper to taste

Place tomatoes and onion in a bowl. In a jar, with a tight-fitting lid, place the remaining ingredients and shake to blend. Pour dressing over the tomatoes and onion and toss to coat well. Cover and refrigerate for several hours to allow flavors to blend. Serves 6.

Red Peppers Vinaigrette with Mushrooms, Onions & Cheese

This salad is colorful and decorative, and by the way, very delicious. It should be prepared in advance and is a grand addition to an antipasto.

    6 red peppers. Remove seeds and stems and cut into 1-inch slices.
    2 cloves garlic, minced
1/4 cup oil

1/2 pound button mushrooms, cleaned and stemmed
    1 cup (about 4 ounces) frozen small white onions, blanched in boiling water until tender
    1 cup diced Mozzarella cheese (about 4 ounces)

Vinaigrette:
1/2 cup oil (can use part olive oil)
1/4 cup red wine vinegar
1/4 cup minced chives
1/2 teaspoon Dijon mustard
1/2 teaspoon sweet basil flakes
      salt and pepper to taste

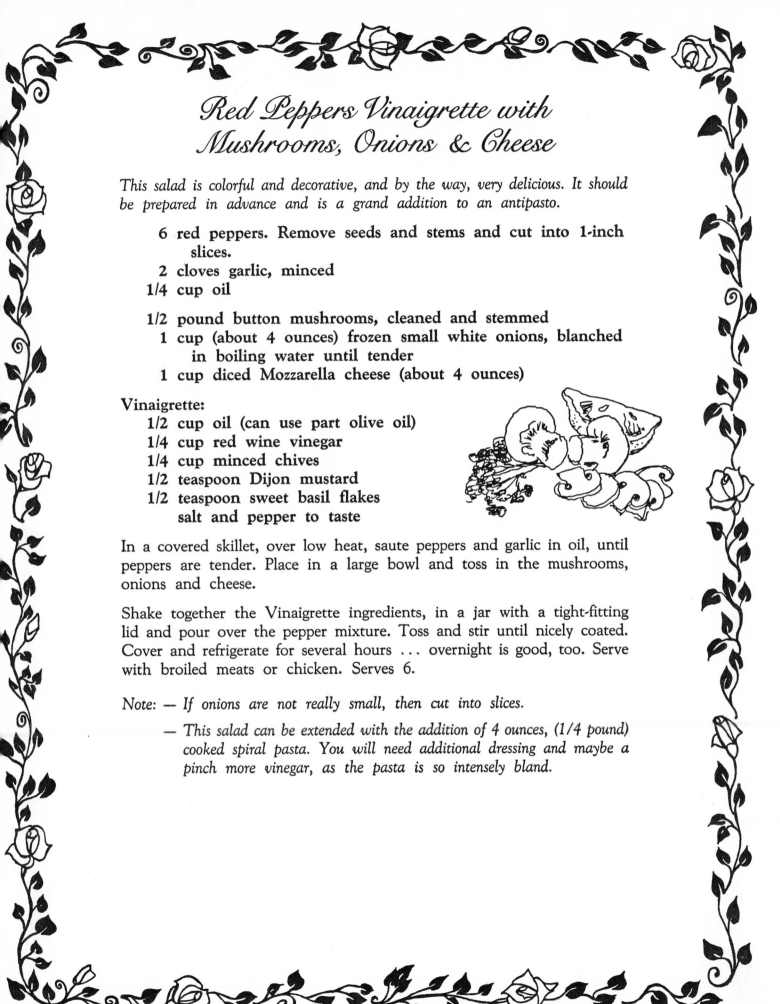

In a covered skillet, over low heat, saute peppers and garlic in oil, until peppers are tender. Place in a large bowl and toss in the mushrooms, onions and cheese.

Shake together the Vinaigrette ingredients, in a jar with a tight-fitting lid and pour over the pepper mixture. Toss and stir until nicely coated. Cover and refrigerate for several hours ... overnight is good, too. Serve with broiled meats or chicken. Serves 6.

Note: — If onions are not really small, then cut into slices.

    — This salad can be extended with the addition of 4 ounces, (1/4 pound) cooked spiral pasta. You will need additional dressing and maybe a pinch more vinegar, as the pasta is so intensely bland.

Green Bean Salad with
Yogurt & Lemon Honey Dressing

2 cans (1 pound, each) whole green beans, drained

1 cup plain unflavored yogurt
1 tablespoon lemon juice
1 tablespoon honey
3 tablespoons chopped chives
1 tablespoon minced parsley
   salt to taste

On a flat, rectangular plate, lay green beans out, in one direction. Stir together the remaining ingredients until blended and pour over the green beans. Cover pan and refrigerate for several hours before serving. Baste now and again while marinating in the refrigerator. Serves 6.

3-Bean Salad with
Red Wine & Garlic Vinaigrette

1 can (1 pound) red kidney beans, rinsed and drained
1 can (1 pound) cut green beans, drained
1 can (1 pound) cici peas (garbanzos), rinsed and drained
3/4 cup chopped green onions
2 cloves garlic, minced
2 tablespoons minced parsley
1 jar (2 ounces) pimiento strips
1/4 cup red wine vinegar
1/2 cup oil
1/2 teaspoon sugar
   salt and pepper to taste

In a large bowl, toss together all the ingredients until thoroughly mixed. Cover and refrigerate for several hours before serving. Serves 8.

Tomato & Green Bean Salad with Pesto Cream Sauce

This is a rather unusual salad, that is beautiful to serve for a spring buffet ... very different and very "in", with a pesto spirit, all its own.

6 large tomatoes, peeled and sliced
1 package (1 pound) whole green beans, defrosted, and
    blanched in boiling water for 6 minutes and drained.
1 medium red onion, cut into very thin rings

1/2 cup cream
1/2 cup sour cream
2 tablespoons chopped parsley
1 tablespoon Dijon mustard
2 tablespoons lemon juice
1 teaspoon sweet basil flakes
    salt and pepper to taste

In a 9x13-inch porcelain baker, layer tomatoes, green beans and onion rings.

Stir together the remaining ingredients until blended. Allow to stand at room temperature for 30 minutes and then drizzle over the salad. Refrigerate for several hours.

When ready to serve, set tomatoes in a circle on a large platter, arrange green beans in a spoke fashion (like a bicycle wheel), and place onion rings decoratively on top. Spoon sauce over the vegetables and serve with pride. Serves 10.

Note: — *This is a variation of the Creme Fraiche with added depth and character. It does not have to be cultured for the usual 4 hours, because the lemon juice hastens the thickening.*

    — *Make certain that the tomatoes and green beans are well drained so that the sauce does not overly dilute.*

    — *If serving this salad in individual portions, serve it on a bed of lettuce.*

    — *1/2 teaspoon dill weed can be substituted for the basil flakes for a totally different character.*

Salads & Dressings

Pineapple Chicken Salad with Cashews & Pineapple Honey Dressing

    4 cups cooked chicken, cut into cubes
    1 head iceberg lettuce, shredded, about 6 cups
    1/2 cup chopped green onions, including green tops
    1 cup cashew nuts, toasted
    1 can (8 ounces) crushed pineapple, drained. Reserve juice.
    2 tablespoons chopped parsley

Pineapple Honey Dressing:
    1/4 cup pineapple juice (reserved from above)
    2 tablespoons honey
    2 tablespoons lemon juice
    1/4 cup oil
    2 tablespoons sesame oil
    1/4 cup rice vinegar
    1 teaspoon Dijon mustard

In a large bowl, toss together first 6 ingredients. In a glass jar, with a tight-fitting lid, shake together dressing ingredients. Pour dressing over chicken mixture and toss until blended. Place salad on a large platter and decorate with pineapple slices sprinkled with chopped cashews. Serves 6.

Note: — *1/2 cup yellow raisins, is a nice optional.*

— *Dressing can be prepared 1 day earlier and stored in the refrigerator. (Drained pineapple should be stored in refrigerator, also.)*

— *Sesame Popovers with Garlic & Herbs is a nice accompaniment.*

Sesame Popovers with Garlic & Herbs

    4 eggs
    1 cup flour
    1/4 teaspoon salt
    1 cup milk
    2 tablespoons toasted sesame seeds
    2 tablespoons chopped chives
    1/4 teaspoon garlic powder

Beat together all the ingredients until blended. Heavily butter 12 muffin molds. (Use the regular size muffin pan.) Divide mixture evenly into each mold and bake in a 400° oven for 30 to 35 minutes or until popovers are puffed and golden brown. Serve immediately. Yields 12.

French Potato Salad with Mustard Vinaigrette

When you are looking for a change from the traditional potato salad, this is a good one to consider. It is a nice accompaniment to meat loaf. While traditionally served cold, this is very delicious served warm (not hot.)

2 pounds potatoes, scrubbed and cooked in boiling water until tender. Chill immediately under cold water, peel and slice. Toss potatoes with 1 teaspoon sugar and 1 tablespoon wine vinegar.

1/4 cup chopped chives
1/2 cup oil
1/4 cup red wine vinegar
2 tablespoons chopped parsley
2 teaspoons Dijon mustard
1/2 teaspoon thyme flakes
1 clove garlic, minced
salt and pepper to taste

In a large bowl, place potatoes. In a jar, with a tight-fitting lid, shake together the remaining ingredients until blended. Pour dressing over the potatoes and toss and turn until nicely blended. Cover and store in the refrigerator for several hours, turning now and again. Overnight is good, too. Serves 6.

Potato Salad with Horseradish Dressing

2 pounds potatoes, boiled, peeled and sliced
1 carrot, grated
1 tablespoon sugar
1 tablespoon vinegar
salt and pepper to taste

1 cup mayonnaise
4 tablespoons lemon juice
1/4 cup chopped chives or green onions
2 tablespoons chopped parsley
2 tablespoons prepared horseradish

In a bowl, toss together first 5 ingredients until nicely mixed. Stir together the next 5 ingredients and add to the potatoes, tossing and turning until blended. Cover and refrigerate, for several hours or overnight. Serve with cold ham, corned beef, and the like. Serves 6.

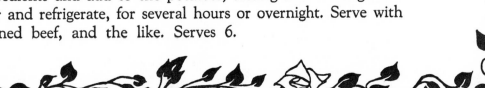

Salads & Dressings

Tabouleh – Bulgur Salad with Tomatoes, Onions & Lemon Vinaigrette

1 cup Bulgur, cracked wheat
2 cups water

1 cup chopped green onions (use the whole onion)
1 tomato, peeled, seeded and chopped
3 tablespoons chopped parsley
salt and pepper to taste

1/4 cup olive oil
1/4 cup lemon juice
1 clove garlic, minced

In a saucepan, bring water to boil and slowly add the bulgur, while water continues boiling. Stir, lower heat and cover saucepan, and cook bulgur at a simmer, until liquid is absorbed, about 10 to 15 minutes. Continue cooking bulgur, stirring, for several minutes, so that grains become dry and fluff up.

Place bulgur into a deep bowl and allow to cool. Toss with the onions, tomato, parsley and seasonings. Shake together oil, lemon juice and garlic and pour dressing over salad. Serve on a bed of lettuce or in small bowls. Serves 6.

Rice Salad Mold with Tomatoes, Carrots & Red Wine Vinaigrette

2 cups cooked white rice (long-grain is better for this dish)
1 can (16 ounces) julienned carrots, drained
1 jar (2 ounces) pimiento strips
1/2 cup finely chopped green onions (use the whole onion)
1 tomato, cut into very fine dice
2 tablespoons chopped parsley
6 tablespoons oil
3 tablespoons red wine vinegar
1 clove garlic, minced
1/2 teaspoon Dijon mustard
salt and pepper to taste

Combine first 6 ingredients in a bowl and toss to mix thoroughly. Stir together the remaining ingredients, until blended. Pour this over the rice and stir until well mixed. Refrigerate for several hours. Before serving, press into a ring mold and invert on serving platter.

Mushroom, Onion & Red Pepper Salad with Lemon Dressing

1 jar (1 pound) roasted sweet red peppers, drained and cut into strips

1 pound button mushrooms, stemmed and caps left whole. Reserve stems for another use.

1/2 pound frozen baby pearl onions, blanched in boiling water for 3 minutes and drained

1/2 cup lemon juice, freshly squeezed

1 cup oil (can use 1/2 olive oil)

1 teaspoon sugar

1/3 cup chopped green onions

1/4 teaspoon garlic powder

1/2 teaspoon each sweet basil flakes and oregano flakes salt and pepper to taste

12 pitted black olives, optional

6 anchovies, optional

In a bowl, toss together peppers, mushrooms and onions. In a glass jar, shake together next 8 ingredients until blended. Pour dressing to taste, over the vegetables. Serve with black olives and anchovies on top. Serves 6.

Pasta Salad al Pesto

1 pound medium-sized pasta, such as penne, ziti or rotini. Cook in a spaghetti cooker until firm but tender and drain. Plunge into cold water until chilled.

1/2 cup sour cream

1/2 cup cream

2 teaspoons dried sweet basil flakes

1/2 cup grated Parmesan cheese

2 cloves garlic, minced

4 tablespoons pine nuts

Place cooked pasta in a large bowl. Combine the remaining ingredients in a food processor and blend until pine nuts are pureed. Pour dressing over cooked pasta and toss to blend. Refrigerate until serving time. Can be prepared earlier in the day and stored in the refrigerator.

Green Bean Salad with Mustard Vinaigrette

1 package (1 pound) frozen whole green beans. Cook in boiling water until firm but tender, about 5 minutes.

1/2 cup oil (can use half olive oil)
3 tablespoons wine vinegar
2 cloves garlic, minced
2 shallots, minced
1/2 teaspoon sweet basil flakes
1/2 teaspoon oregano flakes
1 tablespoon Dijon mustard
1 tablespoon chopped parsley
salt and pepper to taste

Lay green beans in a shallow porcelain server. Combine the remaining ingredients in a jar with a tight-fitting lid and shake until thoroughly blended. Pour dressing to taste over the green beans. Cover and refrigerate overnight. Unused dressing can be stored in the refrigerator. Yields about 3/4 cup dressing.

Cinnamon Carrot Salad with Raisins & Apples & Walnuts

1 pound carrots, scraped clean and grated
3/4 cup yellow raisins
1 apple, cut into small cubes, and dipped into lemon or orange juice to prevent darkening
1/2 cup chopped walnuts

1/2 cup mayonnaise
1/2 cup sour cream
1 tablespoon brown sugar, heaping
1/4 teaspoon cinnamon

In a large bowl, toss together first 4 ingredients. Combine the next 4 ingredients and stir to blend. Pour mayonnaise mixture to taste on the fruits and carrots and toss to blend. Unused dressing can be stored in the refrigerator. Serves 6.

Note: — Now, don't wrinkle you nose for the above salad. It is very unusual, but delicious.

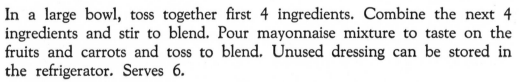

Greek Salad with Lemon Dill Vinaigrette

A Greek salad can be made in any number of ways, but they seem to always include lettuce, tomatoes and cucumbers. The addition of olives and feta cheese makes it a little more festive. And while the anchovies are optional, in this salad, they add depth.

    1 medium head lettuce, cut up, about 4 cups
    4 medium tomatoes, thinly sliced
    1 large cucumber, peeled and cut into thin slices. (If you
        have a few seconds, run a fork down the peeled
        cucumber, and then, when it is sliced, it will look
        faintly scalloped.)
1/4 cup pitted olive slices
    4 ounces feta cheese, crumbled
    3 green onions, finely chopped
    2 tablespoons chopped parsley
      salt and freshly ground pepper to taste
    2 anchovies, mashed (optional)

Toss together all the ingredients in a large bowl and refrigerate. Just before serving pour Lemon Dill Vinaigrette over the salad and toss until evenly coated. Serves 6.

Lemon Dill Vinaigrette:
1/4 cup lemon juice
    1 tablespoon wine vinegar
    1 tablespoon water
3/4 cup oil
1/2 teaspoon dill weed
    1 clove garlic, minced or put through a press
    2 tablespoons grated Parmesan cheese
    1 tablespoon minced parsley
      salt and pepper to taste

Place all the ingredients in a jar with a tight-fitting lid and shake vigorously. Refrigerate dressing until serving time. Yields about 1 cup dressing.

*Note: — Salad can be cut up earlier in the day. Dressing can be prepared
        1 day earlier and stored in the refrigerator.*

Salads & Dressings

Dilled Tomato Mayonnaise
for Fish & Shellfish

1/2 cup mayonnaise
1/2 cup sour cream
  1 tomato, peeled, seeded and chopped
  3 tablespoons lemon juice

1/4 cup chopped chives
  2 tablespoons minced parsley
1/4 teaspoon dill weed
    salt and pepper to taste

In a food processor, blend together first 4 ingredients until tomato is pureed. Stir in the remaining ingredients until blended. Place mayonnaise into a glass bowl, cover and refrigerate until serving time. Serve as an accompaniment to fish or shellfish. Yields 1 1/2 cups sauce.

Garlic & Red Pepper Mayonnaise
with Lemon & Herbs

  1 jar (4 ounces) pimientos, drained
  2 cloves garlic, chopped
  3 tablespoons lemon juice
3/4 cup mayonnaise
1/3 cup sour cream
1/2 teaspoon oregano flakes
    pinch of cayenne pepper

In a food processor, blend together all the ingredients until pimientos are pureed. Place mayonnaise in a glass bowl, cover and refrigerate until serving time. Serve as an accompaniment to fish or shellfish. Yields 1 1/2 cups sauce.

Note: — Both of these sauces can be prepared 1 or 2 days earlier and stored in the refrigerator.

Pesto Mayonnaise for Pasta Salads or Potato Salads

A delicious pesto is one of my favorite sauces for pasta. So, I thought it would be so nice to make a pesto mayonnaise for the cold pasta salads that are so popular today. The mayonnaise can be prepared in a blender or food processor, and the only point to be careful with, is the slow dribble of the oil. Adding the oil too rapidly will result in the separation of the mayonnaise.

> **3** egg yolks
> **1** tablespoon minced shallots
> **1** tablespoon Dijon mustard
> **2** teaspoons dried sweet basil flakes (or **2** tablespoons fresh basil)
> **6** tablespoons lemon juice
> pinch of salt

1 1/2 cups oil (can use part olive oil)

In a blender or food processor, blend together the first 6 ingredients for 10 seconds. Now, start dribbling in the oil, a few drops at a time, (make certain that the oil is incorporating), while the blender keeps running. When the oil is incorporated, mayonnaise is ready. It can be stored in the refrigerator for several days. Yields about 2 cups mayonnaise.

Note: — *Toss mayonnaise over cooked rotelle (spiral shaped pasta), or wide fettuccine. Broccoli, carrots, cauliflower can be cooked, chopped and added to the salad.*

— *Pesto Mayonnaise is lovely tossed into a salad made with cooked potatoes, sliced red onion rings and a good sprinkling of parsley.*

— *Grated Parmesan cheese can be sprinkled and tossed in these salads. However, 1 or 2 tablespoons is adequate. You do not want to overpower the delicate flavor of the basil and lemon.*

— *And finally, 1/4 clove of garlic may be added to the mayonnaise.*

— *Do not store for more than 2 or 3 days, as the flavors will intensify.*

Salads & Dressings

Green Bean, Mushroom & Onion Salad
with Dilled Dressing

1 package (1 pound) frozen whole green beans, cooked in boiling water for 5 minutes or until tender but firm, and drained.
1/2 pound mushrooms, cleaned and sliced
1 medium red onion, thinly sliced

Dilled Dressing:
1/3 cup oil
4 tablespoons red wine vinegar
2 medium green onions (with the green tops), cut into 4 pieces
2 tablespoons chopped parsley
1/2 teaspoon dried dill weed
1 teaspoon Dijon mustard
1 teaspoon honey
salt and pepper to taste

In a shallow porcelain or glass dish, layer green beans, mushrooms and onion slices. In a blender or food processor blend the dressing ingredients until green onions are pureed. Pour dressing over the vegetables and refrigerate for 4 hours. Overnight is good, too.

Serve on a bed of finely chopped lettuce and decorate with thinly sliced cherry tomatoes. Serves 6.

Mixed Green Salad
with Italian Herb Dressing

Compose this salad with a pretty collage of mixed greens, and lots of chives cut into 1-inch strips.

- 1/2 cup oil
- 1/4 cup olive oil
- 1/4 cup red wine vinegar
- 1 shallot, minced
- 1 teaspoon, each, dried oregano and sweet basil flakes
- 1/4 teaspoon thyme flakes
- 2 cloves garlic, put through a press
  salt and freshly ground pepper to taste
- 1/2 teaspoon honey (optional, if the dressing needs a little sweetening)

Combine all the ingredients in a glass jar with a tight-fitting lid and shake vigorously until blended. Refrigerate until ready to use, up to 1 week. (Flavors will intensify after a few days.) Yields about 1 cup dressing.

Mushroom, Cucumber Salad
with Garlic Anchovy Dressing

Try this delicious dressing over a salad composed of mushrooms, cucumbers, very thinly-sliced onion rings, radishes and mixed greens.

- 1/2 cup oil
- 1/4 cup olive oil
- 1/4 cup lemon juice
- 2 anchovy fillets, mashed
- 2 tablespoons chopped chives
- 2 cloves garlic, put through a press
- 1/2 teaspoon Dijon mustard
- 2 tablespoons grated Parmesan cheese
  salt and pepper to taste

Combine all the ingredients in a glass jar with a tight-fitting lid and shake vigorously until blended. Refrigerate until ready to use, up to 1 week. (Flavors will intensify after a few days.) Yields about 1 cup dressing.

Salads & Dressings

Green Bean & Onion Salad with Lemon Creme Fraiche

1 package (1 pound) frozen whole green beans, cooked in boiling water for 5 minutes or until tender but firm, and drained. (Or 1 pound fresh green beans, ends snapped off, and cooked in boiling water for about 7 minutes or until tender, and drained.)

1 medium onion, thinly sliced into rings

Lemon Creme Fraiche:

1/2 cup cream
1/2 cup sour cream
4 tablespoons chopped chives
4 tablespoons lemon juice
2 tablespoons chopped parsley
salt and pepper to taste

In a shallow porcelain or glass dish, layer green beans and onion slices. Stir together the remaining ingredients and spoon over the vegetables, tossing to coat evenly. Refrigerate for 4 hours. Overnight is good, too. Arrange attractively on serving platter and decorate with cherry tomatoes. Serves 4 to 6.

Fish
&
Shellfish

Fish & Shellfish

Baked Spanish Mackerel with Tomato, Currants & Pine Nuts 129
Herbed Orzo with Tomatoes & Onions 129
Mousse of Fillet of Sole with Dilled Spinach & Chive Sauce 130
Fillets of Sole in Herbed Lemon Artichoke Sauce 131
Noodles with Butter & Chives 131
Green Peas with Pearl Onions 131
Fillets of Sole Provencale with Tomatoes, Onions & Cheese 132
Baked Halibut with Artichokes, Tomatoes & Green Onions 132
Baked Fillets of Sole with Caper Anchovy Sauce 133
Mushroom Stuffed Fillets of Sole with Sorrel Sauce 134
Baked Fillets of Sole Persillade with Tomatoes & Cheese 135
Fillets of Sole with Leeks & Lemon Cream Sauce 136
New Orleans Style Hot & Spicy Shrimp 137
Lobster Italienne with Red Pepper & Basil 138
Red Hot Garlic Shrimp with Lemon & Herbs 139
The Best Scampi with Shallots, Garlic & Lemon Sauce 140
Shrimp in Royal Honey Dill Dressing 141
Scallops in Creamy Wine & Cheese Sauce 142
Cioppino—Italian Fisherman's Chowder 143
Easiest & Best American Fish Chowder 144

Baked Spanish Mackerel with Tomato, Currants & Pine Nuts

Black Currants, pine nuts, lemon...all add a marvelous dimension to this dish. Sauce can be prepared 1 day earlier and stored in the refrigerator. Fish can be boned, but ask the butcher to leave the skin on. In this case, bake with skin side down and reduce baking time by 7 or 8 minutes.

    2 onions, finely chopped
    3 cloves garlic, minced
    2 tablespoons butter

    1 can (1 pound) stewed tomatoes, drained and chopped
 1/2 teaspoon sugar
    4 tablespoons dried black currants
    2 tablespoons lemon juice
      salt and pepper to taste

    2 pounds mackerel, cut into 6 slices
 1/4 cup toasted pine nuts

In a saucepan, saute together first 3 ingredients until onions are soft. Stir in the next 5 ingredients and simmer sauce for 10 minutes, uncovered. Place fish into a 9x13-inch baking pan and spoon sauce on top. Bake in a 325° oven for about 45 minutes, or until fish flakes easily with a fork. Sprinkle top with pine nuts before serving. Serve with Herbed Orzo with Tomatoes & Onions. Serves 6.

Herbed Orzo with Tomatoes & Onions

      1 onion, finely chopped
      2 tablespoons oil
 1 1/4 cups orzo (rice-shaped pasta)

      2 cans (10 1/2 ounces, each) chicken broth
      1 tomato, peeled, seeded and chopped
      2 tablespoons tomato sauce
      2 tablespoons dried chopped chives
      2 tablespoons dried parsley flakes
   1/2 teaspoon dried oregano flakes
        salt and pepper to taste

In a Dutch oven casserole, saute onion in butter until onion is soft. Add orzo and saute until orzo is just beginning to color. Stir in the remaining ingredients carefully (liquid will splatter a little), cover pan and simmer orzo until liquid is absorbed and orzo is tender, about 40 minutes. Serves 6 to 8.

Fish & Shellfish

Mousse of Fillet of Sole
with Dilled Spinach & Chive Sauce

If you are preparing for an elegant luncheon, you would do well to consider this simple and very delicious mousse. It also serves well as an hors d'oeuvre or small entree.

1 pound fillets of sole. Sprinkle with salt, white pepper and garlic powder.
1/4 cup dry white wine
1/4 teaspoon dried dill weed

1 tablespoon unflavored gelatin (1 packet)
1/4 cup water

1 cup cream
1 cup sour cream
1/4 cup chopped chives
1/2 teaspoon dried dill weed
4 tablespoons lemon juice

In a large skillet or Dutch oven casserole, evenly place the fillets. Sprinkle with the wine and dill weed. Simmer mixture until fish becomes opaque and flakes easily, about 5 minutes. Do not overcook. Place fish (and any juices) in the bowl of a food processor and blend for about 5 seconds, or until fish is very finely chopped.

In a 1-cup metal measuring cup, soften gelatin in water. Place cup in a pan with simmering water until gelatin is liquefied.

In a large bowl, stir together the remaining ingredients until blended. Stir in the finely chopped fish until blended. Stir in the gelatin until blended. Place mousse in a 4-cup fish mold and refrigerate until firm, about 4 hours. Unmold onto a lovely platter and serve with Spinach & Chive Sauce on the side. Serves 6 to 8.

Spinach & Chive Sauce: Stir together until blended, 1/2 cup sour cream; 1/2 cup mayonnaise; 4 tablespoons chopped chives; 2 tablespoons lemon juice; 1/4 teaspoon dill weed and 1/2 cup chopped frozen spinach (defrosted and well drained) until blended.

Note: — Mousse and sauce can be prepared 1 day earlier and stored in the refrigerator.
— Decorate fish mold with a sliced black olive for the eye and a strip of pimiento for the mouth. (Shape it into a smile.) Garnish platter with a rim of parsley, cherry tomatoes and slices of lemon, decoratively scored and sprinkled with dill weed.

Fillets of Sole
in Herbed Lemon Artichoke Sauce

This simple little dish is a poem of flavors... tangy and delicious. The sauce and fish can be prepared in minutes, making this is a good choice for a night when you are running late.

1 pound fillets of sole. Sprinkle with pepper, garlic powder
    and a pinch of paprika.
2 tablespoons melted butter

1 jar (8 ounces) marinated artichoke hearts, drained
    and chopped
2 shallots, minced
2 tablespoons minced green onions
1 clove garlic, minced
2 tablespoons minced parsley
1 tablespoon lemon juice
1 teaspoon sweet basil flakes
1/2 cup cream
    salt and white pepper to taste

Place fish in one layer in a 9x13-inch pan and drizzle melted butter on top. Bake in a 350° oven for about 10 to 15 minutes, or until fish becomes opaque and flakes easily with a fork. Do not overcook.

Meanwhile, combine the remaining ingredients in a saucepan and simmer mixture for 10 minutes or until sauce is slightly thickened. Place fish on a serving platter and spoon sauce over all. Green Peas with Pearl Onions and Noodles with Butter and Chives are nice accompaniments. Serves 4.

Note: — *Sauce can be prepared earlier in the day and heated at serving time. Bake fish just before serving.*

  — *To make Green Peas with Pearl Onions: Cook together 1 package (10 ounces) frozen peas; 1/2 cup frozen pearl onions, skins removed; 1/2 cup chicken broth; salt and pepper to taste, until vegetables are tender.*

  — *To make Noodles with Butter and Chives: Toss together 8 ounces medium noodles, cooked tender and drained; 4 tablespoons melted butter; 4 tablespoons grated Parmesan cheese; 4 tablespoons chopped chives; salt and pepper to taste.*

Fish & Shellfish

Fillets of Sole Provencale
with Tomatoes, Onions & Cheese

This little dish is amazingly low in calories and quite satisfying, considering its diet qualities. Flavor the fillets generously with pepper, garlic powder and paprika to increase the taste.

- 2 pounds fillets of sole. Sprinkle generously with pepper, garlic powder and paprika.
- 1 can (1 pound) stewed tomatoes, drained and chopped. Reserve juice for another use.
- 1/2 cup chopped green onions
- 4 tablespoons chopped parsley
- 4 tablespoons grated Parmesan cheese

- 8 thin lemon slices

In a 12x16-inch roasting pan, lay fillets in 1 layer. Now, scatter the tomatoes, green onion, parsley and cheese evenly over the fish. Lay lemon slices evenly over all.

Bake in a 350° oven for about 15 to 20 minutes, or until fish flakes easily with a fork. Do not overbake. Serve with the tomato-onion mixture spooned over the top. Serves 6 generously.

Note: — *A nice accompaniment is Brown Rice with Mushrooms & Carrots.*

Baked Halibut with Artichokes,
Tomatoes & Green Onions

- 2 shallots, minced
- 2 tomatoes, peeled, seeded and chopped
- 1 jar (8 ounces) marinated artichoke hearts, drained and chopped
- 1/4 cup chopped green onions
- 2 tablespoons chopped parsley
- 2 tablespoons lemon juice

- 2 pounds halibut steaks (about 6 steaks, 3/4-inch thick) salt and pepper to taste

Stir together first 6 ingredients until blended. Place fish in a 9x13-inch baking pan and spoon sauce on top. Bake at 350° for about 25 minutes, or until fish flakes easily with a fork. Serves 6.

Baked Fillets of Sole with Caper Anchovy Sauce

2 pounds, fillets of sole, sprinkled with salt and white pepper

Caper Anchovy Sauce:
- 1 tablespoon butter
- 2 cloves garlic
- 4 tablespoons chopped chives
- 2 tablespoons chopped parsley
- 2 tablespoons capers, rinsed and drained
- 2 tablespoons lemon juice
- 1 anchovy fillet, mashed
- 1/2 cup cream
- salt and pepper to taste

Bake fillets in 1 layer in a 12x16-inch baking pan for about 15 minutes, or until fish flakes easily with a fork. Meanwhile, in a saucepan, simmer together the sauce ingredients for 5 minutes, or until sauce thickens slightly. Place fish on a serving platter and spoon a little sauce over each. Artichokes with Mushrooms is a nice accompaniment.

Note: — *Sauce can be prepared earlier in the day and stored in the refrigerator. Heat before serving. Fish should be baked before serving.*

Mushroom Stuffed Fillets of Sole
with Sorrel Sauce

Sorrel is becoming more and more available in supermarkets these days. However, if you can find a jar of Sorrel Puree packed in water, you would do well to purchase it. The one I particularly like is imported from Belgium. A little goes a long way, as a single teaspoon flavors a good amount of sauce, and it can be enjoyed throughout the year. To make your own puree, remove the stems and drop the leaves in boiling water for just under a minute. Drain, puree and freeze the sorrel in small quantities in little plastic bags. This is an especially glamorous recipe for sole.

6 fillets of sole, about 1 1/2 pounds. Sprinkle with salt and white pepper and baste with a little melted butter.

Mushroom Stuffing:
- 1/4 pound mushrooms, thinly sliced
- 2 shallots, minced
- 1 clove garlic, minced
- 4 tablespoons butter
- salt and pepper to taste

- 3/4 cup fresh bread crumbs
- 1 tablespoon chopped parsley
- 1 egg white

Saute together first 5 ingredients until shallots are softened. In a bowl, stir together mushroom mixture and remaining stuffing ingredients until blended. Place 2 tablespoons stuffing on the cut side of each fillet and roll it up. Place in a 9x13-inch baking pan, seam side down. Sprinkle tops with Cheese Topping and bake in a 350° oven for about 20 minutes, or until fish flakes easily. Serve surrounded with a little Sorrel Sauce.

Sorrel Sauce:
- 1 tablespoon melted butter
- 1 teaspoon sorrel puree
- 4 tablespoons chopped chives
- 2 tablespoons dry white wine
- 1/2 cup cream
- 1 teaspoon lemon juice
- 3 egg yolks

In a saucepan, heat first 6 ingredients. Beat yolks and gradually beat in half the cream mixture. Return this to the saucepan, and cook, over low heat, stirring all the while, until sauce thickens. DO NOT ALLOW TO BUBBLE OR BOIL or sauce will curdle. Remove from heat and allow to cool. Before serving, place sauce in the top of a double boiler and heat it over hot, not simmering water. Again, do not allow to bubble or boil. This is also delicious served cold as one would serve mayonnaise.

Cheese Topping: Stir until blended 2 tablespoons fresh bread crumbs, 2 tablespoons grated Parmesan cheese and 1 tablespoon melted butter.

Baked Fillets of Sole Persillade with Tomatoes & Cheese

A persillade is basically a parsley and crumb coating which is especially fine on meats and fish. This persillade can be prepared earlier in the day. Fish should be baked before serving.

    1 pound fillets of sole, sprinkled with salt and white pepper

    1 can (1 pound) stewed tomatoes, drained and chopped

Persillade:

    1/2 cup fresh bread crumbs

    2 tablespoons chopped parsley

    2 green onions, finely chopped

    2 cloves garlic, minced

    1/4 cup butter, melted

    2 tablespoons lemon juice

    1/4 cup grated Parmesan cheese

    pinch of cayenne (optional)

    salt and pepper to taste

In a 9x13-inch baking pan, lay fillets in one layer. Place tomatoes around the fillets. In a bowl, stir together the remaining ingredients. Sprinkle crumb mixture on the fillets and bake in a 350° oven for 15 minutes, or until fish flakes easily with a fork. Broil for 1 minute to brown top. Serves 4.

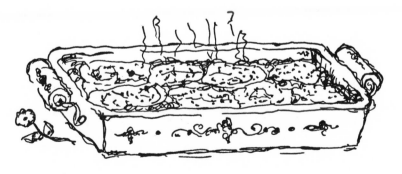

Fish & Shellfish

Fillets of Sole with Leeks & Lemon Cream Sauce

Leeks, shallots and garlic in a delicate lemon cream sauce elevate this dish to gastronomic heights. Sauce can be prepared 1 day earlier and stored in the refrigerator. Fish should be baked before serving. As this only takes minutes, it is a good dish to serve after a busy day.

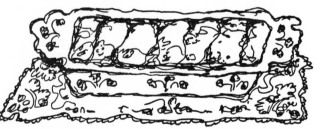

- 2 tablespoons butter
- 2 leeks, chopped. (Use only the white and soft green parts.) Wash thoroughly to remove every trace of sand.
- 2 shallots, minced
- 3 cloves garlic, minced

- 2 tomatoes, peeled, seeded and chopped (fresh or canned)
- 1/4 cup dry white wine

- 1/2 cup cream
- 2 tablespoons lemon juice
- salt and white pepper to taste

- 2 pounds fillets of sole, sprinkled with salt, white pepper and paprika
- 2 tablespoons chopped parsley

In a saucepan, saute together first 4 ingredients until leeks are soft. Add the tomatoes and wine and cook until most of the liquid is evaporated. Add cream, lemon juice and seasonings and simmer sauce for 10 minutes. Can be held at this point in the refrigerator.

Place fillets in one layer in a greased baking pan and bake in a 350° oven for about 10 minutes or until fish flakes easily with a fork. Spoon sauce on top and heat through. This is nice to serve with small boiled potatoes that have been rolled in butter and sprinkled with parsley. Serves 6.

New Orleans Style Hot & Spicy Shrimp

If you are stout of heart and enjoy hot, fiery dishes, this is a nice one to consider. This is very "hot" for me, although blazing palates will find this mild. Increase the amount of cayenne, if you enjoy bringing tears to your eyes.

- 2 onions, chopped
- 6 cloves garlic, minced
- 1/2 cup finely chopped celery
- 1 medium green bell pepper, cut into strips
- 3 tablespoons oil

- 1 can (1 pound) stewed tomatoes, chopped. Do not drain.
- 1 can (8 ounces) tomato sauce
- 1 tablespoon sugar
- 1 teaspoon sweet basil flakes
- 1 teaspoon thyme flakes
- 1/4 teaspoon, each, cayenne pepper, paprika and dry mustard salt and pepper to taste

- 2 pounds cooked shrimp, shelled and deveined

In a Dutch oven casserole, saute together first 5 ingredients until vegetables are soft. Add the next 7 ingredients and simmer sauce for 15 minutes. Add the shrimp and heat through. Serve over a bed of Spiced Rice. Cornbread Muffins are a nice accompaniment. Serves 6.

Spiced Rice:
- 1 1/2 cups long-grain rice
- 3 cups chicken broth
- 2 tablespoons oil
- 1/2 teaspoon sweet basil flakes
- 1/2 teaspoon thyme flakes
- 1/4 teaspoon, each, cayenne pepper and paprika salt and pepper to taste

In a saucepan, stir together all the ingredients. Cover pan and simmer rice for about 30 minutes, or until rice is tender and liquid is absorbed. Serves 6.

Lobster Italienne with Red Pepper & Basil

Lobster served with a delicate cream sauce, sparkled with red pepper and basil makes a fine combination. The sauce can also be served over cooked fillets of sole. It is not a lot of sauce. Just enough to coat the lobster and add its distinct flavor.

- 1 medium sweet red bell pepper, cut into strips
- 1/2 cup chopped green onions
- 2 cloves garlic, minced
- 2 shallots, minced
- 2 tablespoons butter

- 1/4 cup dry white wine

- 2 tablespoons chopped parsley
- 2 tablespoons lemon juice
- 1 teaspoon dried sweet basil flakes
- 1/2 cup cream
  salt and white pepper to taste

- 1 pound cooked lobster meat, cut into chunks

In a saucepan, saute together first 5 ingredients until pepper is softened. Add the wine, and cook until wine has evaporated. Add the next 5 ingredients, and simmer sauce for 10 minutes. Add the cooked lobster meat and heat through. Serve with rice, sprinkled with chives and grated Parmesan cheese. Serves 4.

Note: — *Sauce can be prepared earlier in the day and heated before serving. Add the lobster just before serving.*

— *This is a lovely small entree. In this case, serve on toast points or puffed pastry patty shells. Serves 6.*

— *Roasted red pepper strips, sold in jars, are being featured more and more in supermarkets. 1/2 cup of red pepper strips can be substituted for the fresh red bell pepper.*

Red Hot Garlic Shrimp
with Lemon & Herbs

This dish can be prepared in minutes and is a good choice on a night when you are running late. Sauce can be prepared earlier in the day, or even 1 day earlier, and heated before cooking the shrimp.

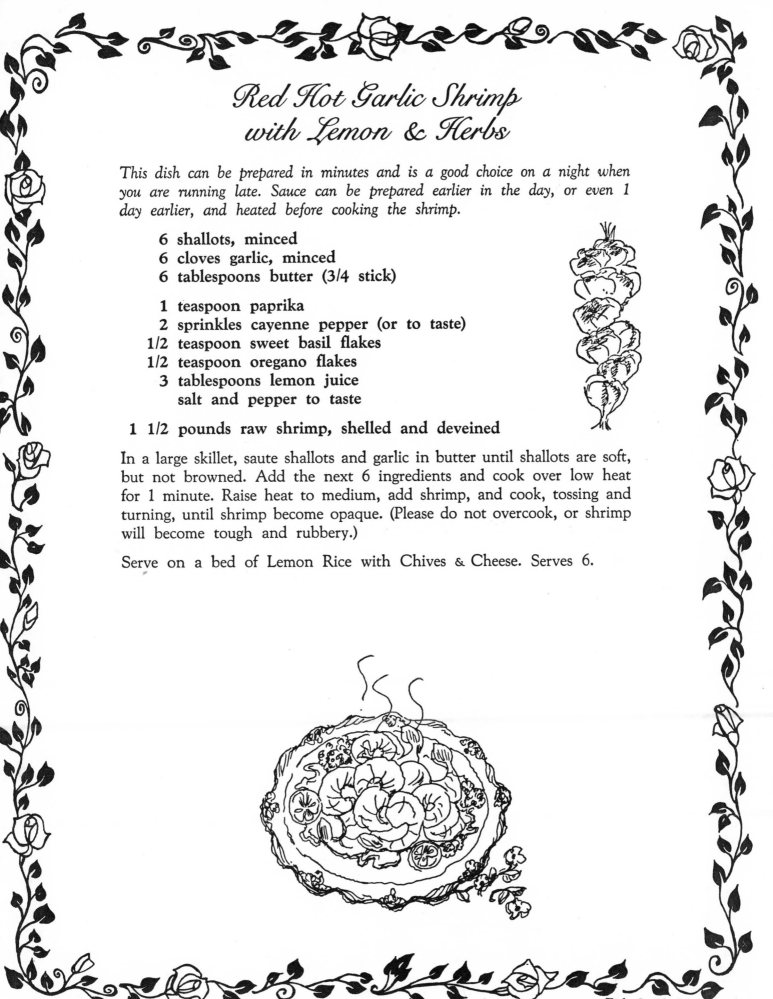

- 6 shallots, minced
- 6 cloves garlic, minced
- 6 tablespoons butter (3/4 stick)

- 1 teaspoon paprika
- 2 sprinkles cayenne pepper (or to taste)
- 1/2 teaspoon sweet basil flakes
- 1/2 teaspoon oregano flakes
- 3 tablespoons lemon juice
- salt and pepper to taste

1 1/2 pounds raw shrimp, shelled and deveined

In a large skillet, saute shallots and garlic in butter until shallots are soft, but not browned. Add the next 6 ingredients and cook over low heat for 1 minute. Raise heat to medium, add shrimp, and cook, tossing and turning, until shrimp become opaque. (Please do not overcook, or shrimp will become tough and rubbery.)

Serve on a bed of Lemon Rice with Chives & Cheese. Serves 6.

The Best Scampi with Shallots, Garlic & Lemon Sauce

Perhaps one of the easiest and best ways to prepare shrimp is to broil them for a few minutes in a rich garlic, butter and lemon sauce. Serve with a loaf of crusty Italian bread to dip in the delicious sauce.

1 1/2 pounds large shelled shrimp, peeled and deveined. (If you can leave the tails on, it's especially attractive.)

1/4 cup (1/2 stick) butter, melted
1/4 cup olive oil
4 cloves garlic, minced
3 shallots, minced
4 tablespoons lemon juice
3 tablespoons minced parsley
salt and pepper to taste

Place shrimp in one layer in a 8x12-inch baking pan. Stir together the remaining ingredients until blended. Pour sauce over the shrimp, making certain they are nicely coated.

Broil shrimp about 6-inches from the heat, a few minutes on each side, and only until shrimp turn pink and become opaque. Watch carefully so that shrimp are not over-cooked. Serve at once with the sauce spooned over the top. Serves 6 as a first course or 4 as a main dish.

Note: — Sauce ingredients can be mixed together earlier in the day. Entire dish can be assembled 30 minutes before broiling. Broil just before serving.

Shrimp in Royal Honey Dill Dressing

There are few hors d'oeurves you can make that are simpler or more elegant than this one. The dressing is delicate and subtle with a lot of solid character. Serve in a beautiful, shallow silver bowl with some lovely cocktail forks.

Royal Honey Dill Dressing:

- 1/4 cup mayonnaise
- 3/4 cup sour cream
- 1/4 cup lemon juice
- 1/4 cup honey
- 1 green onion
- 2 tablespoons fresh dill weed or 1/2 teaspoon dried dill weed
- salt to taste

Place all the ingredients in a blender or food processor and blend until onion is pureed. Yields 1 1/2 cups sauce.

To Prepare: In a large bowl, place 2 pounds shrimp with dressing to taste and refrigerate for several hours.

To Serve: Place shrimp and sauce in a shallow silver bowl and keep toothpicks or cocktail forks close by. (For this lovely dish, I recommend the pretty, carved cocktail forks that are sold in party shops.)

Note: — If you are serving this as a small entree on a bed of lettuce, you can substitute cooked crabmeat or lobster chunks.

Fish & Shellfish

Scallops in a Creamy Wine & Cheese Sauce

This is a simplified version of Coquilles St. Jacques. It is a delicious main course and an excellent small entree.

- 1/2 **cup cream**
- 1/2 **cup sour cream**
- 1/2 **cup grated Swiss chesse**
- 2 **tablespoons grated Parmesan cheese**
- 2 **tablespoons lemon juice**
- 4 **tablespoons chopped chives**
- 1/2 **teaspoon dried dill weed, or to taste**

- 2 **tablespoons butter**
- 6 **cloves garlic, minced**
- 3 **shallots, minced**

- 1/4 **cup dry white wine**
- **salt and white pepper to taste**
- 2 **pounds small bay scallops. (Sea scallops are larger and should be cut in half.)**

In a bowl, stir together first 7 ingredients until blended. Refrigerate for several hours or overnight. (You will be making Creme Fraiche.)

In a skillet, saute together next 3 ingredients until shallots are softened. Add the wine, seasonings and scallops and cook over medium heat until scallops become opaque. Do not overcook. Remove scallops and continue cooking until all the liquid has evaporated. Now, stir everything together, and place mixture into a buttered oval porcelain baker. Sprinkle top with Buttered Crumbs and heat through in a 350° oven. Serves 6.

To make Buttered Crumbs: Mix together 6 tablespoons soda cracker crumbs, 2 tablespoons grated Parmesan cheese and 2 tablespoons melted butter, until blended.

Note: — This can serve 12 as a small entree, and is lovely served in individual scallop shells.

Cioppino – Italian Fisherman's Fish Chowder

You will hardly believe that this deep, rich and flavorful chowder is so low in calories. Serving 6, it is an ample portion and serves well as a main course. As this dish is only a little over 200 calories, a slice or 2 of crusty Italian bread, will still keep the total low. And no need to butter the bread, for it can be dipped into the marvelous sauce.

2 onions, chopped
6 cloves garlic, minced
2 cans (10 1/2 ounces, each) chicken broth
2 cups tomato juice
1 can (8 ounces) tomato sauce
1 can (7 ounces) chopped clams (do not drain)
1 teaspoon sugar
1 teaspoon oil
1 teaspoon Italian Herb Seasoning Flakes
1 teaspoon sweet basil flakes
1 teaspoon ground turmeric
1 tablespoon dried parsley flakes
  pinch of cayenne pepper
  salt and pepper to taste

2 pounds fillets of sole, cut into 1 1/2-inch chunks

In a Dutch oven casserole, place all the ingredients, except the fish, and simmer soup base for 20 minutes. Bring soup to a rolling boil and add the fish. Lower heat, and simmer fish for about 4 to 5 minutes, or until it becomes opaque. Do not overcook. Serve in deep bowls, with a slice of crusty Italian bread for dipping. Italian Flat Bread with Tomatoes, Onions & Cheese, is an incredible accompaniment. Serves 6.

Note: — *Soup base can be prepared earlier in the day and stored in the refrigerator. However, do not cook the fish until a few minutes before serving.*

Fish & Shellfish

Easiest and Best American Fish Chowder with Green Onion Flatbread

This lovely dish is not quite a stew, nor a soup. It lies somewhere in-between and it is filled with all manner of good things. The soup base is rich and flavorful, with just the mildest "bite."

Soup Base:
- 2 tablespoons oil
- 2 large onions, chopped
- 3 shallots, chopped
- 6 cloves garlic, minced
- 1 can (1 pound) stewed tomatoes, chopped. Do not drain.
- 3 cups tomato juice
- 1 tablespoon parsley flakes
- 1 teaspoon thyme flakes
- 1 teaspoon sweet basil flakes
- 2 teaspoons sugar
- 3 threads of saffron
- 1/2 teaspoon turmeric
- 1/4 teaspoon red pepper flakes
  - salt and pepper to taste

- 2 cans (7 ounces, each) minced clams. Do not drain.

In a Dutch oven casserole, combine first 14 ingredients, and simmer mixture for 20 minutes. Add the clams with the broth, and simmer mixture for 5 minutes. Bring soup to a rolling boil and add:

- 2 pounds of fileted fish, cut into 1-inch pieces. Sole, perch, flounder, halibut are good. Can also use a mixture of fish and shellfish, i.e., cod, snapper, haddock, scallops, clams, crab or lobster. There are no rules.

- 1 can (1 pound) sliced potatoes

Cook for about 5 minutes, at a steady bubble, or until fish becomes opaque. Serve in deep bowls with some Green Onion Flatbread. Serves 6 to 8.

Note: — Soup base can be made earlier in the day, and refrigerated. Bring to a boil and cook the fish just before serving.

Poultry
&
Dressing

Poultry & Dressing

Baked Chicken Breasts with Tomato Artichoke Sauce 147
Roast Chicken with Hazelnut Dressing & Raisin Sauce 148
Chicken in a Delicate Mushroom & Lemon Dill Sauce 149
Roast Chicken with Cinnamon, Orange & Honey Glaze 150
Herbed Chicken with Lemon Garlic & Cheese 150
Baked Chicken with Carrots, Apples & Prunes 151
Chicken Mimosa with Apple, Orange & Raisin Wine Sauce 152
Oven-Fried Chicken Dijonnaise with Garlic & Cheese 153
Chicken Breasts with Ricotta Stuffing in Tomato Sauce 154
Chicken Romano with Tomatoes, Onions & Peppers 155
Black Raspberry Glazed Chicken with Wild Rice & Almond Stuffing 156
Sweet & Sour Chicken with Red Cabbage, Apples & Raisins 157
Orange Chicken with Hot Honey Currant Glaze 158
Chicken Romano with Garlic Butter Lemon Sauce 159
Family Oven-Fried Chicken, Southern Style 160
Country Cream Gravy 160
Honey Buttermilk Chicken with Honey Pecan Glaze 161
Orange Honey Baked Apples 161
Poulet Dijonnaise with Garlic, Peppers & Tomato Sauce 162
Honey Cinnamon Glazed Rock Cornish Hens 163
Spiced Apple & Raisin Stuffing 163
Roast Turkey with Apple & Chestnut Raisin Bread Stuffing 164
Herbed Stuffing with Ground Pork, Apples & Onions 165
Royal Herbed Cornbread Stuffing with Chestnuts, Apples & Raisins 166
Cinnamon Rice Stuffing with Raisins & Pine Nuts 167
Herbed Cornbread Stuffing with Cranberries & Pecans 167
Sausage & Ground Beef Stuffing with Mushrooms & Onions 168

Baked Chicken Breasts with Tomato & Artichoke Sauce

This dish is especially easy to prepare and it has good, deep, solid character. The sauce is light and full of flavor. Everybody loved it and welcomed the subtle balance of tomato and artichokes.

> 4 boned chicken breasts, skinned, boned and cut into halves. Sprinkle with garlic powder and paprika, (about 4 ounces, each)
>
> 1 can (1 pound) stewed tomatoes, chopped. Do not drain.
> 1 jar (6 ounces) marinated artichokes, drained and chopped
> 1 clove minced garlic
> 1 teaspoon sugar
> 1 tablespoon lemon juice
> salt and pepper to taste

In a 9x13-inch pan, place the chicken breasts in one layer. Bake in a 350° oven for about 20 minutes or until breasts are cooked through. Do not overbake.

Meanwhile, in a saucepan, heat together the remaining ingredients and simmer mixture for 10 minutes. Pour sauce over the chicken breasts and bake for another 5 minutes. Serve with angel hair pasta, cooked al dente, and spoon a little sauce on top. Serves 8.

Note: — Sauce can be prepared earlier in the day and heated at serving time. However, bake chicken breasts just before serving to make certain they are not overcooked.

— Angel hair pasta is delicious with this dish. 8 ounces of pasta will produce about 4 cups cooked pasta.

Roast Chicken with Hazelnut Dressing & Orange Raisin Sauce

If you are looking for a new and delicious way to serve chicken, try this lovely dish some evening soon. The sauce is tart and fruity and the combination of raisins and hazelnuts is simply marvelous.

1 onion, chopped
1 stalk celery, finely chopped
1/2 cup (1 stick) butter

1/2 cup chopped hazelnuts
1/4 cup yellow raisins
1/4 teaspoon ground poultry seasoning
1/4 teaspoon sage leaves
salt and pepper to taste

6 slices egg bread, crusts removed and cut into cubes
chicken broth

1 roasting chicken (about 3 to 4 pounds)
salt, pepper, garlic powder and paprika
4 tablespoons melted butter

Saute onion and celery in butter until onions are soft. In a bowl, combine onion mixture, hazelnuts, raisins and seasonings and toss to blend. Toss in the egg bread until well mixed. Add chicken broth, a little at a time, until stuffing holds together. (Stuffing should not be soggy nor too dry.)

Place chicken in a roasting pan. Fill chicken cavity with stuffing and close the opening with skewers or poultry pins. Sprinkle chicken with salt, pepper, garlic powder and paprika to taste. Baste with the melted butter, and bake in a 350° oven for 1 hour 30 minutes or until chicken is tender. Baste now and again with the juices in the pan. Remove the skewers and serve with Orange Raisin Sauce on the side. Serves 4.

Orange Raisin Sauce:
1/2 cup yellow raisins
2 tablespoons finely grated orange (use fruit, juice and peel)
1 tablespoon grated lemon (use fruit, juice and peel)
1/2 cup orange juice
1/4 cup dry white wine
1/2 cup currant jelly

In a saucepan, combine all the ingredients and simmer sauce for 15 minutes, over very low heat. Sauce is like a jellied relish. Add a little more white wine, if sauce is too thick.

Chicken in a Delicate Mushroom & Lemon Dill Sauce

This is one of the simplest, most elegant dishes you can serve for the most discriminating dinner party. Yet it is simple enough to prepare for family and friends some Sunday night, soon. The sauce is subtle and delicate with a good deal of depth and character. And it can be prepared, from beginning to end, in 30 minutes.

4 chicken breasts, boned and cut in halves. Sprinkle lightly with salt and garlic powder. Dust lightly with flour and brush lightly with 3 tablespoons melted butter.

Mushroom & Lemon Sauce:

- 1/2 pound mushrooms, sliced
- 2 cloves garlic, minced
- 2 shallots, minced
- 2 tablespoons butter

- 1/4 cup dry white wine
- 1/2 cup rich chicken broth
- 1 tablespoon chopped parsley
- 1/2 teaspoon dried dill weed
  - salt to taste
- 1 cup cream
- 1 tablespoon lemon juice

Place chicken in 1 layer in a 9x13-inch roasting pan and bake in a 325° oven for about 20 to 25 minutes, or until breasts are just cooked through. Do not overcook, or chicken will toughen up.

Meanwhile, saute together, mushrooms, garlic, shallots in butter until mushrooms are tender, but not browned, and all the liquid rendered is absorbed. Add the wine and cook until the wine is evaporated. Add the remaining ingredients and simmer sauce for about 10 to 15 minutes, uncovered, or until it is slightly thickened.

Place the warm chicken on a lovely platter and spoon a little sauce on the top. Pass the remaining sauce at the table. Serves 8.

Note: — Sauce can be prepared earlier in the day and heated before serving. Chicken can be sprinkled with seasoning and flour earlier in the day, but bake before serving.

Roast Chicken with Cinnamon, Orange & Honey Glaze

2 fryer chickens (about 3 pounds each), cut into serving
    pieces. Sprinkle with salt, pepper, garlic powder and
    paprika to taste.
4 tablespoons melted butter

Cinnamon, Orange & Honey Glaze:
1 cup honey
1/2 cup orange juice
1 tablespoon grated orange peel
1/2 teaspoon cinnamon
    pinch of powdered cloves

Place chicken, in one layer, in a 12x16-inch roasting pan, and bake in
a 350° oven for 40 minutes. Meanwhile, in a saucepan, heat together
the glaze ingredients, until mixture is nicely combined, about 3 minutes.

Brush glaze on chicken, and continue baking until chicken is tender, about
30 minutes. Baste 3 or 4 times during this period. Chicken will be highly
glazed and golden brown. Serve with Brown Rice with Mushrooms, Carrots
and Onions, as a lovely accompaniment. Serves 6.

Herbed Chicken with Lemon, Garlic & Cheese

*The simplicity of this dish in no way indicates its subtle and divine flavor.
It is light and delicate.*

1/4 cup butter, melted
1/4 cup oil
1/4 cup lemon juice
4 cloves minced garlic
1 teaspoon sweet basil flakes
    salt and pepper to taste

2 frying chickens, (about 2 1/2 pounds, each) cut into
    serving pieces

4 tablespoons grated Parmesan cheese

Stir together the first 6 ingredients. In a 12x16-inch pan, place chicken
in one layer. Pour lemon-butter mixture evenly over the chicken. Bake
in a 350° oven for 30 minutes, basting now and again. Sprinkle chicken
with grated cheese and continue baking and basting for about 40 minutes,
or until chicken is tender. Serves 6.

Baked Chicken with Carrots, Apples & Prunes

This is a dish, fit for a king, full-bodied and very flavorful. It also delivers quite a nice sized portion. The vegetables and fruit are a lovely medley of colors.

2 fryer chickens (about 2 1/2 pounds, each), cut into fourths. Sprinkle with salt, pepper and garlic powder to taste.

1 cup dry white wine
1 can (10 1/2 ounces) chicken broth
1 medium apple, peeled, cored and grated
2 onions, finely chopped
4 carrots, peeled and sliced
6 pitted prunes, coarsely chopped
6 medium potatoes (4 ounces, each), peeled and sliced
1 teaspoon paprika
1 teaspoon grated orange peel
1/2 teaspoon thyme flakes

In a 12x16-inch baking pan, place chicken in 1 layer. Stir together the remaining ingredients and place evenly over the chicken. Cover pan with foil and bake in a 350° oven for 40 minutes. Remove foil and continue baking until chicken and vegetables are tender, about 40 minutes. Remove skin from chicken and serve with the vegetables and fruit. Serves 8.

Poultry & Dressing

Chicken Mimosa with Apple, Orange & Raisin Wine Sauce

The inspiration for this dish came from a drink we often serve our guests. Mimosas are delicious and made by combining equal parts of orange juice and champagne (or white wine) in a stemmed goblet. The combination of orange juice and champagne (or white wine) works wonders in this lovely fruited chicken dish.

> **2 fryer chickens, (about 2 1/2 to 3 pounds, each), cut into serving pieces. Sprinkle chicken with salt, pepper and garlic powder and dust lightly with flour.**
> **4 tablespoons melted butter**
> **1/3 cup toasted slivered almonds**

In a 12x16-inch pan, place chicken pieces in one layer, and drizzle with melted butter. Bake in a 350° oven for about 40 minutes. Pour Apple, Orange & Raisin Wine Sauce evenly over the top and continue baking for about 30 minutes or until chicken is tender. Just before serving sprinkle with almonds.

Serve chicken and fruit with a simple pilaf. Serves 6 to 8 depending on other courses served.

Apple, Orange & Raisin Wine Sauce:
> **1 cup orange juice**
> **1 cup champagne (or dry white wine)**
> **1/2 cup orange marmalade**
> **1/2 cup yellow raisins**
> **2 tablespoons butter**
> **2 large apples, peeled and thinly sliced**
> **1 teaspoon cinnamon, 1/4 teaspoon nutmeg, 1/8 teaspoon powdered cloves (optional, but very good, indeed)**

In a saucepan, stir together all the ingredients and simmer mixture for about 20 to 25 minutes or until apples are softened (not mushy). Pour sauce evenly over partially cooked chicken. Almonds should be sprinkled on before serving (to retain crispness).

Note: — Sauce can be prepared earlier in the day and stored in the refrigerator.

— Entire dish can be prepared earlier in the day and heated at serving time.

Oven-Fried Chicken Dijonnaise with Garlic & Cheese

This is a homey dish and a good choice for a warm evening. It is easily assembled and quick to prepare. The crumb coating keeps the breasts juicy and succulent.

> **4 chicken breasts (about 1 pound, each) boned and cut in half**

Dipping Mixture:
> **1/2 cup butter, melted (1 stick)**
> **1 tablespoon Dijon mustard**
> **1/4 teaspoon garlic powder**
> **salt and pepper to taste. (Use the salt very sparingly as the coating has grated Parmesan.)**

Coating Mixture:
> **1 cup cracker crumbs. (Use a tasty cracker like French Onion or the like.)**
> **1/2 cup grated Parmesan cheese**

In a bowl, combine the ingredients for the Dipping Mixture. In another bowl, stir together the ingredients for the Coating Mixture.

Heavily butter a 9x13-inch baking pan. Dip chicken into Dipping Mixture and then roll in the Coating Mixture, making certain that the chicken is well covered on all sides. Place chicken pieces in one layer in prepared pan (teflon is good for this dish) and bake in a 325° oven for about 1 hour or until chicken is cooked through. Serve with spiced peaches or apricots and buttered broccoli. Serves 4 to 6 depending on appetites.

Note: — Chicken can be dipped and coated earlier in the day and stored in the refrigerator. This is best served right after baking.

Chicken Breasts with Ricotta Stuffing in a Light Tomato Sauce

The inspiration for this dish came from the old-fashioned lasagna. Only, in this case, the pasta was substituted with chicken breasts. This dish is quite unusual and you are probably the first ones in the country (maybe the world) to try it. (Leftover stuffing can be crumbled on chicken breasts the last 10 minutes of baking.)

4 **chicken breasts,** (about 1 pound, each) **cut into halves.** (Ask butcher to remove the bones and to gently flatten.) Sprinkle lightly with salt, white pepper, garlic powder and paprika.

2 cups fresh white bread crumbs (about 6 slices, minimum)
2 tablespoons grated onion
1/2 cup Ricotta cheese
1/2 cup grated Mozzarella cheese
1/3 cup grated Parmesan cheese
1 teaspoon sweet basil flakes
1/4 teaspoon oregano flakes
1 tablespoon chopped parsley
1 egg
3 tablespoons melted butter
   salt and pepper to taste

Prepare chicken breasts. Beat the remaining ingredients together until blended. Stuffing will be very stiff. Place 1 heaping tablespoon stuffing in center of chicken breasts, roll and secure with tooth picks. Roll stuffed breasts in flour. (Can be held at this point in refrigerator.)

In pan you will bake breasts, melt 4 tablespoons butter. Roll stuffed breasts in butter and bake at 325° for about 1 hour, basting frequently with the butter, until chicken is tender.

Place chicken on a serving platter and spoon Light Tomato Sauce on top. Pass remaining sauce at the table. Serve with Italian green beans laced with butter and garlic. Serves 8.

Light Tomato Sauce — In a Dutch oven casserole, stir together, 1 can (1 pound 12 ounces) crushed tomatoes in tomato puree; 2 teaspoons sugar; 1/2 medium onion, minced; 1 clove garlic, minced; 1 teaspoon sweet basil flakes; 1/2 teaspoon Italian Herb Seasoning Flakes; 1 tablespoon chopped parsley; salt and pepper to taste; 1 tablespoon oil. Simmer sauce for 20 minutes. (Can be prepared earlier in the day and refrigerated. Heat before serving.)

Chicken Romano with Tomatoes, Onions & Peppers

We enjoyed a dish very similar to this at Tre Scallini's in Rome. Even a non-fancier of peppers (like me) would have to love this succulent dish.

6 cloves garlic, finely chopped
1 medium onion, finely chopped
1 large red pepper, cut into 1-inch slices
1 medium green pepper, cut into 1/2-inch slices
2 tablespoons olive oil

1 can (1 pound) stewed tomatoes, coarsely chopped. Do not drain.
4 tablespoons tomato paste
1 teaspoon sweet basil flakes
    salt and pepper to taste

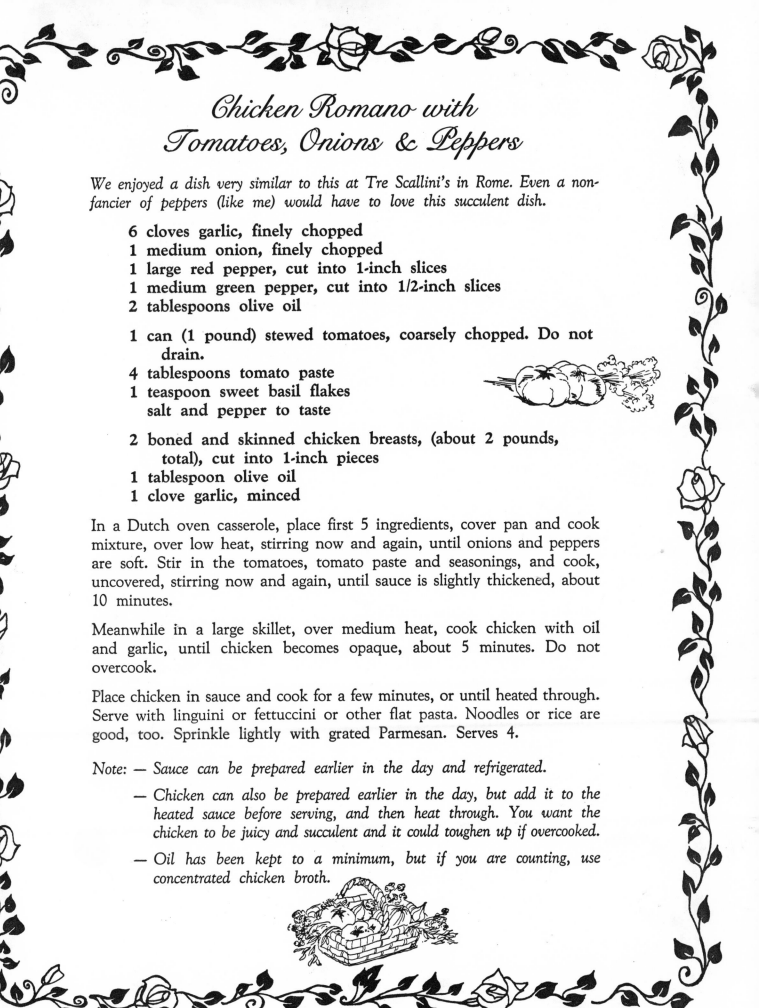

2 boned and skinned chicken breasts, (about 2 pounds, total), cut into 1-inch pieces
1 tablespoon olive oil
1 clove garlic, minced

In a Dutch oven casserole, place first 5 ingredients, cover pan and cook mixture, over low heat, stirring now and again, until onions and peppers are soft. Stir in the tomatoes, tomato paste and seasonings, and cook, uncovered, stirring now and again, until sauce is slightly thickened, about 10 minutes.

Meanwhile in a large skillet, over medium heat, cook chicken with oil and garlic, until chicken becomes opaque, about 5 minutes. Do not overcook.

Place chicken in sauce and cook for a few minutes, or until heated through. Serve with linguini or fettuccini or other flat pasta. Noodles or rice are good, too. Sprinkle lightly with grated Parmesan. Serves 4.

Note: — *Sauce can be prepared earlier in the day and refrigerated.*

— *Chicken can also be prepared earlier in the day, but add it to the heated sauce before serving, and then heat through. You want the chicken to be juicy and succulent and it could toughen up if overcooked.*

— *Oil has been kept to a minimum, but if you are counting, use concentrated chicken broth.*

Black Raspberry Glazed Chicken Breasts with Wild Rice & Almond Stuffing

This is a grand dish to serve for a formal dinner party, yet simple enough to serve family and friends on an evening when preparation time is limited. Serve with additional wild rice as an accompaniment, or buttered vegetables and spiced apricots ... DELICIOUS!

> **8 halved chicken breasts (about 6 to 8 ounces, each, after boning.) (Ask butcher to remove skin and bones and to gently flatten.) Sprinkle with salt, paprika and garlic powder.**
>
> **Wild Rice & Almond Stuffing**
>
> **Black Raspberry Honey Glaze**

Place 1 part stuffing in center of each (half) breast. Roll and secure with a wooden toothpick. Dust stuffed breasts lightly with flour. Melt 1/2 cup butter (1 stick) in a 9x13-inch baking pan and roll stuffed breasts in melted butter. Bake in a 325° oven for 40 minutes.

Now, baste with Black Raspberry Honey Glaze and continue baking and basting until chicken is tender and highly glazed, about 30 minutes. (Baste 2 or 3 times during the final baking period.)

Serve with additional wild rice, a simple buttered vegetable, or spiced fruit. Carrots, glazed with raisins, is especially nice. Serves 8.

Wild Rice & Almond Stuffing:
Cook 1 package (7 ounces) Herb Seasoned Wild and Long Grain Rice according to the directions on the package, except substitute 2 cups chicken broth for the 2 cups water. When rice is tender, and all the liquid is absorbed, stir in 1/2 cup toasted slivered almonds.

Black Raspberry Honey Glaze:
> 1/2 cup seedless black raspberry jam
> 1/2 cup honey
> 2 tablespoons frozen orange juice concentrate. Do not dilute.
> 1 teaspoon finely grated orange peel

In a saucepan, heat all the ingredients together and stir until blended.

Note: — Entire dish can be prepared earlier in the day, but shorten baking time by 10 minutes. Continue baking and glazing just before ready to serve.

Sweet & Sour Chicken with Red Cabbage, Apples & Raisins

Here's a delicious chicken recipe for informal dinners with family and friends. It's deeply flavorful and bursting with good taste. Potato pancakes, dumplings or home-fried potatoes are all nice accompaniments.

> 2 fryer chickens (2 1/2 to 3 pounds, each) cut into serving portions. Sprinkle with salt and pepper and garlic powder.
>
> 2 jars (1 pound, each) sweet and sour red cabbage
> 1/2 cup yellow raisins
> 2 apples, peeled, cored and grated
> 4 tablespoons honey
> 3 tablespoons lemon juice
> 1 can (10 1/2 ounces) chicken broth
> salt and pepper to taste

Place chicken in one layer in a 12x16-inch roasting pan and bake in a 350° oven for 40 minutes.

Meanwhile, in a Dutch oven casserole, cook together the remaining ingredients for 30 minutes. Pour cabbage mixture over the chickens, cover pan loosely with foil, and continue baking for 40 minutes, or until chicken is tender. Transfer to a serving platter.

Serve chicken surrounded with cabbage. Potato pancakes are a delicious accompaniment.

Note: — If gravy is a little loose, thicken it with 1 or 2 tablespoons gingersnap cookie crumbs.

— If you care to splurge and add 1 can (1 pound) chestnuts, drained, be assured of a standing ovation.

— Fresh red cabbage can be used if you have a little extra time. To prepare Sweet & Sour Red Cabbage, place in a Dutch oven casserole 1 small red cabbage, grated (about 1 pound); 2 tablespoons butter; 1 apple, peeled, cored and grated; 1/4 cup currant jelly; 2 tablespoons vinegar; salt and pepper to taste; 1/2 cup chicken broth. Simmer everything together for about 30 to 40 minutes, or until cabbage is tender and most of the liquid is absorbed. Continue recipe as above.

— Entire dish can be prepared earlier in the day and stored in the refrigerator. Heat carefully before serving as red cabbage has a tendency to scorch.

Poultry & Dressing

Orange Chicken with Hot Honey Currant Glaze

2 fryer chickens (about 2 1/2 pounds, each), cut into serving pieces. Sprinkle with salt, pepper and garlic powder.

Hot Honey Currant Glaze:
- 1/2 cup honey
- 1/2 cup currant jelly
- 1/2 orange, grated. (Use peel, fruit and juice and remove any large pieces of membrane.)
- 1 shallot, minced
- 2 tablespoons lemon juice
- 1/2 teaspoon ground ginger
- 1/8 teaspoon cayenne pepper (or more to taste)

Place chicken pieces in a 9x13-inch baking pan and bake in a 350° oven for 40 minutes.

Meanwhile, combine all the glaze ingredients in a saucepan and simmer mixture for 2 or 3 minutes or until ingredients are nicely blended. Baste chicken with glaze and continue baking and glazing for 25 to 30 minutes or until chicken is tender and a deep golden color.

Serve with Brown Rice with Onions & Lentils as a lovely accompaniment. Serves 6 to 8.

Note: — If you are preparing only 1 chicken, unused glaze can be stored in the refrigerator for 1 week.

— Chicken can be prepared earlier in the day, but bake it for 1 hour. Continue baking and glazing before serving.

Chicken Romano with Garlic Butter Lemon Sauce

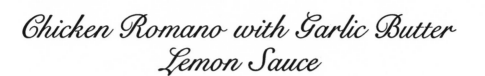

8 half chicken breasts (about 6 ounces, each) boned,
    skinned and gently pounded to flatten, Sprinkle with
    garlic powder.
8 thin slices prosciutto ham
8 thin slices Mozzarella cheese

Place one slice of ham and cheese over each half of breast. Roll up and secure with a wooden toothpick. Roll chicken in Seasoned Bread Crumbs and place in a baking pan.

Bake in a 325° oven for 20 minutes. Now, baste with Garlic Butter Lemon Sauce. Continue baking for another 30 minutes, basting now and again (use all the sauce) or until chicken is cooked. Serve at once. Serves 8.

Seasoned Crumbs:
    3/4 cup bread crumbs
    1/4 cup flour
    1/2 cup grated Parmesan cheese
    2 teaspoons garlic powder
    2 teaspoons paprika
    1 teaspoon salt

Combine the ingredients in a plastic bag and shake until blended. Store unused crumbs in the freezer. Can be kept for several months and very good to use with fish or chicken.

Garlic Butter Lemon Sauce:
    1/2 cup butter, (1 stick)
    2 cloves garlic, put through a press
    2 tablespoons lemon juice
    1 teaspoon parsley flakes

Heat together all the ingredients until butter is melted. Use to baste on chicken. Yields about 1/2 cup sauce.

Note: — Entire dish can be assembled earlier in the day and refrigerated. However, please bake this just before serving.

Family Oven-Fried Chicken, Southern Style, with Country Cream Gravy

2 fryer chickens (about 3 pounds, each), cut into 8 pieces.
(Legs, thighs, and breasts cut into 4 pieces). Reserve
backs and necks for broth.*

3/4 cup cream

1 cup cornflake crumbs
1/2 teaspoon garlic powder
1/2 teaspoon paprika
    salt to taste

Dip chicken pieces in cream and roll in mixture of crumbs, garlic powder, paprika and salt. Place in a 12x16-inch roasting pan and bake in a 350° oven for 1 hour and 15 minutes or until tender.

Serve with biscuits and honey and Country Cream Gravy on top. Serves 6 to 8.

Country Cream Gravy

2 tablespoons butter
2 tablespoons flour

1 cup rich chicken broth*
1 cup cream
    salt and pepper to taste

In a saucepan, cook together butter and flour for 2 minutes, stirring all the while. Add the remaining ingredients and continue cooking and stirring until gravy is thickened. Yields about 2 cups gravy.

*Rich Chicken Broth

Chicken backs and necks from above
1 can (10 1/2 ounces) chicken broth
1/4 cup minced onions
1/4 cup grated carrots
    salt to taste

In a saucepan, combine all the ingredients and simmer mixture for 45 minutes to 1 hour. Broth will be rich and concentrated. Strain broth. (The little bits of chicken and vegetables can be reserved for another use or discarded.)

Note: — Entire dish can be prepared earlier in the day and heated at serving
    time. Spoon gravy on chicken just before serving.

Honey Buttermilk Chicken with Honey Pecan Glaze

Chicken on Sunday is an old American tradition. But serving it glazed with honey and pecans adds a new touch to an old favorite. Chicken can be prepared earlier in the day, but sprinkle pecans the last 10 minutes of reheating.

2 fryer chickens, cut up into serving pieces. Sprinkle with salt, pepper and garlic powder.

2 tablespoons honey
1 egg
1/2 cup buttermilk

1/2 cup cracker crumbs. (Use a savory cracker, like Ritz or Waverly.)

1/2 cup honey, heated
1/2 cup chopped pecans

Beat together honey, egg and buttermilk until blended. On a flat plate, place cracker crumbs. Dip chicken pieces into buttermilk mixture and then roll lightly into cracker crumbs. Place chicken pieces in 1 layer in a 12x16-inch baking pan.

Bake in a 350° oven for 40 minutes. Baste chicken lightly with warm honey and continue baking for 30 minutes. Now, baste with honey again and sprinkle chicken with chopped pecans. Bake for another 10 minutes or until pecans are toasted. (Watch carefully so that pecans do not burn.)

Serve at once with warm Buttery Raisin Scones, buttered broccoli and Orange Honey Baked Apples. Wonderful! Serves 6 to 8.

Orange Honey Baked Apples

6 baking apples, peeled, cored and sliced
1/4 cup butter, melted
1/4 cup honey
1/2 cup orange juice
2 tablespoons grated orange peel
1 cup brown sugar
1/4 cup yellow raisins

Place apples in a buttered porcelain baker. Stir together the remaining ingredients and pour evenly over the apples. (Bury the raisins into the juice, to prevent their browning too readily.) Bake in a 350° oven for about 40 minutes or until apples are tender. Serves 6 to 8.

Poulet Dijonnaise with Garlic Peppers & Tomato Sauce

Often are the times, when we want to elevate a "chicken-in-a-pot" to gastronomical heights. This is a welcomed change to roast or braised chicken. It is especially delicious, sparkled with a sauce made with wine, onions, tomatoes and peppers.

2 fryer chickens, (about 2 1/2 pounds, each), cut into serving pieces. Brush chicken with 2 tablespoons Dijon mustard and sprinkle with salt, pepper and garlic powder.

4 tablespoons melted butter (1/2 stick)

In a 12x16-inch pan, place chicken pieces in one layer, and drizzle with melted butter. Bake in a 350° oven for about 40 minutes. Pour Garlic, Pepper & Tomato Sauce over the top and continue baking for about 30 minutes, or until chicken is tender.

Serve chicken and vegetables on a bed of brown rice. Serves 6 to 8, depending on appetites.

Garlic, Pepper & Tomato Sauce:
   1/2 pound mushrooms, sliced
   2 medium onions, chopped
   4 cloves garlic, minced
   1 medium red bell pepper, cut into strips
   1 medium green bell pepper, cut into strips
   4 tablespoons butter (1/2 stick)

1/4 cup dry white wine

   1 can (1 pound) stewed tomatoes, finely chopped. Do not drain.
   1 tablespoon paprika
1/4 cup cream
   salt and pepper to taste

In a skillet, saute together first 6 ingredients until vegetables are soft and liquid rendered is evaporated. Add the wine and simmer mixture until wine is evaporated. Add the remaining ingredients and simmer mixture for 5 minutes. Pour sauce over partially cooked chicken.

Note: — Sauce can be prepared earlier in the day and stored in the refrigerator. Entire dish can be prepared earlier in the day and heated at serving time.

Honey & Cinnamon Glazed Rock Cornish Hens with Spiced Apple & Raisin Stuffing

This is one of the most delicious stuffings for these succulent little hens. It is spicy and fruity and a lovely blend of flavors. The stuffing can be assembled in advance, but stuff the hens just before baking.

4 Rock Cornish Hens (about 1 to 1 1/4 pounds, each).
Sprinkle with salt and garlic powder.

Stuff hen cavities 3/4 full with Spiced Apple & Raisin Stuffing and skewer openings with wooden picks or metal skewers. Place hens in a roasting pan and bake in a 325° oven for 45 minutes, basting with a little butter and pan juices.

Now start basting with Honey & Cinnamon Glaze, every 10 minutes, for about 30 minutes, or until hens are a rich, golden color. (Total cooking time is about 1 hour 15 minutes.)

To serve, remove skewers and place hens on a bed of Brown Rice with Onions and Mushrooms. Delicious! Serves 4.

Spiced Apple & Raisin Stuffing:
- 2 medium apples, peeled, cored and grated
- 1/4 cup orange juice
- 1/2 cup yellow raisins
- 1/4 cup honey
- 1 teaspoon cinnamon
- 1/4 teaspoon ground cloves
- 1/4 teaspoon nutmeg
- 1/2 cup chopped walnuts or pecans
- 1/4 cup butter (1/2 stick)

- 1 cup fresh bread crumbs

In a saucepan, combine first 9 ingredients and heat until apples are wilted, about 3 minutes. Stir in the crumbs until blended. (If apples render a lot of juice, you may need another tablespoon of bread crumbs. Stuffing should not be too dry, or soggy.)

Honey & Cinnamon Glaze:
- 1/2 cup butter
- 1/2 cup honey
- 1 teaspoon cinnamon

Heat together all the ingredients until blended.

Roast Turkey with Apple & Chestnut Raisin Bread Stuffing

This is a glorious stuffing, filled with all manner of good things ... apples, chestnuts, cinnamon, raisin bread. I prefer to make stuffing in a separate pan, and thereby, avoid the problem of harmful bacteria forming. If you prefer to stuff the turkey, then stuff it just before baking. Figure about 3/4 cup stuffing for each pound of turkey.

    1 turkey about 15 to 16 pounds, ready to cook, but not
        butter basted

Basting Mixture:
    1 cup melted butter
    1 tablespoon paprika
    1 teaspoon salt
    1/4 teaspoon pepper
    6 cloves garlic
    1/4 teaspoon onion powder
    1 teaspoon poultry seasoning

Place all the ingredients in a blender and blend until garlic is pureed. Baste turkey generously, inside and out, with basting mixture. Roast at 325°, tented loosely with foil, and basting occasionally, until turkey tests done, about 5 to 6 hours. Test for doneness by moving the drumstick up and down. If it gives easily, turkey is done. Or, during the last hour of roasting, insert a meat thermometer in the center of the inside thigh muscle. Thermometer should register between 185° and 190°. Yields about 14 servings.

Apple & Chestnut Raisin Bread Stuffing:
    2 onions, chopped
    2 apples, peeled, cored and grated
    1 can (15 1/2 ounces) chestnuts, packed in water, not
        syrup, drained and chopped
  1/2 cup butter
    6 tablespoons sugar
1 1/2 teaspoons cinnamon

    2 loaves (1 pound, each) raisin bread, cut into cubes
    2 cups apple juice, or enough to moisten bread
    2 eggs, beaten
      salt to taste

In a large skillet, over low heat, saute together first 6 ingredients until apples are soft. Meanwhile, soften bread in apple juice, not too dry, nor soupy. Combine bread and apple mixtures and mix until blended. Mix in the beaten eggs and salt to taste. Place mixture in a greased 10x3-inch round baking pan, and bake at 350°, for about 40 minutes or until top is browned. Yields 12 cups stuffing, enough to stuff a 16-pound turkey.

Herbed Stuffing with Ground Pork, Apples & Onions

2 onions, chopped
1 stalk celery, chopped
2 cloves garlic, minced
1 apple, peeled, cored and grated
4 tablespoons butter

1 pound lean ground pork
   salt and pepper to taste
1/4 teaspoon poultry seasoning
1 package (8 ounces) herb-seasoned stuffing mix
2 eggs, beaten
   chicken broth (about 3/4 cup)

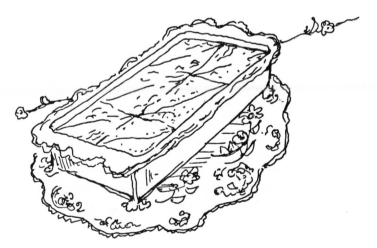

Saute together first 5 ingredients until vegetables are soft. Add the pork and seasonings and continue, cooking and stirring until meat loses its pinkness. (If the pork is fatty, do this in a separate pan, drain, and add to vegetable mixture.) Toss in stuffing mix and beaten eggs. Stir in the chicken broth, a little at a time, until stuffing holds together, not too dry, nor let it get soggy.

Place mixture into a 10-inch porcelain baker and bake in a 350° oven for about 30 minutes or until stuffing is set. Serves 8.

Royal Herbed Cornbread Stuffing with Chestnuts, Apples & Raisins

2 stalks celery, chopped
1 onion, chopped
2 cloves garlic, minced
4 shallots, chopped
1 apple, peeled, cored and grated
1/2 cup butter

1 can (15 ounces) chestnuts, drained and chopped
1/2 cup yellow raisins
2 tablespoons chopped parsley
1 package (8 ounces) herbed cornbread stuffing
2 eggs, beaten
chicken broth, about 1/2 to 3/4 cup
1/2 teaspoon dried sage flakes
salt and pepper to taste

In a large skillet, saute together first 6 ingredients until vegetables are soft. Toss mixture in a large bowl with chestnuts, raisins, parsley and stuffing.

Stir in the eggs and chicken broth, until stuffing is moist, but not soggy. Stir in seasonings.

Place stuffing in a porcelain baker and bake in a 350° oven for about 30 minutes or until stuffing is set and lightly browned. Serves 8.

Note: — *The above stuffing can be further glamorized with the addition of several dried fruits and nuts. Add any or all of the following:*

6 pitted prunes, soaked in orange juice, and chopped
1/2 cup black currants, soaked in orange juice
1/2 cup yellow raisins, soaked in orange juice
6 dried apricot halves, soaked in orange juice
1/3 cup walnuts, coarsely chopped
1/3 cup pecans, coarsely chopped

Cinnamon Rice Stuffing with Raisins & Pine Nuts

1 cup rice
2 cups chicken broth
2 tablespoons butter
   salt to taste

2 onions
2 tablespoons butter
1 tablespoon sugar

1 cup yellow raisins
3/4 cup pine nuts
1/4 teaspoon cinnamon

In a saucepan, place first 4 ingredients. Cover pan and simmer rice, until liquid is absorbed and rice is tender, about 30 minutes. In a skillet, saute onions in butter with sugar until onions are soft. Stir in raisins, pine nuts and cinnamon and cook and stir for 1 minute. Stir together cooked rice and onion mixture until well mixed. Place mixture into a 2-quart souffle dish and cover tightly with foil. At serving time, heat in a 325° oven until heated through, about 25 minutes. Serves 6.

Herbed Cornbread Stuffing with Cranberries & Pecans

1 onion, chopped
1 stalk celery, finely chopped
1/2 cup (1 stick) butter

1 package (8 ounces) herb-seasoned Cornbread Stuffing Mix
1 cup whole berry cranberry sauce, broken-up
3/4 cup chopped pecans
1/4 teaspoon poultry seasoning — salt and pepper to taste
1 egg
   chicken broth (about 3/4 to 1 cup)

Saute onion and celery in butter until onions are soft. In a bowl, combine all the ingredients, adding enough chicken broth to hold stuffing together. Place stuffing in a 10-inch porcelain baker and bake in a 350° oven for 30 minutes or until set. Serves 6.

Poultry & Dressing

Sausage & Ground Beef Stuffing with Mushrooms & Onions

1/2 pound ground beef
1/2 pound sausage

 2 onions, chopped
 2 cloves garlic, minced
1/2 pound mushrooms, sliced
1/2 cup butter (1 stick)

 1 package (8 ounces) herb-seasoned stuffing mix
 3 eggs, beaten
 1 teaspoon sage leaves (or 1/4 teaspoon powdered sage)
   salt and pepper to taste
   chicken broth (about 1 cup)

In a skillet, saute ground beef until meat loses its pinkness. Drain and set aside. Cut sausage into thin slices, and place in another skillet, covered with water. Cover pan and cook for about 20 minutes, or until liquid is evaporated. Uncover pan and continue cooking sausage, tossing and turning, until meat is lightly browned and crumbled. Set aside.

In a skillet, saute together onions, garlic and mushrooms in butter until onions are soft.

In a large bowl, place beef, sausage and sauteed vegetables. Add the stuffing mix, beaten eggs and seasonings. Add enough chicken broth to hold stuffing together, not too dry, nor too soggy.

Place mixture into an 8x12-inch baker and bake in a 350° oven for about 30 minutes or until stuffing is set. Serves 8.

Meats

Meats

Braccioli all Salsa Marinara 171
Meat Loaf Dijonnaise with Tomatoes & Cheese 172
Barbecued Brisket wth Honey Barbecue Sauce 173
Linguine & Beef Casserole with Onions & Cheese 174
Greek-Styled Lamb Shanks in Tomato Garlic Wine Sauce 175
Roast Leg of Lamb with Spiced Ruby Currant Glaze 176
Dilled Lamb with Yogurt, Lemon & Garlic Sauce 177
Honey Baked Ham with Cinnamon Apple Rings 178
Sweet & Sour Pork with Sauerkraut & Apples 179
Apricot Glazed Canadian Bacon with Honey Spiced Apricots 180
Honey Barbecued Loin of Pork 181
Baked Apples & Raisins 181
Cinnamon Roast Loin of Pork with Apricots, Prunes & Carrots 182
All-American Country Ribs with Honey Barbecue Sauce 183
Pate of Veal & Red Peppers with Herbed Tomato Sauce 184
Veal Shanks with Tomatoes, Garlic & Peppers 185
Veal Meatloaf with Brandied Apple Rings 186
Rice Pilaf with Herbs 186
Veal & Peppers with Tomatoes, Onion & Garlic 187
Sweet & Sour Veal Roast with Pearl Onions & Mushrooms 188
Paprikash of Veal with Mushrooms & Creme Fraiche 189
Veal & Vegetable Loaf with Tomato Sauce 190
Herb Stuffed Breast of Veal in Currant Wine Sauce 191
Veal Roast Stuffed with Vegetable Pesto in Tomato Sauce 192

Braccioli alla Salsa Marinara
(Roulades of Beef with Herbed Stuffing, Bacon & Pine Nuts)

Incredibly easy and very delicious are these tender, succulent beef rolls, stuffed with an easy to prepare stuffing that is sparkled with bacon and pine nuts. The sauce is scented with basil and garlic.

24 slices spencer steaks. (Ask your butcher to slice these
    from the small end and not more than 1/4-inch thick.)

  1 package chicken flavored stuffing mix (6 ounces)
  1 egg, beaten
1/2 cup toasted pine nuts
  3 strips bacon, cooked crisp, drained and crumbled

1/2 cup (1 stick) butter, about
1/4 cup Cognac or brandy

Prepare stuffing mix according to the directions on the package, substituting beef broth for the water. Stir in the beaten egg, pine nuts and bacon.

Place 1 tablespoon stuffing on end of each steak, roll it up, and fasten it with a toothpick. Roll these in Seasoned Flour and saute the rolls in butter, until meat loses its pinkness. Do not overcrowd the pan and do not overcook. (Steaks are exceedingly tender.)

Warm Cognac in a brandy warmer, ignite and carefully pour over beef rolls. (Can be held at this point in the refrigerator.) Before serving, bring to room temperature and heat in a 300° oven until heated through. Serve hot and pass the sauce. Serves 12.

Seasoned Flour: Combine in a plastic bag and shake until blended, 1 cup flour; 2 teaspoons garlic powder; 1 tablespoon paprika; 1/2 cup grated Parmesan cheese; and 1 teaspoon salt. Store unused flour in the refrigerator.

Salsa Marinara: Combine and simmer for 10 minutes, 1 can (1 pound 12 ounces) crushed tomatoes in tomato puree; 2 cloves garlic, minced; 1 small onion, grated; 2 teaspoons sugar; 2 tablespoons chopped parsley; 1 teaspoon sweet basil flakes; 1 teaspoon Italian Herb Seasoning flakes; 1 tablespoon olive oil; and salt and pepper to taste. Sauce can be prepared earlier in the day and stored in the refrigerator. Heat before serving.

Meat Loaf Dijonnaise with Tomatoes & Cheese

What a wonderful blend of flavors. Mustard, tomatoes and cheese serve to elevate a simple meat loaf. This can be baked in a ring mold or loaf pan. A 1 1/2 quart souffle dish is also nice, but will take a few minutes extra baking time.

1 1/2 pounds lean ground beef
   1 cup fresh bread crumbs
   2 eggs
   2 tablespoons grated Parmesan cheese
   1 small onion, grated
 1/3 cup tomato sauce
   1 tablespoon Dijon mustard
   1 teaspoon sweet basil flakes
      salt and pepper to taste

   1 tablespoon Dijon mustard
 2/3 cup tomato sauce
   1 tablespoon grated Parmesan cheese

In a bowl, combine first 9 ingredients and mix until blended. Pack mixture into a 9x5-inch loaf pan. Spread mustard on top of loaf, cover with tomato sauce and sprinkle with grated cheese.

Bake in a 350° oven for about 1 hour or until meat is cooked through. Remove every trace of fat and unmold onto a lovely platter. Brush top with the little sauce that has collected. Yields 6 servings.

Note: — *This can be prepared earlier in the day and heated before serving.*

     — *This is also very delicious served cold, with a light brushing of mustard.*

     — *Try this as a sandwich between slices of crusty Italian bread.*

Barbecued Brisket with Honey Barbecue Sauce

Brisket is a very flavorful, cut of meat. It is especially good braised in this very tasty barbecue sauce. Use the sauce on chicken or pork or other barbecued meats.

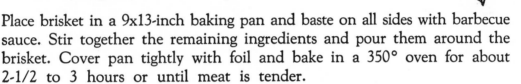

1 brisket of beef, about 4 pounds, trimmed of fat. Sprinkle
    with salt, pepper, paprika and lots of garlic powder

1 cup Honey Barbecue Sauce
1 can (10 1/2 ounces) beef broth
1 cup dry white wine
3 teaspoons beef stock base
2 tablespoons brown sugar

Place brisket in a 9x13-inch baking pan and baste on all sides with barbecue sauce. Stir together the remaining ingredients and pour them around the brisket. Cover pan tightly with foil and bake in a 350° oven for about 2-1/2 to 3 hours or until meat is tender.

Remove meat from pan and cut into thin slices. Place in porcelain baker and drizzle top with 3/4 cup of the gravy, from which every trace of fat has been removed. Can be held at this point.

When ready to serve, baste top with additional barbecue sauce to taste, and heat in a 350° oven for about 30 minutes, or until heated through. Serves 6.

Honey Barbecue Sauce:
    1 cup ketchup
    1 cup chili sauce
    1/2 cup honey
    1/4 cup vinegar
    2 tablespoons lemon juice
    2 teaspoons Dijon mustard
    2 to 3 sprinkles of cayenne pepper
        salt and pepper to taste

In a saucepan, heat together all the ingredients and simmer sauce, stirring, now and again, for 5 minutes. Sauce will keep for several weeks in the refrigerator. Yields 3 cups sauce.

Linguine & Beef Casserole with Onions & Cheese

This is a rather pleasant dish to serve for a luncheon or light dinner. It is also nice to take along for a pot luck supper or any informal occasion. It is very tasty, not terribly expensive and will serve a generous number of people.

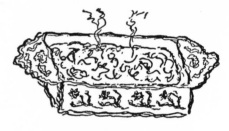

- 1 1/2 pounds lean ground beef
- 1 medium onion, grated
- 2 cloves garlic, minced

- 1/2 pound ricotta cheese (8 ounces)
- 1 cup sour cream
- 1/2 cup cream
- 4 eggs
- 1/2 cup grated Parmesan cheese
- salt and pepper to taste

- 1 package (8 ounces) linguine, cooked al dente and drained
- 1/3 cup butter, melted

In a skillet, saute together the first 3 ingredients until beef loses its pinkness and onions are softened.

In a large bowl, stir together the ricotta, sour cream, cream, eggs, Parmesan cheese and seasonings.

Toss together the cooked linguine and melted butter.

In a 9x13-inch pan, layer half the noodles, beef mixture and then the remaining noodles. Pour the egg mixture over all and ease the noodles, so that the egg mixture is even.

Bake in a 350° oven for about 50 minutes, or until casserole is set and top is lightly browned. Cut into squares and serve warm. Serves 8 for lunch and 12 as a side dish.

Note: — Entire casserole can be prepared earlier in the day and stored in the refrigerator. Cover pan with foil to reheat.

— Add 1 package (10 ounces) frozen chopped spinach, defrosted and drained, to the cheese mixture if you wish a one-pot meal for family dining.

Greek-Styled Lamb Shanks in a Tomato Garlic Wine Sauce

This is an adaptation of the classic Italian Osso Bucco. The lamb gives the sauce a totally different character and flavor. Orzo, a rice-shaped pasta, is an especially good accompaniment.

6 lamb shanks (about 3/4 pound, each) trimmed of any visible fat. Sprinkle with salt, pepper and a faint dusting of flour.

6 medium onions, thinly sliced

2 cans (1 pound each) stewed tomatoes, chopped. Discard seeds

1 can (6 ounces) tomato paste

1 cup dry white wine

1 can (10 1/2 ounces) beef broth

3 carrots, finely grated

1 tablespoon sugar

3 tablespoons olive oil

6 cloves garlic, minced

1/2 teaspoon each, oregano, basil and thyme flakes
salt and pepper to taste

Place lamb shanks in a 12x16-inch baking pan and scatter onions over lamb. Stir together the remaining ingredients and pour sauce evenly over the lamb. Cover pan tightly with foil and bake in a 350° oven for 1 1/2 hours, or until lamb is almost tender. Remove foil and bake for another 30 minutes. Sauce should be quite thick and lamb, very tender. Remove every trace of fat.

Serve on a bed of Orzo and ladle sauce over all. A little grated Parmesan on top is optional, but very nice. Serves 6.

To make Orzo: In a Dutch oven casserole, place 1 1/2 cups orzo, 3 cups chicken broth, 3 tablespoons oil and salt and pepper to taste. Stir mixture, cover pan and simmer mixture for about 40 minutes, or until liquid is absorbed and orzo is tender. (If you use the very large sized orzo, you may need another 1/4 cup chicken broth).

Roast Leg of Lamb with Spiced Ruby Currant Glaze

This is a rather unusual manner of preparing lamb, yet the results are surprisingly delicious. It is an exceptionally good glaze that is fragrant with the peels of orange and lemon.

1 leg of lamb (about 5 to 6 pounds), boned and tied. Sprinkle with salt and pepper. Make a paste with 6 cloves garlic and 3 tablespoons butter and spread over the meat.

Spiced Ruby Currant Glaze:
- 2 tablespoons butter
- 2 shallots, minced

- 1 cup currant jelly
- 1/3 cup port wine
- 3 tablespoons grated orange (use fruit, juice and peel)
- 1 tablespoon grated lemon (use fruit, juice and peel)
- 1/2 teaspoon cinnamon
- 1/8 teaspoon powdered cloves
- 1/8 teaspoon ground ginger

Place meat thermometer in center of roast. Roast lamb in a 350° oven, until meat thermometer registers 120°.

Meanwhile, in a saucepan, saute shallots in butter until they are soft, but not browned. Add the remaining ingredients and simmer sauce for 5 minutes.

Baste lamb with Spiced Currant Glaze, every now and again, until meat thermometer registers 140° for medium rare or 160° for medium doneness. (If you like lamb well-done, meat thermometer should register 175°, but it is not recommended.)

To serve, arrange slices of lamb on a platter and serve with 1 teaspoon of glaze on the side. Wild and brown rice is a nice accompaniment.

Note: — Glaze can be prepared days ahead and stored in the refrigerator. Heat before using.

Dilled Lamb with Yogurt, Lemon & Garlic Sauce

Lamb is so nice around the Easter holidays. Marinated in a mixture of yogurt and lemon juice and then cooked with tomatoes and dill is a special delight.

- 3 pounds boneless lamb, cut from the leg and into 3/4-inch cubes
- 2 tablespoons lemon juice
- 2 tablespoons oil
- 1/4 cup yogurt

- 2 onions, chopped
- 6 cloves garlic, minced
- 1 can (1 pound) stewed tomatoes, chopped. Do not drain
- 1 can (10 1/2 ounces) chicken broth
- 1/2 teaspoon dried dill weed
- salt and pepper to taste

In a large bowl, toss together lamb, lemon juice, oil and yogurt. Allow to stand at room temperature for 2 hours, turning and tossing every now and again. (Refrigerate, if marinating for a longer period.)

In a 9x13-inch pan, toss together meat and the remaining ingredients until blended. Cover pan tightly with foil and bake in a 350° oven for about 1 1/2 hours or until lamb is tender.

Transfer to a porcelain casserole and remove every trace of fat. Heat through before serving. Serve with Brown Rice with Mushrooms and Onions as a hearty accompaniment. Serves 6 to 8.

Honey Baked Ham
with Cinnamon Apple Rings

Mustard, brown sugar and cloves is the traditional coating for baked ham. This coating is enhanced with the addition of apple juice, honey and cinnamon. Serve it thinly sliced with hot biscuits and honey.

1 ready-to-eat ham, about 12 pounds, with bone in. With a sharp knife, remove the skin and fat, leaving a thin layer of fat to keep meat moist while baking. Score surface of ham in a diamond pattern, without cutting into the meat. Place a whole clove in half of the diamonds, but don't overdo it. We do not want the cloves to overpower the taste. Brush top with 3 tablespoons Dijon mustard. Place ham in a roasting pan.

1 cup brown sugar
1/2 cup honey
1 teaspoon cinnamon

1 1/2 cups apple juice

3 apples, cored and sliced into rings
1/2 cup honey
3/4 cup apple juice
1/2 teaspoon cinnamon
1/8 teaspoon nutmeg

1 cup finely chopped pecans

Combine sugar, honey and cinnamon and spread mixture over the ham. Pour apple juice into the pan. Roast in a 325° oven for about 1 1/2 hours, basting now and again with the juices in the pan, or until a meat thermometer, set in the thickest part (not touching the bone), registers 160°.

Meanwhile, in another roasting pan, lay apple rings. Combine honey, apple juice and spices and drizzle over the apples. Bake in a 350° oven for 20 minutes, sprinkle top with pecans and continue baking for 10 minutes.

Serve ham surrounded with apple rings, and cut into thin slices to serve.

Note: — Apples can be prepared earlier in the day and heated before serving.
— Ham can be decorated with apple rings with cherries in the core. In this instance, bake apples for 20 minutes to keep them firm.

Sweet & Sour Pork with Sauerkraut & Apples

1 pound pork loin chops, sliced thin, (about 8 to the pound)
2 large apples, peeled, cored and sliced
1 large onion, chopped
1 tablespoon oil
1 tablespoon paprika
1 cup sauerkraut, undrained
2 tablespoons brown sugar
2 tablespoons granulated sugar
1 can (10 1/2 ounces) chicken broth
2 tablespoons lemon juice
   salt and pepper to taste

Trim chops of every trace of fat and lay flat in a Dutch-oven casserole. In a large bowl, combine the remaining ingredients and place mixture into Dutch-oven. Bring to a boil, cover pan, and reduce heat to a simmer. Cook for about 1 1/2 hours, or until pork is tender.

Serve with buttered noodles, sprinkled with a little lemon juice. And a thick, crusty dark rye or pumpernickel with raisins would be just lovely to soak up the delicious gravy. Serves 4.

Note: — *Entire dish should be prepared earlier in the day and stored in the refrigerator. Remove any congealed fat. Heat carefully, so as not to scorch. Gravy is thick.*

— *Can be prepared 1 day earlier.*

— *Roasted Potatoes & Onions is another nice accompaniment.*

Roast Potatoes & Onions: In a 9x13-inch pan toss together 4 medium potatoes, unpeeled, and cut into 3/4-inch dice; 1 onion, chopped; 2 teaspoons paprika; 6 tablespoons melted butter; and salt to taste until nicely combined. Bake in a 350° oven, for about 40 minutes, turning now and again, until potatoes are tender.

179

Apricot Glazed Canadian Bacon
with Honey Spiced Apricots

2 pounds Canadian bacon or boneless ham round (ready to eat). Brush top with 1 tablespoon spicy hot mustard.
1/2 cup apricot jam
1/2 cup brown sugar
1/2 teaspoon ground cloves
1/4 cup apricot syrup (reserved from below)

Place Canadian bacon in an 8x12-inch baking pan. Stir together the remaining ingredients and spread mixture over the meat. Bake in a 375° oven for about 30 minutes, brushing now and again, until meat is glazed. Allow to cool.

Thinly slice the meat and place in a porcelain baker. Drizzle a little glaze on top. (Can be held at this point.) Just before serving, warm in a 350° oven for 20 minutes, or until heated through. Do not overheat. Serve warm, garnished with warm Honey Spiced Apricots.

Honey Spiced Apricots:
2 tablespoons butter
1/4 cup sugar
1/4 cup honey
1/4 cup apricot syrup (reserved from below)
1 teaspoon cinnamon
1/4 teaspoon ground nutmeg
1/4 teaspoon ground cloves
2 tablespoons chopped pecans
1 can (1 pound 12 ounces) apricot halves in syrup, drained. Reserve syrup. Place apricot halves, cut side down, in a porcelain baker.

In a saucepan, heat together first 8 ingredients and cook sauce for about 2 to 3 minutes, or until sugar is totally dissolved. Pour mixture over the apricots. (Can be held at this point, covered, in the refrigerator.) Before serving, warm in a 350° oven for about 20 minutes or until heated through. Serve apricots warm, not hot.

Note: — If this is served for breakfast or brunch, it can serve from 6 to 12, depending on how many courses served.

— Canadian bacon and apricots can be prepared earlier in the day or 1 day earlier and stored in the refrigerator. Warm before serving.

Honey Barbecued Loin of Pork with Baked Apples & Raisins

1 loin of pork roast, about 4 to 5 pounds. Ask butcher to remove the chine bone and any excess fat. Sprinkle with salt and pepper and garlic powder to taste. Brush top with 2 tablespoons Dijon mustard. Place meat thermometer into the thickest part of the meat, making certain it rests in the center and does not touch the bone.

Place roast in a shallow baking pan, bone side down, and bake in a 325° oven for about 2 1/2 hours, or until meat thermometer registers 160°. Now, brush Honey Barbecue Glaze over the roast, and continue baking and basting until pork is tender and meat thermometer registers 175°. Serve with Baked Apples & Raisins. Serves 6.

Honey Barbecue Sauce:
  2 tablespoons butter
  1/2 cup honey
  1/2 cup ketchup
  2 tablespoons lemon juice
  2 tablespoons brown sugar
  1 clove garlic, minced

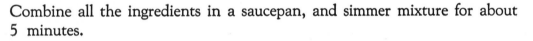

Combine all the ingredients in a saucepan, and simmer mixture for about 5 minutes.

Baked Apples & Raisins

1/2 cup yellow raisins
  6 medium apples, peeled, cored and cut into 1-inch rings

1/2 cup apple cider
1/2 cup orange juice
1/2 cup sugar
  4 tablespoons butter
  4 tablespoons grated orange (use fruit, juice and peel)
  2 thin slices lemon

In a 9x13-inch porcelain baker, scatter raisins. Place apple rings over the raisins. Stir together the remaining ingredients and pour over the apples. Bake in a 350° oven for about 30 minutes, or until apples are tender, but firm. (Do not allow to get mushy.) Serves 6.

Cinnamon Roast Loin of Pork with Apricots, Prunes & Carrots

This is a nice homey dish to serve family and friends. Succulent pork, surrounded by a bed of fruits and vegetables and faintly seasoned with cinnamon, will transform an average dinner into a celebration.

1 loin of pork (about 4 pounds). Ask the butcher to loosen the chine bone. Sprinkle meat with salt, pepper, garlic powder and paprika. Insert meat thermometer into thickest part of the meat, and not touching the bone.

12 pitted prunes
12 dried apricots
6 medium carrots, peeled, and cut into 1-inch slices
6 medium potatoes, peeled and cut into 1-inch slices

1 can (10 1/2 ounces) beef broth, or more as necessary
1 thin slice lemon
1/4 cup (1/2 stick) butter, melted
1/4 teaspoon cinnamon
salt and pepper to taste

Place roast in a 9x13-inch roasting pan and bake in a 350° oven for 40 minutes. Remove roast to a clean pan or drain any fat that has accumulated.

Now, place prunes, apricots, carrots and potatoes, evenly around the roast. Combine the remaining ingredients and pour mixture over the fruits and vegetables. Tent pan loosely with foil.

Return roast to oven and continue baking for about 1 1/2 hours or until meat thermometer registers 175°. Baste from time to time with pan juices, and add a little beef broth, if the juices are evaporating. Turn the fruits and vegetables once or twice during baking time. Remove roast from baking pan and place on serving platter. Arrange fruits and vegetables evenly around the roast and spoon some of the sauce on top. Carve at the table and serve 6.

All-American Country Ribs with Honey Barbecue Sauce

3 to 4 pounds country-style pork ribs, sprinkle with salt, pepper and garlic powder.

Honey Barbecue Sauce:
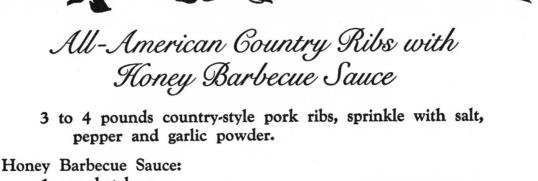
- 1 cup ketchup
- 1 cup chili sauce
- 1/2 cup honey
- 1/2 cup brown sugar
- 2 teaspoons dry mustard
- 1/4 cup vinegar
- 1/4 teaspoon cayenne pepper
- 1/4 cup (1/2 stick) butter
- salt and freshly ground pepper to taste

Lay ribs in a 12x16-inch roasting pan and bake in a 350° oven for about 45 minutes. Remove ribs from pan and drain of all fat that has been rendered. Return ribs to cleaned pan.

Stir together the Barbecue Sauce ingredients until blended, and baste ribs with sauce. Return ribs to 350° oven and continue baking and basting until ribs are tender and highly glazed. (Turn ribs now and again so they are sauced on all sides.) Unused sauce can be stored in the refrigerator for several weeks. Serves 4 to 6.

Note: — *Ribs can be prepared earlier in the day, but reduce cooking time by 15 minutes. Continue baking and basting before serving.*

— *Now, there is an alternate way of making ribs that I thought you should know about. Pork ribs are sometimes quite fatty and a greasy rib is less than satisfactory. So either way you choose to prepare ribs, make certain that you remove as much excess fat.*

Alternate Preparation:
Place ribs in a stock pot with enough water to cover them. Bring to a boil, lower heat, and simmer ribs for about 45 minutes or until ribs are almost tender. Drain thoroughly. Now place ribs in a 12x16-inch baking pan, brush on all sides with Honey Barbecue Sauce and continue baking and basting until tender and glazed.

Note: — *Ribs made in this fashion can be completed on the barbecue, but make certain that the heat is low or the honey will burn.*

Pate of Veal and Red Peppers with Herbed Tomato Sauce

Veal and peppers are a wonderful blend of flavors. This elegant pate is much too grand to call "meat loaf". It is nice for an informal dinner and the sauce, so easy and delicious, can be served with many other dishes. If you are using the sauce for another purpose, it must be simmered for 20 minutes.

- 2 sweet red peppers, cleaned and cut into fourths
- 3 cloves garlic, minced
- 2 tablespoons oil

- 2 pounds ground veal
- 1 large onion, grated (must be grated, not chopped)
- 2 eggs, beaten lightly
- 1 cup fresh bread crumbs
- 1/3 cup chicken broth
- salt and pepper to taste

In a skillet, saute peppers and garlic in oil, over low heat, stirring now and again, until peppers are soft but not browned.

Combine the remaining ingredients and mix until thoroughly blended. Press half the meat mixture into a foil-lined 9x5-inch loaf pan. Lay the red peppers and garlic on top and press remaining meat mixture over the peppers.

Spread Herbed Tomato Sauce over the top and bake in a 350° oven for 1 hour 15 minutes or until meat is cooked through. Serve with Brown Rice with Onions & Mushrooms as a lovely accompaniment. Serves 6.

Note: — Can be prepared in advance and stored in the refrigerator. Heat before serving.

Herbed Tomato Sauce:
- 1 can (8 ounces) tomato sauce
- 1 small onion, minced (about 1/4 cup)
- 2 cloves garlic, minced
- 1 tablespoon minced parsley
- 2 teaspoons sugar
- 1 teaspoon sweet basil flakes (not ground)
- 1/2 teaspoon Italian Herb Seasoning flakes (not ground)
- 2 teaspoons oil
- salt and pepper to taste

Stir together all the ingredients until blended. (If you are preparing the sauce for another use, simmer it for 20 minutes.)

Veal Shanks with Tomatoes, Garlic & Peppers
(Osso Bucco)

Oh! what a delicious dish to serve family and friends for an informal dinner. This is a wonderful blend of flavors and textures. Be sure to have some crusty bread close by, to soak up the delicious gravy.

3 veal shanks (also called shinbones), about 6 pounds. Ask butcher to saw them into 3-inch pieces. Sprinkle with salt, pepper and a little flour.

6 medium onions, coarsely chopped

1 green bell pepper, cut into strips

2 cans (1 pound, each) stewed tomatoes, chopped. Discard seeds.

1 can (6 ounces) tomato paste

1 cup dry white wine

1 tablespoon grated lemon (use fruit, juice and peel)

1 large carrot, grated

1 tablespoon sugar

6 cloves garlic, minced

1 1/2 teaspoons Italian Herb Seasoning

salt and pepper to taste

Place veal shanks in a 12x16-inch roasting pan (marrow side up) and scatter onions and pepper over all. Stir together the remaining ingredients and pour sauce evenly over the veal. Cover pan tightly with foil and bake in a 350° oven for about 2 hours, or until veal is tender. (Sauce is perfect and does not need to be thickened.)

Allow veal to cool and then refrigerate for several hours to allow flavors to blend. Overnight is good, too. To serve, heat in a 350° oven for 20 minutes or until heated through. Serve with Lemon Rice with Parmesan. Serves 6.

Veal Meatloaf with Brandied Apple Rings in Cream & Herbed Rice

Meat loaf can be elevated quite a few notches, with the addition of apples and cream. The Herbed Rice is a lovely accompaniment.

- 1 pound ground veal
- 1 pound lean ground pork
- 1 small onion, grated
- 1 apple, peeled, cored and grated
- 3 slices egg bread, crusts removed. Soak in water and squeeze dry.
- 2 eggs
- 1 tablespoon chopped parsley
  salt and pepper to taste

In a large bowl, combine all the ingredients and mix until thoroughly blended. Place mixture into a loaf pan and bake in a 350° oven for 1 hour 15 minutes or until meat is cooked through. Serve with Brandied Apple Rings in Cream and Rice Pilaf with Herbs.

Brandied Apple Rings in Cream:
- 4 tablespoons butter
- 4 tablespoons cinnamon sugar
- 3 apples, cored and sliced into 1/2-inch thick slices. Do not peel.
- 1 tablespoon brandy

- 1/2 cup cream

In a large skillet, saute apple slices in butter, cinnamon sugar and brandy until apples are tender. Remove apples from skillet and add cream. Simmer cream for 2 or 3 minutes or until well blended with the syrup formed in the pan. Pour creamy syrup over the apples and serve with the veal loaf. Serves 6.

Rice Pilaf with Herbs:
- 1 1/2 cups long grain rice
- 2 tablespoons chopped chives
- 1 tablespoon chopped parsley
- 2 cans (10 1/2 ounces, each) chicken broth
- 1/2 cup water
- 4 tablespoons butter
  salt and pepper to taste

In a Dutch oven casserole, combine all the ingredients and simmer mixture, covered, until rice is tender and liquid is absorbed. Serves 6.

Veal & Peppers with Tomatoes, Onion & Garlic

This is a nice homey dish to serve family and friends. Serve it with Pink Rice and crusty Italian bread to soak up the delicious gravy.

3 pounds boneless veal, cut from the leg into 3/4-inch cubes. Sprinkle with salt, pepper and garlic powder to taste.

3 large onions, coarsely chopped

2 bell peppers, seeded and cut into 1/2-inch strips

3 cloves garlic, minced

1 can (1 pound 12 ounces) crushed tomatoes in tomato puree

1 cup dry white wine

1 can (10 1/2 ounces) beef broth

1 carrot, finely grated

1 tablespoon sugar

1 1/2 teaspoons Italian Herb Seasoning

2 tablespoons olive oil

Place veal in a 9x13-inch baking pan. In a large bowl, stir together the remaining ingredients and pour evenly over the veal. Cover pan tightly with foil and bake in a 350° oven for about 2 hours or until veal is tender.

Serve with Pink Rice with Parmesan as a delicious accompaniment. Serves 6.

Sweet & Sour Veal Roast with Pearl Onions & Mushrooms

This is such a lovely dish to serve some evening when you are dining with friends and are looking for a dish that is exciting, yet very easy to prepare and serve. As you have probably guessed, I have included it, so that you will be tempted to try the Sauerkraut Bread, which is a wonderful accompaniment.

> **2 pounds boneless veal, cut from the leg into 1-inch cubes. Sprinkle with salt, pepper and garlic powder and dust very lightly with flour.**
> **1 tablespoon oil**
>
> **1 can (1 pound) stewed tomatoes, chopped. Do not drain.**
> **1/2 cup dry red wine**
> **1 can (10 1/2 ounces) chicken broth**
> **3 cloves garlic, minced**
> **1 onion, very finely chopped**
> **4 tablespoons vinegar**
> **4 tablespoons brown sugar**
> **1 bay leaf**
> **1/8 teaspoon powdered cloves**
> **salt and pepper to taste**
>
> **1/2 pound frozen pearl onions, do not defrost**
> **1/2 pound mushrooms, sliced**

In a 9x13-inch pan spread 1 tablespoon oil and place the meat. Stir together the next 10 ingredients and spread evenly over the veal. Scatter mushrooms and pearl onions over all.

Cover pan tightly with foil and bake in a 350° oven for about 1 hour 20 minutes, or until veal is tender. (If you use a less tender cut of veal, baking time will be longer.)

Allow to cool and refrigerate for several hours. Overnight is preferred. Remove bay leaf. Reheat in a 350° oven for about 30 minutes or until heated through. Serves 6.

Note: — After baking, entire dish could be transferred to a porcelain baker, for storing, reheating and serving.

— Dumplings are a delicious accompaniment. And of course, the Sauerkraut Bread. Enjoy!

Paprikash of Veal with Mushrooms & Creme Fraiche

This is much too elegant to be called a veal stew. It is an elegant and subtle dish and just lovely, served on a bed of herbed rice or lightly buttered noodles. Cooking time will depend on the cut of veal used. Veal, cut from the leg, will cook in less time than veal cut from the shoulder.

3 pounds boneless veal, cut from the leg and into 3/4-inch cubes
2 tablespoons oil
2 onions, chopped
3 shallots, chopped
3 cloves garlic, minced
3 medium carrots, sliced
2 tablespoons paprika
1 can (1 pound) stewed tomatoes, chopped, Do not drain.
1 can (10 1/2 ounces) chicken broth
1/2 cup dry white wine
salt and pepper to taste

1/2 pound mushrooms
1 tablespoon butter
1 tablespoon lemon juice
1/3 cup cream
1/3 cup sour cream

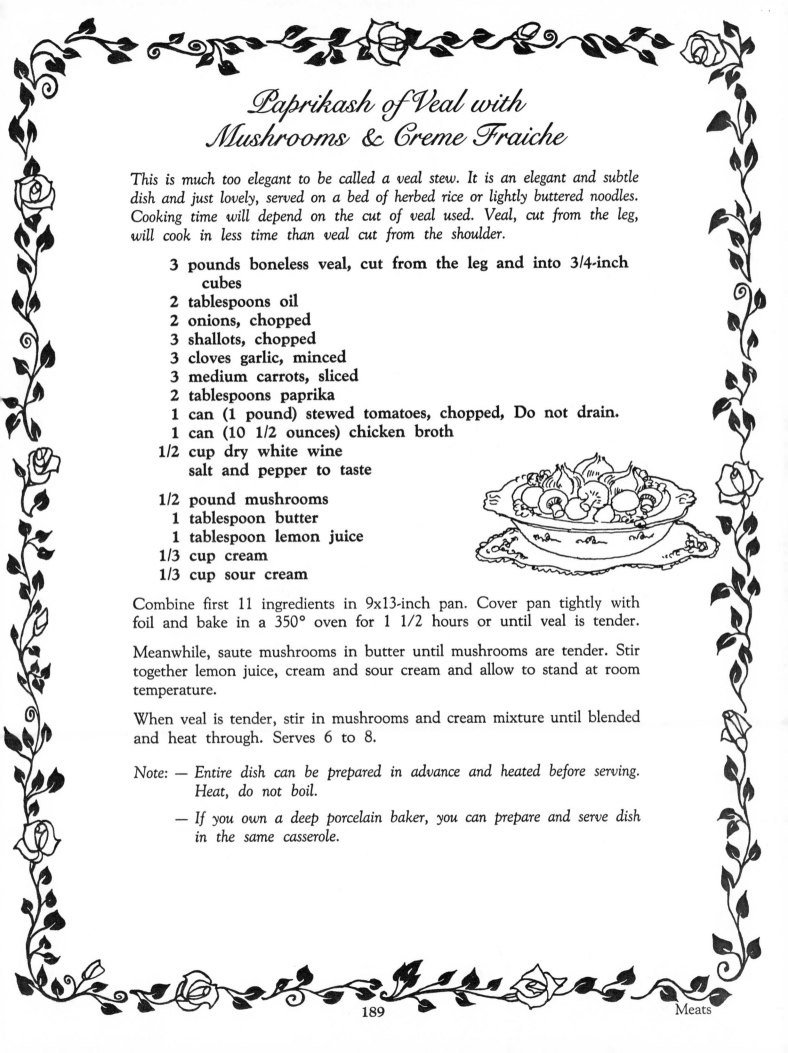

Combine first 11 ingredients in 9x13-inch pan. Cover pan tightly with foil and bake in a 350° oven for 1 1/2 hours or until veal is tender.

Meanwhile, saute mushrooms in butter until mushrooms are tender. Stir together lemon juice, cream and sour cream and allow to stand at room temperature.

When veal is tender, stir in mushrooms and cream mixture until blended and heat through. Serves 6 to 8.

Note: — *Entire dish can be prepared in advance and heated before serving. Heat, do not boil.*

— *If you own a deep porcelain baker, you can prepare and serve dish in the same casserole.*

Veal & Vegetable Loaf with Tomato Sauce

You could say that this little dish is almost a complete food. It contains meat, vegetables, eggs and bread. Basically, veal is lean, but be especially certain this is, or the calories will mount.

      2 carrots, peeled and cut into fourths
      1 medium red pepper, cored, seeded and cut into fourths
      1 medium onion, peeled and cut into fourths
      3 sprigs parsley, remove the stems
      2 eggs

      1 pound lean ground veal
  1/2 cup fresh bread crumbs (1 1/2 slices)
      1 package (10 ounces) frozen chopped spinach, defrosted
          and drained
          salt, pepper and garlic powder to taste
  1/2 cup tomato sauce

In the bowl of a food processor, place first 5 ingredients and blend until vegetables are finely chopped.

In a large bowl, mix together chopped vegetables, veal, bread crumbs, spinach and seasonings until very well blended. Pat mixture into a 9x5-inch loaf pan and pour tomato sauce over the top.

Bake in a 350° oven for about 1 hour or until meat is cooked through. Serves 6.

Note: — This is delicious served hot or cold. Serve any leftovers cold, with an interesting mustard.

Herb Stuffed Breast of Veal in Currant Wine Sauce

A delicious herb stuffing sparkles the breast of veal and the Currant Wine Sauce is the perfect balance. This is truly delicious and a marvelous choice for dinner with family and friends. Veal can be served immediately after baking, but it is a little more difficult to slice. By allowing it to chill, it cuts into the most attractive slices.

    1 breast of veal (about 6 to 7 pounds), boned and trimmed
        of any fat. (This will yield about 5 pounds, net
        weight.) Sprinkle with garlic powder on both sides.

    2 onions, finely chopped
    2 carrots, grated
    2 stalks celery, finely chopped
    6 cloves garlic, minced
    1/2 cup (1 stick) butter

    1/2 teaspoon sage flakes
    1 package (8 ounces) herb-seasoned stuffing mix
    1 can (10 1/2-ounces) chicken broth
        salt and pepper to taste

In a skillet, saute onions, carrots and celery in butter until vegetables are tender. Place vegetables in a bowl and toss with sage and stuffing mix. Add the chicken broth and toss and turn until blended. (Stuffing should be moist, but not soggy.)

Lay veal out flat and place stuffing down the center of the longer side. Pick up the sides to enclose the stuffing, overlapping about 1-inch. Close the seam with metal skewers. Place in a 9x13-inch baking pan and pour Currant Wine Sauce over the top. Cover pan tightly with foil and bake in a 350° oven for about 2 1/2 hours, or until veal is tender. Allow to cool and then refrigerate.

Remove metal skewers and any trace of fat from the gravy. Slice the veal into 1-inch slices and place in a porcelain baker with the gravy. Cover pan with foil and refrigerate until serving time. Heat in a 350° oven before serving. Serves 8.

Currant Wine Sauce:
    1 cup dry white wine
    6 tablespoons ketchup
    1/3 cup red currant jelly
    1 onion, grated
    1 can (10 1/2 ounces) chicken broth

In a saucepan, heat together all the ingredients until blended.

Veal Roast Stuffed with Vegetable Pesto in Tomato Wine Sauce

If you are planning to serve this for a formal dinner party, then, I suggest making the roast early in the day and firming it up in the refrigerator. Slice the roast cold, but leave it assembled. Spoon a little sauce on top, cover pan with foil, and heat through.

Vegetable Pesto Stuffing:

- 1/2 cup butter (1 stick), melted
- 6 cloves garlic
- 1/4 cup pine nuts
- 1 carrot, cut into 1-inch pieces
- 1 onion, cut into 8 pieces
- 2 tablespoons chopped parsley
- 1 teaspooon sweet basil flakes

- 1/2 cup fresh bread crumbs
- salt and pepper to taste

- 1 leg of veal, about 4 pounds, boned and butterflied

Place first 7 ingredients in food processor and blend for 30 seconds. Scrape down the sides and blend for another 15 seconds or until carrots are very finely chopped. Place mixture in a skillet, and cook, covered, over low heat, until carrots are tender. Stir in the bread crumbs and seasonings.

Lay the veal flat, cut side up and spread the stuffing mixture on top. Reassemble the roast and skewer it or tie it securely with string. Place roast in a 9x13-inch pan and pour Tomato Wine Sauce over the top. Bake in a 350° oven for about 1 hour 15 minutes or until meat is tender. (Baste every 15 minutes with the juices in the pan). Remove skewers or strings and carve into 1/2-inch slices. Serve with a spoonful of sauce. Serves 6 to 8.

Tomato Wine Sauce:
- 1 can (1 pound) stewed tomatoes, finely chopped
- 1/2 cup dry white wine
- 1 teaspoon sweet basil flakes
- 2 cloves garlic, minced
- 2 teaspoons sugar
- 2 teaspoons lemon juice
- 6 tablespoons melted butter
- salt and pepper to taste

Stir together all the ingredients until blended.

Noodles, Rice
&
Pastas

Noodles & Rice

Casserole of Wild Rice with Carrots, Apples & Onions 195
Pink Rice with Parmesan 195
Timbales of Rice & Carrots 196
Green Rice with Lemon & Herbs 196
Lemon Rice with Peas & Parmesan Cheese 197
Rice with Tomato, Parsley & Chives 197
Rice with Onions, Carrots & Cici Peas 198
Pink Rice with Chili Beans 199
Brown Rice with Onions & Lentils 200
Country Brown Rice with Mushrooms, Carrots & Onions 200
Casserole of Brown Rice with Cabbage & Onions 201
Brown Rice with Mushrooms & Onions 201
Noodle Pudding with Sweet Red Peppers & Cheese 202
Lemon Rice with Chives & Cheese 202
Timbales of Noodles with Red Peppers & Cheese 203
Noodle & Broccoli Ring Mold with Mushrooms & Cheese 204
Royal Crown Noodle & Apple Pudding 205
Orzo with Tomatoes, Onions & Peas 206
Orzo with Raisins & Pine Nuts 206
Lasagna Rolls with Spinach & Cheese in Light Tomato Sauce 207
Florentines with Instant Tomato Sauce 208
Linguini Primavera with Creme Fraiche Lemon Dill Dressing 209
Spaghetti alla Bolognese 210
Angel Hair Pasta in Zucchini Tomato Sauce 211
Fettuccini alla Romano with Onions, Pepper & Cheese 212

Casserole of Wild Rice with Carrots, Apples & Onions

2 onions, chopped
2 carrots, grated
1 apple, peeled, cored and grated
2 cloves garlic, minced
4 tablespoons butter

1 cup wild rice
1 cup long grain brown rice
4 cups chicken broth
   salt and pepper to taste

In saucepan you will cook rice, saute together first 5 ingredients until vegetables are soft. Add the remaining ingredients and simmer mixture until liquid is absorbed and rice is tender, about 40 to 45 minutes. Stir now and again to prevent sticking. Serve with roasted cornish hens or roast pork. Serves 12.

Note: — Casserole can be prepared earlier in the day and heated at serving time

Pink Rice with Parmesan

1 cup long-grain rice
1 can (10 1/2 ounces) chicken broth
3/4 cup water
2 tablespoons oil
1 tomato, peeled, seeded and chopped. (Can use 1 canned stewed tomato.)
1 tablespoon tomato sauce
2 tablespoons chopped chives
1 tablespoon chopped parsley

1/4 cup grated Parmesan cheese

In a saucepan, combine first 8 ingredients and stir until nicely mixed. Cover pan and simmer mixture until rice is tender and liquid is absorbed, about 30 to 35 minutes. Stir in the cheese just before serving. Serves 6.

Note: — Rice can be prepared earlier in the day and heated at serving time. Stir in the cheese just before serving.

Timbales of Rice & Carrots

1 cup cooked long-grain rice
1/2 pound carrots, cooked in water with a pinch of sugar
  until tender and drained. Reserve 1 carrot for garnish
  and coarsely chop the remaining carrots in a food
  processor. (Can be mashed with a fork.) Slice reserved
  carrot decoratively.
2 eggs, beaten
3/4 cup cream
2 tablespoons chopped chives
  pinch of sugar
  salt and white pepper to taste

Place rice and carrots in a bowl. Beat together the remaining ingredients until blended and add to rice and carrot mixture. Stir until blended. Butter 6 muffin molds and sprinkle with dry bread crumbs until nicely coated. Divide mixture between the molds. Place pan in a larger pan with simmering water and bake in a 400° oven for about 40 to 45 minutes or until timbale is set. Remove muffin pan from water and allow to set for 10 minutes before unmolding. Decorate top with carrot slices. Serves 6.

Green Rice with Lemon & Herbs

1 small onion, finely chopped
2 tablespoons butter
1 tablespoon lemon juice
1 cup long-grain rice
1 can (10 1/2 ounces) chicken broth
3/4 cup water
2 tablespoons finely chopped parsley
2 tablespoons finely chopped chives
  salt and pepper to taste

In a saucepan, saute onion in butter until onion is transparent. Stir in the remaining ingredients, cover pan and simmer rice until liquid is absorbed and rice is tender. Serves 6.

Lemon Rice with Peas & Parmesan Cheese
(Risotto di Limone)

This is a nice dish to serve with Osso Bucco. It is especially attractive flecked with peas and sparkled with Parmesan.

        1 small onion, finely chopped
        4 tablespoons butter
    1 1/2 cups rice

        2 cans (10 1/2 ounces, each) chicken broth
    1/2 cup water
        2 tablespoons lemon juice
          salt to taste

        1 package (10 ounces) frozen peas, cooked in 1/4 cup water
              for 5 minutes, and drained
        4 tablespoons grated Parmesan cheese

In a Dutch oven casserole saute onion in butter until onion is soft. Add the rice and saute for 2 minutes, stirring and turning. Carefully stir in the broth (it will splatter for a few seconds), water, lemon juice and salt. Cover pan and simmer rice for about 30 minutes, or until rice is tender and liquid is absorbed. Stir in cooked peas and heat through. Just before serving, toss with grated Parmesan cheese. Serves 6.

Rice with Tomato, Parsley & Chives

        2 cans (10 1/2 ounces, each) chicken broth
        3 tablespoons butter
        1 tomato, peeled, seeded and chopped
        1 tablespoon tomato sauce
        1 tablespoon chopped parsley
        1 tablespoon chopped chives
    1 1/4 cups rice

Combine all the ingredients in a saucepan and stir until nicely mixed. Cover pan and simmer rice for 30 minutes, or until rice is tender and liquid is absorbed. Serves 5 to 6.

Rice with Onions, Carrots and Cici Peas

This is an unusual casserole that is especially pretty for a buffet. It is a lovely blend of tastes, textures and colors.

- **2** medium carrots, grated
- **1** large onion, chopped
- **1** clove garlic, minced
- **2** tablespoons butter

- **1** can (1 pound) cici peas (also known as garbanzo beans), drained

- **1** cup rice
- **2** cups chicken broth, homemade or canned
- **1** tablespoon minced parsley
- **2** tablespoons butter
  salt and pepper to taste

In a skillet, over low heat, saute together first 4 ingredients until onion is soft, but not browned. Add the cici peas and continue cooking, over low heat, stirring now and again, until cici peas are softened.

Meanwhile, in a saucepan, stir together rice, broth, parsley, butter and seasonings, cover pan and simmer mixture until rice is tender and liquid is absorbed, about 30 minutes. Fluff rice with a fork as you stir in onion mixture.

Serve with roasted meats or poultry. Serves 6, generously.

Note: — *Casserole can be prepared earlier in the day and stored in the refrigerator. Sprinkle with a few drops water before reheating over low heat. Stir now and again to prevent rice from sticking to the bottom of the pan.*

— *If you use canned chicken broth, then use 1 can (10 1/2 ounces) chicken broth mixed with 3/4 cup water.*

Pink Rice with Chili Beans

This is a nice dish to consider for a barbecue or a backyard picnic. It is a great accompaniment to broiled meats.

2 cups rice
4 cups chicken broth (homemade or canned)
4 tablespoons butter
1 tablespoon tomato sauce
salt and pepper to taste

1 onion, chopped
2 shallots, minced
3 cloves garlic, minced
3 tablespoons butter

1 can (1 pound) stewed tomatoes, chopped. Do not drain.
1 can (8 ounces) tomato sauce. (Use 1 tablespoon for the rice.)
2 cans (1 pound, each) kidney beans, rinsed and drained
2 tablespoons chili powder, or to taste
salt and pepper to taste

In a Dutch oven casserole, place first 5 ingredients, cover pan and simmer mixture until rice is tender and liquid is absorbed, about 35 minutes.

Meanwhile, in a saucepan, saute onion, shallots and garlic in butter until onion is soft, but not browned. Add the remaining ingredients and simmer mixture for 20 minutes, uncovered or until kidney beans are softened and mixture is thickened.

Add the bean mixture to the rice and toss and turn until everything is nicely blended. Serves 10 to 12.

Note: — *Casserole can be prepared earlier in the day and stored in the refrigerator. Reheat over low heat, stirring now and again to prevent rice from sticking to the bottom of the pan.*

— *If you use canned chicken broth, then use 2 cans (10 1/2 ounces, each) chicken broth and 1 1/2 cups water.*

Noodles, Rice & Pastas

Brown Rice with Onions & Lentils

1 medium onion, chopped
3 tablespoons butter

3/4 cup brown rice
1/2 cup lentils
2 cans (10 1/2 ounces, each) chicken broth
   salt and pepper to taste

In a saucepan, saute onion in butter until onion is transparent. Stir in the remaining ingredients, (carefully, as broth could splatter), cover pan, and simmer mixture for about 40 to 45 minutes or until rice and lentils are tender and liquid is absorbed. Serves 6.

Country Brown Rice with Mushrooms, Carrots & Onions

1/4 pound mushrooms, thinly sliced
2 medium carrots, grated
1 onion, finely chopped
2 tablespoons butter

1 cup brown rice
   salt to taste
2 cans (10 1/2 ounces, each) chicken broth
2 tablespoons butter

In a skillet, saute first 4 ingredients together, until onions are transparent. Do not allow onions to brown.

In a saucepan, combine remaining ingredients, cover pan and simmer mixture for 40 minutes, or until liquid is absorbed and rice is tender. Stir in mushroom mixture and heat through. Serves 6.

Note: — *Rice can be prepared earlier in the day and stored in the refrigerator. Heat before serving.*

Casserole of Brown Rice with Cabbage & Onions

This is a rather unusual combination but it is very delicious, and a lovely accompaniment to roast goose or pork. Add a little leftover poultry or meat, and it does well for a light supper.

- 4 tablespoons butter
- 1 onion, chopped
- 2 shallots, minced
- 1 clove garlic, minced
- 1 cup finely shredded cabbage

- 2 cans (10 1/2 ounces, each) chicken broth
- 1 cup brown rice
  salt and pepper to taste

In saucepan you will cook rice, place first 5 ingredients and cook mixture, over low flame, until vegetables are soft. Stir every now and again to prevent sticking.

Add the remaining ingredients, cover pan, and simmer mixture until liquid is absorbed and rice is tender, about 40 to 45 minutes. Fluff rice with a fork and serve. Serves 6.

Note: — This can be prepared earlier in the day and heated at serving time.

— Can be used as an excellent stuffing. Will stuff a 4-pound chicken.

Brown Rice with Mushrooms & Onions

- 1 1/2 cups brown rice
- 2 tablespoons oil
- 3 cups chicken broth
  salt and pepper to taste

- 1/4 pound mushrooms
- 1 small onion, chopped
- 2 tablespoons butter

In a saucepan, simmer together first 4 ingredients, covered, until rice is tender and liquid is absorbed, about 35 to 40 minutes. Meanwhile, saute mushrooms and onions in butter until onions are soft. When rice is cooked through, stir in the mushrooms and onions. Serves 6 to 8.

Note: — Both dishes can be prepared earlier in the day and heated before serving.

Noodles, Rice & Pastas

Noodle Pudding with Sweet Red Peppers & Cheese

This is a beautiful dish to serve on a buffet for a lovely luncheon. It is also a grand accompaniment to dinner with a simple roast of veal. Roast chicken is very good, too.

    1/2 pound medium noodles, cooked in boiling water and 1 tablespoon oil, until tender but firm and drained.

    1 jar (15 ounces) sweet red peppers, drained and chopped (pimientos)

    4 eggs

1 1/2 cups cream

    1/2 cup Ricotta cheese

    1/2 cup chopped green onions

    2 tablespoons parsley

    1/2 cup grated Parmesan cheese

    salt to taste

In a buttered 9x13-inch pan toss the cooked noodles with the chopped pimientos. Beat together the remaining ingredients until blended. Pour mixture over the noodles and mix and toss until everything is nicely blended.

Bake in a 350° oven for about 1 hour or until pudding is set and top is nicely browned. Cut into squares to serve. Serves 10.

Lemon Rice with Chives & Cheese

1 1/4 cups rice

2 1/2 cups chicken broth

    2 tablespoons butter

    salt and pepper to taste

    4 tablespoons chopped chives

    2 tablespoons lemon juice

    4 tablespoons grated Parmesan cheese

In a covered saucepan, simmer together first 4 ingredients until rice is tender and liquid is absorbed. Toss rice with remaining ingredients until blended. Serve at once. Serves 6.

Note: — Rice can be prepared earlier in the day but do not add the lemon, chives and cheese. Toss these in after reheating the rice and just before serving.

Timbales of Noodles with Red Peppers & Cheese

This is a divine tasting and glamorous accompaniment to roast chicken or veal. It is an especially good choice for a dinner with an Italian mood.

1 package (8 ounces) fine egg noodles, cooked until firm-tender and drained

1 jar (8 ounces) roasted sweet red peppers, drained and chopped

3 eggs
1 cup cottage cheese
1 cup sour cream
1/4 cup grated Parmesan cheese
1/4 cup chopped chives
2 tablespoons chopped parsley
pinch cayenne
salt and pepper to taste

Toss together noodles and red peppers until combined. Beat together the remaining ingredients and stir with noodle mixture until nicely blended. Divide between 8 heavily greased 6-ounce custard cups and place in a pan with 1-inch boiling water.

Bake in a 350° oven for about 30 minutes, or until eggs are set and a knife, inserted in center, comes out clean. Gently loosen timbales, by running a knife around the edge and invert onto a buttered porcelain baker. Sprinkle tops with Cheese & Chive Crumbs and heat through before serving. Serves 8.

Cheese & Chive Crumbs: Stir together 1 tablespoon grated Parmesan cheese, 1 tablespoon chopped chives and 1 tablespoon cracker crumbs, until blended.

Note: — Can be prepared earlier in the day and stored in the refrigerator. Heat before serving.

Noodle & Broccoli Ring Mold with Mushrooms & Cheese

This is a delicious and festive combination of flavors and textures. Baking it in a ring mold adds a touch of glamor It can also be baked in a 9x9-inch pan and cut into squares to serve

- 1/4 pound mushrooms, sliced
- 2 cloves garlic, minced
- 4 tablespoons butter

- 2 eggs
- 1/4 cup cream
- 1/4 cup sour cream
- 1/4 cup grated Parmesan cheese
- 2 tablespoons finely chopped green onions
- 1/2 teaspoon Italian Herb Seasoning Flakes
  salt and pepper to taste

- 1 package (8 ounces) medium noodles, cooked firm-tender and drained
- 1 package (10 ounces) frozen broccoli, defrosted

Saute mushrooms and garlic in butter until mushrooms are tender. Beat together the next 7 ingredients until blended. In a large bowl, stir together all the ingredients until blended.

Place mixture into a 2-quart ring mold that has been heavily greased and sprinkled with cracker crumbs. Place mold on a cookie sheet and bake in a 350° oven for about 1 hour, or until custard is set and top is lightly browned. Loosen mold from pan by running a knife along the edge. Invert onto a serving platter and fill the center with glazed carrots or sauteed mushroom caps. Serves 6 to 8.

Note: — Can be prepared earlier in the day and gently loosened from the sides of the pan. Not necessary to remove from pan. Reheat in pan placed on a cookie sheet, and invert onto a serving platter before serving.

Royal Crown Noodle & Apple Pudding with Cinnamon & Pecans

Noodle pudding is a homey, family dish, but when baked in a ring mold, masked with cinnamon and pecans, it is dressed for the most formal occasions. The apples, baked in the custard, are especially appealing. To facilitate unmolding, be sure to generously butter the mold.

- 3 tablespoons melted butter
- 3 tablespoons cinnamon sugar
- 1 cup pecan halves

- 1 apple, peeled, cored and grated
- 1/4 cup melted butter (1/2 stick)
- 4 tablespoons cinnamon sugar
- 1 package (8 ounces) medium noodles, cooked tender but firm

- 2 eggs
- 1/2 cup sour cream
- 1/2 cup sugar
- 1/2 teaspoon vanilla

Generously butter a 2-quart ring mold. Drizzle bottom of mold with melted butter, sprinkle with cinnamon sugar, and evenly place pecans.

Toss together apple, butter, cinnamon sugar and cooked noodles and place evenly over the pecans.

Beat together eggs, sour cream, sugar and vanilla until blended and pour this over the noodles so that it is distributed evenly. Place mold on a cookie pan and bake in a 350° oven for 1 hour, or until top is golden and custard is set. Unmold onto a serving platter and decorate with spiced peaches or spiced apricots. Serves 8.

Note: — *If you prepare this earlier in the day, store, in the mold, in the refrigerator. However, it must be reheated in a pan with 1-inch water, for about 25 minutes, or until heated through... or pecans will burn.*

Orzo with Tomatoes, Onions & Peas

Orzo is a nice variation to the more traditional rice. Everyone seems to enjoy this rice-shaped pasta, flavored with broth and tomatoes. The addition of peas makes it especially attractive for buffet serving.

    1 cup orzo (rice-shaped pasta)
    1 can (10 1/2 ounces) chicken broth
    1 cup water
    2 tablespoons oil
      salt and pepper to taste

    1 small onion, chopped
    2 cloves garlic, minced
    2 tomatoes, peeled, seeded and chopped
    1 tablespoon butter
    1 package (10 ounces) frozen peas

In a saucepan, stir together the first 5 ingredients, cover pan and simmer mixture for about 40 minutes, or until orzo is tender and liquid is absorbed.

Meanwhile in a covered saucepan, cook together the remaining ingredients until onions are soft. Remove cover and cook for several minutes, or until liquid is evaporated. Toss together orzo and tomato mixture until blended. Heat through before serving. Sprinkle with a little grated Parmesan before serving (optional). Serves 4 to 6.

Orzo with Raisins & Pine Nuts

    1 cup orzo (rice-shaped pasta)
    1 can (10 1/2 ounces) chicken broth
    1 cup water
    2 tablespoons oil
      salt and pepper to taste

    1/2 cup toasted pine nuts
    1/2 cup plumped yellow raisins

In a saucepan, stir together first 5 ingredients, cover pan and simmer mixture for about 40 minutes, or until orzo is tender and liquid is absorbed. Just before serving, stir in the pine nuts and plumped raisins. Serves 4 to 6.

Lasagna Rolls with Spinach & Cheese & Light Tomato Sauce

This is a more festive and glamorous lasagna. Traditionally served layered and flat, the noodles in this dish are filled and rolled with a savory spinach and cheese filling. A delicate tomato sauce is ladled on top. The green noodles and red sauce make a beautiful presentation.

- 1 pound lasagna noodles, cooked tender but firm (al dente). (Green lasagna noodles are especially nice, but not essential.)
- 2 packages (10 ounces, each) frozen chopped spinach, defrosted and drained very dry
- 1 pound Ricotta cheese
- 1 package (8 ounces) cream cheese, at room temperature
- 1 cup grated Parmesan cheese
- 1 package (8 ounces) Mozzarella cheese, grated coarsely
- 1/2 teaspoon sweet basil flakes
- 1/4 teaspoon oregano flakes
  salt and pepper to taste

Prepare lasagna noodles and set aside. In a large bowl, beat together the remaining ingredients until blended.

Lay out each lasagna noodle and spoon about 1/2 cup filling on the top of the noodle. Roll it up, jelly-roll fashion. Place rolls in a 9x13-inch pan, coiled side up. Continue with remaining noodles.

Pour Light Tomato Sauce over the rolls and sprinkle top with additional grated Parmesan cheese. Bake in a 350° oven for about 30 minutes or until heated through. (Make certain the Mozzarella is melted.) Yields 10 to 12 rolls, depending on the length of the noodles.

Light Tomato Sauce:
- 1 can (1 pound 12 ounces) crushed tomatoes in tomato puree
- 1 can (8 ounces) tomato sauce
- 1 tablespoon sugar
- 1 tablespoon oil
- 2 tablespoons dried onion flakes
- 1/2 teaspoon coarsely ground garlic powder
- 1 teaspoon sweet basil flakes
- 1/2 teaspoon Italian Herb Seasoning
  pinch of red pepper flakes
  salt and pepper to taste

Combine all the ingredients and simmer sauce for 10 minutes.

Noodles, Rice & Pastas

Florentines with Instant Tomato Sauce

1 package (12 ounces) florentines, (spinach pasta, stuffed with spinach and cheese.) Cook in boiling water with 2 tablespoons oil, until firm but tender. Drain. (These can be purchased in Italian groceries. Use the frozen florentines, not the dried ones.)

Instant Tomato Sauce:

    1 can (1 pound 12 ounces) crushed tomatoes in tomato puree
1 1/2 tablespoons sugar
    2 tablespoons instant minced onions
    1 teaspoon Italian Herb Seasoning
1/2 teaspoon sweet basil flakes
1/4 to 1/3 teaspoon coarse grind garlic powder
    1 bay leaf
1/4 teaspoon seasoned pepper
    salt to taste
    dash or more of red hot pepper flakes

Combine all the ingredients in a Dutch oven and simmer mixture for 10 minutes. Remove bay leaf, and serve over pastas.

Note: — This is a grand sauce to serve over pastas. It can be prepared earlier in the day or even 1 day before serving.

— Florentines can be served as a small entree or a main course.

— Tortellinis are a good substitution.

Linguini Primavera with Creme Fraiche Lemon Dill Dressing

Using the frozen mixed vegetables makes this marvelous salad available at a moment's notice. The dressing can be used on any number of salads. It is very delicate and flavorful.

1 package (1 pound) frozen Del Sol Vegetables. (This is a mixture of carrot sticks, cauliflower and broccoli, all neatly cut up.) Cook vegetables in boiling water for a few minutes until tender but firm.

1 package (8 ounces) linguini, cooked tender but firm and drained.

Creme Fraiche Lemon Dill Dressing:

1 cup sour cream
1/2 cup cream
2 green onions, cut up
3 tablespoons lemon juice
1/2 teaspoon dried dill weed
1/8 teaspoon garlic powder
1 teaspoon sugar
4 sprigs parsley (remove stems)
salt and pepper to taste

In a large bowl, toss together cooked vegetables and linguini. In a blender or food processor, place all the dressing ingredients and blend, until dressing is flecked with green. Store dressing in a jar, with a tight-fitted lid, and refrigerate for several hours. Overnight is good, too. (Flavor will intensify, if kept much longer.) Yields 1 3/4 cups dressing.

Pour dressing to taste over the vegetables and linguini and toss mixture until nicely blended. Refrigerate until serving time. (Unused dressing can be stored in the refrigerator.) Serves 6 as a first course.

Note: — *You can substitute 1 teaspoon dried sweet basil for the dill weed. This will give dressing a totally different character.*

Noodles, Rice & Pastas

Spaghetti alla Bolognese
(Spaghetti with Meat & Tomato Sauce)

This rich and flavorful spaghetti sauce is one of the best-loved sauces in all of Italy. It is a good basic sauce to be used over veal, eggplant and various pastas.

- 1 onion, finely chopped
- 1/2 cup finely grated carrots
- 3 cloves garlic, minced
- 2 tablespoons olive oil

- 1 pound lean ground beef

- 2 cans (1 pound, each) stewed tomatoes, chopped. Do not drain.
- 1 can (6 ounces) tomato paste
- 1/2 cup dry white wine
- 4 tablespoons minced parsley
- 1 teaspoon, each, Italian Herb Seasoning and sweet basil flakes
- 1 bay leaf
- 2 teaspoons sugar
  salt and freshly ground pepper to taste

In a Dutch oven or large saucepan, saute onion, carrots and garlic in oil until onion is transparent. Add the ground beef and continue sauteing until the meat loses its pinkness.

Add the remaining ingredients, and stir until mixture is nicely blended. Simmer the sauce, uncovered, for about 30 minutes. Remove bay leaf and adjust seasonings. Yields about 1 quart sauce, enough for about 1 pound of spaghetti.

To cook spaghetti: Use a spaghetti cooker for pastas. The strainer facilitates draining and can be used to keep the pasta warm for a short while. Also, just before serving, pasta can be plunged into boiling water for a few minutes, to be heated through and then drained. In absence of a spaghetti cooker, use a large pot, allowing about 3 quarts of water for each pound of pasta. Add 2 tablespoons oil to the water to help prevent pasta from sticking. Bring water to a boil, add 1 teaspoon salt, and gradually add pasta so that the water keeps boiling briskly. Do not break the spaghetti, but place it in the water, and as it softens, it will sink into the pot. Stir occasionally with a wooden spoon. Cook fresh pasta for 2 to 3 minutes. Commercially prepared pasta can take as long as 12 minutes to cook tender, but firm. Drain in a collander.

Angel Hair Pasta
with Zucchini Tomato Sauce

Angel hair pasta, tossed with a delicate blend of zucchini, shallots, tomatoes and cheese is practically a complete meal.

- 2 tablespoons olive oil
- 1 onion, chopped
- 3 cloves garlic, minced
- 2 shallots, minced
- 4 medium Italian zucchini, peeled and grated

- 1 can (1 pound) stewed tomatoes, chopped. Do not drain.
- 4 tablespoons tomato paste
- 1 tablespoon chopped parsley
- 1 teaspoon, each, Italian Herb Seasoning and sweet basil flakes
- salt and pepper to taste

- 1 package (8 ounces) angel hair pasta, cooked tender but firm and drained
- 1/3 cup grated Parmesan cheese

In a saucepan, saute together first 5 ingredients until vegetables are softened and most of the liquid rendered is evaporated. Add the tomatoes, tomato paste and seasonings and simmer sauce, uncovered, for 30 minutes. Toss pasta with sauce and pass grated cheese at the table. Serves 6 as a small entree, or 4 as a main course.

Note: — Sauce can be prepared earlier in the day and heated before serving.

— Pasta can be prepared 1 hour before serving and held in the strainer of a spaghetti cooker. Just before serving, plunge the strainer in boiling water for 2 minutes and drain.

Noodles, Rice & Pastas

Fettuccini alla Romano with Onions, Pepper & Cheese

Let me say, right at the start, that while I am not overly fond of bell peppers (or is it that they are not fond of me), in this dish, they are delicious. This sauce should be fresh and flavorful, and not simmered for hours... 20 to 30 minutes is about all I recommend.

      2 onions, chopped
      1 green bell pepper, cut into strips
      1 red bell pepper, cut into strips
      4 cloves garlic, minced
    1/2 pound mushrooms, sliced
      4 tablespoons oil

    1/4 cup dry red wine
      2 cans (1 pound, each) stewed tomatoes, finely chopped.
          Do not drain.
      2 cans (8 ounces, each) tomato sauce
      1 teaspoon sweet basil flakes
      1 teaspoon Italian Herb Seasoning
      2 teaspoons sugar
          pinch of cayenne pepper
          salt and pepper to taste

      1 pound cooked fettuccini, cooked firm but tender
          and drained
          grated Parmesan cheese

In a Dutch oven casserole, saute together first 6 ingredients until onions and peppers are tender. Add the next 8 ingredients and simmer sauce for 20 minutes, uncovered.

Meanwhile, cook the pasta, drain it and place it in a large bowl. Place the hot sauce in another bowl and pass it at the table. Serve with a generous spoonful of grated Parmesan on top. Serves 6, depending on accompaniments.

Note: — *When the vegetables are sauteed, do this over medium high heat. If the heat is too low, vegetables will render a great deal of liquid, and then you must continue cooking until liquid is evaporated.*

   — *Sauce can be prepared earlier in the day and heated carefully at serving time. Prepare the pasta before serving. If you use fresh pasta, remember that it cooks up in 2 or 3 minutes.*

Vegetables

Vegetables

Mini-Souffle with Artichokes, Spinach & Cheese 215
Artichokes with Mushrooms & Cheese Crumb Topping 215
Asparagus in Lemon Cheese Sauce 216
Asparagus with Lemon Garlic Caper Sauce 216
Casserole of Broccoli, Mushrooms & Tomatoes 217
Brussel Sprouts with Bacon, Lemon & Garlic Crumbs 218
Brussel Sprouts with Mushrooms, Shallot & Garlic 218
Casserole of Cabbage, Apples & Noodles 219
Cabbage & Apples in Honey Cream Sauce 220
Sweet & Sour Red Cabbage with Apples & Raisins 220
Cabbage with Apples & Raisins 221
Honey Carrots with Onions, Yogurt & Dill 222
Pureed Carrot Casserole with Onions & Cheese 222
Molded Ramekins with Carrots, Onions & Cream 223
Carrots Glazed with Maple Butter 223
Cauliflower & Onion Frittata with Bacon & Cheese 224
Cauliflower Mini-Souffle with Tomatoes & Swiss Cheese 224
Cauliflower Casserole with Tomatoes, Chiles & Cheese 225
Cauliflower with Apples & Onions 226
Chestnut Pudding with Raisins, Carrots & Prunes 227
Compote of Chestnuts, Apricots & Prunes 227
Linguini Provencal with Eggplant, Tomato & Onion Sauce 228
Eggplant Dumplings with Onions & Cheese in Tomato Sauce 229
Herbed Eggplant Casserole with Ricotta & 5-Minute Tomato Sauce 230
Italian Green Beans with Potatoes & Onions 231
Italian Green Beans with Tomato, Onions & Cheese 231
Green Beans with Tomatoes, Onions, Chiles & Bacon 232
Glazed Onions with Cinnamon & Raisins 233
Honey Baked Onions in Butter & Broth 233
Peas in Mushroom & Onion Sauce 234
Peas with Parsley & Shallots 234
Italian-Style Stuffed Green Peppers with Beef & Rice 235
Spinach & Red Pepper Dumplings with Onions & Cheese 236
Potato & Onion Pancake in Casserole 237
Orange Applesauce 237
Spinach with Tomatoes, Onions & Cici Peas 238
Molded Ramekins with Spinach, Noodles & Cheese 239
Spiced Sweet Potatoes with Cinnamon, Honey & Walnuts 239
Candied Sweet Potatoes with Glazed Walnuts 240
Stuffed Sweet Potatoes with Cinnamon Topping 240
Old-Fashioned Tomatoes Stuffed with Rice, Tomatoes & Garlic 241
Baked Tomatoes with Chiles & Cheese 242
Herbed Zucchini Mold with Cheese, Onions & Garlic 243
Timbales of Zucchini, Tomatoes & Onions with Cheese 244
Zucchini & Onion Fritatta 244

Mini-Souffle with Artichokes, Spinach & Cheese

1 jar (15 ounces) marinated artichoke hearts, drained and cut into fourths. Place in 1 layer in a greased 12-inch oval au gratin dish.

5 eggs
1 cup half and half
1 package (8 ounces) cream cheese, at room temperature and cut into 8 pieces
1 cup grated Swiss cheese
1/2 cup grated Parmesan cheese

1 package (10 ounces) frozen chopped spinach, defrosted and drained
1/3 cup chopped green onions
salt and pepper to taste

Prepare artichokes. In a food processor, blend the eggs, cream and cheeses until blended. Stir in the remaining ingredients. Pour egg mixture over the artichokes, and bake in a 350° oven for about 25 minutes, or until top is browned and souffle is puffed. Serve at once. Serves 6.

Artichokes with Mushrooms & Cheese Crumb Topping

1/2 pound mushrooms, sliced
1 onion, minced
2 shallots, minced
4 cloves garlic, minced
3 tablespoons butter

1/4 cup cream
1 tablespoon lemon juice
1 jar (15 ounces) marinated artichoke hearts, drained

Saute together first 5 ingredients until mushrooms are softened. Add the cream and lemon juice and cook for 2 minutes. In a 10-inch oval porcelain baker, stir together mushroom mixture and artichokes and sprinkle top with Cheese Crumb Topping. Bake in a 350° oven for 25 minutes or until crumbs are browned. Serves 6.

Cheese Crumb Topping: Toss together until blended 2 tablespoons fresh bread crumbs, 2 tablespoons grated Parmesan cheese and 1 tablespoon melted butter.

Asparagus in Lemon Cheese Sauce
& Cheese Crumbs

2 pounds asparagus, washed to remove every trace of sand. Snap or cut off the twiggy bottoms. (I like to run a vegetable peeler over the remaining bottoms, to assure tender stalks, but this is optional.) Asparagus should be tied into bundles and steamed upright. Boiling may leave the tips too soft. They can also be cooked (vertically) in 1-inch boiling water. Cook asparagus for about 8 to 10 minutes, or until tender but firm, and drain.

1/2 cup grated Swiss cheese
1/4 cup cream
1/4 cup sour cream
1/3 cup chopped chives
2 tablespoons lemon juice

2 tablespoons bread crumbs
2 tablespoons grated Parmesan cheese

Lay cooked asparagus in an 8x12-inch baking pan. Stir together next 5 ingredients and spread over the asparagus. Sprinkle top with mixture of crumbs and cheese. (Can be held at this point in the refrigerator.)

Before serving, heat in a 350° oven until heated through and cheese is melted. Brown top for 1 minute under the broiler. Serves 6.

Asparagus with Lemon Garlic Caper Sauce

2 pounds asparagus, cooked tender but firm. (See above recipe.)

4 tablespoons butter
4 cloves garlic, minced
3 tablespoons lemon juice
2 tablespoons capers, rinsed and drained
salt and pepper to taste

3 tablespoons grated Parmesan cheese

Lay cooked asparagus in an 8x12-inch baking pan. Heat together next 5 ingredients for 2 minutes and drizzle over the asparagus. Sprinkle top with grated cheese. (Can be held at this point in the refrigerator.) Before serving, heat in a 350° oven until heated through. Serves 6.

Casserole of Broccoli, Mushrooms & Tomatoes with Cheese Crumbs

2 packages frozen chopped broccoli, defrosted
1 can (1 pound) stewed tomatoes, drained and chopped. Use juice for another use.
1/4 pound mushrooms, cleaned and chopped
1/2 onion, chopped
2 eggs
1 cup Ritz cracker crumbs
salt and pepper to taste

Combine all the ingredients in a bowl and mix until blended. Place mixture into a heavily oiled (use 2 tablespoons oil) 9x13-inch baking pan, and sprinkle top with Cheese Crumbs.

Bake in a 350° oven for about 40 minutes or until casserole is set and top is browned. Serve warm as a vegetable accompaniment. Serves 6.

Cheese Crumbs:
1/4 cup Ritz cracker crumbs
1/4 cup grated Parmesan cheese

Combine crumbs and cheese and toss until blended.

Note: — Entire dish can be prepared earlier in the day and heated at time of serving.

— Drained tomatoes, mushrooms, onion and eggs can be chopped together in the food processor until mixture is coarsely chopped.

— Frozen chopped spinach can be substituted for the chopped broccoli.

Vegetables

Brussel Sprouts with Bacon, Lemon & Garlic Crumbs

2 packages (10 ounces, each) frozen Brussel sprouts
1/2 cup chicken broth

2 cloves garlic, minced
2 tablespoons butter
1/3 cup fresh bread crumbs
2 strips bacon, cooked crisp, drained and crumbled
1 tablespoon lemon juice
salt and pepper to taste

In a saucepan, simmer Brussel sprouts in chicken broth until they are tender, and drain.

Meanwhile in a skillet, saute garlic in butter for 2 or 3 minutes, but do not let garlic brown. Toss in the bread crumbs, bacon, lemon juice and seasonings.

Toss crumb mixture with sprouts and heat through. Serves 6.

Brussel Sprouts with Mushrooms, Shallot & Garlic

2 packages (10 ounces, each) frozen Brussel sprouts
1/2 cup chicken broth

1/4 pound mushrooms, thinly sliced
3 shallots, finely minced
3 cloves garlic, minced
2 tablespoons butter

2 tablespoons chopped chives
salt and pepper to taste

In a saucepan, simmer Brussel sprouts in chicken broth until they are tender, and drain.

In a skillet, saute together mushrooms, shallots and garlic in butter until mushrooms are tender and all the liquid rendered is evaporated. Add sprouts, chives and seasonings and heat through. Serves 6.

Note: — Both of the above may be prepared earlier in the day and heated before serving.

— 1/4 teaspoon dried dill weed may be added to the mushroom mixture. It imparts a delicate flavor, but does change the character of the dish.

Casserole of Cabbage, Apples & Noodles with Buttered Crumbs

Even those who are not fond of cabbage will enjoy this delicious casserole. Cabbage, flavored with apples, onions and buttered crumbs is a nice accompaniment to pot roast or meat loaf.

> 1 cabbage (about 1 pound), cored and cut into 1/4-inch shreds
>
> 1 onion, chopped
> 2 apples, peeled, cored and thinly sliced
> 2 teaspoons sugar
> 4 tablespoons butter
>
> 1/4 pound medium egg noodles, cooked al dente and drained
> 1 tablespoon lemon juice
> salt and pepper to taste
>
> 1/3 cup dry bread crumbs, tossed with
> 1 tablespoon melted butter

Plunge cabbage in boiling water and cook for about 7 to 8 minutes or until cabbage is tender, but firm. Drain thoroughly in a collander.

Saute together the next 4 ingredients until onion and apples are soft, but not mushy.

In a Dutch oven casserole, place cabbage, onion mixture, noodles, lemon juice and seasonings and toss to blend. Sprinkle mixture with buttered bread crumbs. Heat through carefully, over low heat, so that cabbage does not scorch. (A few drops of water will help.) This is a nice family dish and great for informal dinners with friends. Serves 6.

Note: — *Entire dish can be prepared earlier in the day and heated at serving time. Again, be careful in reheating so that cabbage does not scorch.*

Cabbage & Apples in Honey Cream Sauce

For those who feel that cabbage is a "country" dish, please know that this is an exception. It is sparkled with apples and wine and honey. Shred the cabbage into very thin strips, for a more delicate presentation.

- 2 tablespoons butter
- 1 onion, minced
- 2 shallots, minced
- 2 tablespoons honey
- 2 apples, peeled, cored and grated

- 1 small cabbage, cored and finely shredded (about 1 pound)
- 1/2 cup Reisling wine (or other semi-dry wine)
- 3/4 cup cream
- 1 tablespoon lemon juice
  salt and pepper to taste

In a Dutch oven casserole, saute together first 5 ingredients until onions are transparent. Add the remaining ingredients, and simmer mixture, for about 45 minutes, with cover slightly ajar, until cabbage is tender. Serve with roast capon, turkey or goose and a delicious Chestnut Pudding. Serves 6.

Sweet & Sour Red Cabbage with Apples & Raisins

- 1 small onion, minced
- 4 tablespoons butter

- 1 small red cabbage (about 1 1/4 pounds), cored and finely shredded
- 2 apples, peeled, cored and grated
- 1/2 cup raisins
- 1 cup apple juice
- 3 tablespoons sugar
- 3 tablespoons lemon juice
- 2 strips bacon, cooked crisp, drained and crumbled
  salt and pepper to taste

In a Dutch oven, saute onion in butter until onion is transparent. Stir in the remaining ingredients, cover pan, lower heat and simmer mixture for about 45 minutes, stirring now and again, until cabbage is tender. Add a little apple juice, if necessary, to avoid scorching. Serve with a hearty roast pork or roasted capon. Serves 6.

Cabbage with Apples & Raisins in Lemon Cream Sauce

Even if cabbage is not your preferred vegetable, you will enjoy this delicious combination of cabbage, apples, raisins in a lemony cream sauce. Sprinkle top with buttered crumbs just before serving.

1 onion, chopped
2 tablespoons sugar
2 tablespoons butter

1/2 cup chicken broth
1 small cabbage (about 1 pound), grated

1 apple, peeled and grated
1/2 cup yellow raisins
1/2 cup cream
2 teaspoons lemon juice
salt and pepper to taste

buttered crumbs

In a Dutch oven casserole, saute onion in sugar and butter until onion is transparent. Add the chicken broth and cabbage, cover pan, and simmer mixture for 30 minutes, or until cabbage is almost tender. Add the apple, raisins, cream, lemon juice and salt, cover pan, and continue simmering until cabbage is soft, about 15 minutes. Serve warm with a sprinkling of Buttered Crumbs. Serves 6.

To make Buttered Crumbs: In a skillet, melt 3 tablespoons butter. Add 1 1/4 cups cracker crumbs and cook and stir until crumbs are coated with butter and lightly toasted. Unused crumbs can be stored in the refrigerator.

Note: — Entire dish can be prepared earlier in the day and stored in the refrigerator. Heat carefully before serving.

Vegetables

Honey Carrots with Onions, Yogurt & Dill

1 onion, chopped
3 shallots, minced
2 tablespoons butter

1 package (1 pound) frozen baby carrots
2 teaspoons honey
1 tablespoon chopped parsley
1/4 cup chicken broth
salt and pepper to taste

1/2 cup yogurt
1/2 teaspoon dill weed

In a skillet, saute onion and shallots in butter until onions are transparent. Add the carrots, honey, parsley, broth and seasonings. Cover pan and cook over low heat, until carrots are tender. Stir in the yogurt and dill and heat through. Do not allow to boil. Serves 4 to 5.

Pureed Carrot Casserole with Onions & Cheese

1 pound carrots, cooked in water until tender and drained
1 slice onion, about 1/2-inch thick, cut from a medium-sized onion
2 eggs
1 cup Ricotta cheese
2 slices egg bread, roughly torn
salt and pepper to taste

Combine all the ingredients in the bowl of a food processor and blend until mixture is coarsely pureed. Place mixture into a buttered, scalloped 10-inch quiche pan and bake in a 350° oven until set and top is lightly browned, about 35 minutes.

Molded Ramekins with
Carrots, Onions & Cream

1 pound carrots, cleaned and cut into 1-inch slices
1 onion, chopped
2 tablespoons butter

3 eggs
1/2 cup cream
    salt to taste
    pinch of nutmeg

Cook carrots in boiling water to cover for about 15 minutes or until carrots are soft. Drain carrots and discard cooking liquid. Saute onion in butter until onion is soft, but do not brown.

Place onion and cooked carrots in a food processor and blend until mixture is coarsely chopped. Add the remaining ingredients to processor and blend for 10 seconds or until mixture is finely chopped

Divide mixture between 6 buttered porcelain ramekins. Place ramekins in a pan with 1-inch hot water and bake in a 375° oven for about 20 to 25 minutes, or until a cake tester, inserted 1/2-inch off center, comes out clean. Serve directly from ramekins; no need to unmold. Serves 6.

Carrots Glazed with Maple Butter

2 pounds frozen baby carrots, cooked in boiling salted water
    until tender and drained

1/4 cup butter
1/4 cup maple syrup
1/2 cup yellow raisins
    salt to taste

Prepare whole baby carrots, and set aside. In a large skillet, heat together butter and maple syrup. Add carrots and cook, stirring for 5 minutes. Add the raisins and continue cooking for about 5 minutes, or until carrots are lightly browned and glazed. Watch carefully so that the raisins do not brown. Serves 8 to 10.

    Vegetables

Cauliflower and Onion Frittata
with Bacon & Cheese

    3 onions, chopped
    3 tablespoons butter

    3 eggs
    1 cup cream or half and half
    1 cup grated Swiss cheese
1/2 cup grated Parmesan cheese
    1 package (10 ounces) frozen cauliflower, cut into small
        florets
    6 strips bacon, cooked crisp, drained and crumbled
        salt and pepper to taste

    1 tomato, cut into 6 very thin slices and seeded

Saute onions in butter, until onions are very soft, but not browned. (About 20 minutes, over low heat.) Beat together remaining ingredients until blended. Beat in onions. Pour batter into a greased 10-inch porcelain baker and place tomato slices on top. Bake in a 350° oven for about 30 minutes, or until custard is set and top is browned. Serves 4 to 6.

Cauliflower Mini-Souffle with
Tomatoes & Swiss Cheese

    2 packages (10 ounces, each) frozen cauliflower, cut into
        small florets
    1 can (1 pound) stewed tomatoes, drained and chopped
2/3 cup grated Swiss cheese

    5 eggs
    1 package (8 ounces) cream cheese, at room temperature
        and cut into 8 pieces
3/4 cup half and half
    6 tablespoons grated Parmesan cheese
        salt and pepper to taste

Butter Crumb Topping:
    2 tablespoons fresh bread crumbs
    1 tablespoon grated Parmesan cheese
    1 tablespoon melted butter

Toss together cauliflower, tomatoes and cheese and place in a greased 12-inch oval porcelain baker. In a food processor, blend together next 5 ingredients until mixture is pureed, and pour this evenly over the cauliflower mixture. Combine topping ingredients and sprinkle on top. Bake in a 350° oven for 25 to 30 minutes or until casserole is puffed and golden. Serves 6.

Cauliflower Casserole with Tomatoes, Chiles & Cheese Crumb Topping

This is a nice vegetarian casserole that is filled with all manner of good things ... eggs, vegetables, cheese. It is exceptionally easy to prepare as it can be assembled in literally minutes.

1/4 cup	chopped chives
2	packages (10 ounces, each) frozen cauliflower, cut into florets
2	tomatoes, peeled, seeded and diced
1	can (3 1/2 ounces) diced green chiles
1 1/2 cups	grated Swiss cheese
3	eggs
1 cup	half and half
1/2 cup	grated Parmesan cheese
3 tablespoons	cracker crumbs
3 tablespoons	grated Parmesan cheese

Toss together first 5 ingredients until nicely mixed and place in a greased 9x13-inch porcelain baker. Beat together eggs, half and half, and grated Parmesan until blended. Pour this over the vegetables in the pan and spread evenly. Sprinkle top with cracker crumbs and Parmesan cheese.

Bake casserole in a 350° oven for about 45 to 50 minutes, or until custard is set and topping is browned. Cut into squares to serve. Serves 6 for lunch, or 12 as an accompaniment to lunch or dinner.

Note: — If you are assembling this earlier in the day, follow this plan. Place vegetables in the porcelain baker and refrigerate. Eggs can be beaten with half and half and cheese, earlier in the day, and stored in the refrigerator. Have crumbs and cheese ready. Just before baking, pour egg mixture over the vegetables, sprinkle crumbs on top, and bake as described above.

Vegetables

Cauliflower with Apples & Onions

This is a rather unusual way to prepare cauliflower ... but, it is very good, indeed. Make certain that the florets are cut into small pieces to better blend the flavors.

- **1** large onion, chopped
- **2** medium apples, peeled, cored and grated
- **2** teaspoons sugar
- **3** tablespoons butter

- **2** packages (10 ounces, each) frozen cauliflower, cut into small florets and cooked in boiling water until very tender

- **1/2** cup bread crumbs
- **2** tablespoons butter
- **1** tablespoon chopped parsley

- salt and pepper to taste

In a Dutch oven casserole, saute together first 4 ingredients until onion and apples are very tender. Add the cooked cauliflower and toss until blended.

In a skillet combine crumbs, butter and parsley and cook until mixture is nicely blended. Add to cauliflower and toss until mixture is well combined. Season with salt and pepper to taste.

Serve with roast chicken or veal. Serves 6.

Note: — This can be prepared earlier in the day and heated at serving time.

— Reheat carefully, with a drop or two of water to prevent cauliflower from scorching.

Chestnut Pudding with Raisins, Carrots & Prunes

This recipe can also double as a stuffing for roast capon or Cornish hens. I prefer to bake this separately and serve it in a silver platter.

- 1 onion, chopped
- 2 medium carrots, grated
- 4 tablespoons butter

- 1 can (15 1/2 ounces) chestnuts, drained and coarsely chopped
- 1/2 cup chopped prunes
- 1/4 cup yellow raisins
- 1 package (8 ounces) herb-seasoned stuffing mix
- 2 eggs, beaten
- salt and pepper to taste
- 3/4 cup chicken broth

In a skillet, saute together first 3 ingredients until onions are soft. In a large bowl, place onion mixture and remaining ingredients, adding only enough broth to hold stuffing together. Place mixture into a greased 9-inch deep-dish pie plate and bake in a 350° oven for 30 minutes or until pudding is set. Serves 6.

Compote of Chestnuts, Apricots & Prunes

- 1 can (15 1/2 ounces) chestnuts, drained and sliced
- 1 cup soft pitted prunes
- 1 cup dried apricots
- 1/2 cup yellow raisins
- 1/2 orange, grated (about 3 tablespoons fruit, juice and peel)
- 1/2 cup orange juice
- 1/4 cup sugar
- 2 tablespoons butter
- 1/2 teaspoon vanilla

- 1/2 cup chopped walnuts

Simmer together first 8 ingredients for 30 minutes, or until mixture is syrupy. (Add a little orange juice, if mixture is getting sticky.) Stir in chopped walnuts. Serve warm or at room temperature with roast pork. Serves 6.

Note: — **To Prepare Fresh Chestnuts:** These dishes are enhanced with the use of fresh chestnuts. You will need 1 pound of chestnuts. With a very sharp knife, cut an "X" on the round side of each chestnut. Cover chestnuts with water and simmer for 25 minutes. Drain. Allow to cool until you are able to handle them, and remove the shell and brown skin covering. Chestnuts can now be chopped. Do not mash.

Vegetables

Linguini Provencal with Eggplant, Tomato & Onion Sauce

As you probably already know, eggplant acts like a sponge with oil, and frying one eggplant can sometimes use as much as 1 to 1 1/2 cups of oil... (a staggering 2000 to 2500 calories.) This recipe can be prepared with as little as 1 tablespoon, or it can be omitted altogether. This is a good vegetarian dish and quite substantial for dinner.

1 eggplant (about 1 pound), peeled and thinly sliced
1 tablespoon oil (optional)

1 large onion, finely chopped
4 cloves garlic, minced
1 tablespoon olive oil

1 can (1 pound, 12 ounces) crushed tomatoes in
   tomato puree
1 can (1 pound) stewed tomatoes, chopped. Do not drain.
2 tablespoons chopped parsley
1 teaspoon sweet basil flakes
1 teaspoon Italian Herb Seasoning
2 teaspoons sugar
   pinch of cayenne pepper
   salt and pepper to taste

1 pound linguini, cooked tender but firm and drained
   grated Parmesan cheese

In a 9x13-inch roasting pan, place eggplant slices, and drizzle with the optional oil. Cover pan tightly with foil and bake in a 400° oven for 25 to 30 minutes, or until eggplant is soft. Break it up into small pieces.

Meanwhile, saute onion and garlic in olive oil until onions are transparent. Add the next 8 ingredients and the eggplant, and simmer sauce, uncovered, for about 20 to 25 minutes. (Sauce will have thickened slightly.) Serve tossed with linguini and a generous spoonful of grated Parmesan.

Note: — Sauce can be prepared earlier in the day and reheated at serving time.

Eggplant Dumplings with Onions & Cheese & Light Tomato Sauce

This is a lovely vegetarian dish filled with so many good things, that are good for you, too. Serve these dumplings with a little Light Tomato Sauce on the side and with rice, flavored with a little lemon juice and grated Parmesan cheese.

- 1 small eggplant, about 3/4 pound, peeled and cut into 1/4-inch slices
- 1 tablespoon oil

- 1/2 cup Ricotta cheese
- 2/3 cup fresh bread crumbs (whole wheat)
- 1/4 cup chopped green onions
- 2 eggs
- 1/2 cup grated Parmesan cheese
- 1 tablespoon chopped parsley
- 1/2 teaspoon sweet basil flakes
- pepper to taste (cheese is salty, enough)

In a 9x13-inch pan, place the eggplant slices and drizzle with oil. Cover pan tightly with foil and bake in a 350° oven for about 25 minutes or until eggplant is soft. Remove from pan, drain and place in the large bowl of an electric mixer. Beat in the remaining ingredients until blended.

Shape eggplant mixture into 2-inch patties, and saute in an oiled teflon skillet until browned on both sides, adding a little oil as necessary. (These can also be baked in a 9x13-inch oiled teflon baking pan, about 10 minutes on each side.) Drain on paper towelling.

Before serving, heat in a 350° oven for about 10 minutes, or until heated through. Serve with Light Tomato Sauce on the side. Yields about 18 dumplings and serves 4 to 6.

Light Tomato Sauce:
- 1 can (1 pound) stewed tomatoes, drained and chopped
- 1/4 cup tomato sauce
- 2 tablespoons minced onion
- 1 tablespoon lemon juice
- 1 teaspoon sugar
- 2 teaspoons oil
- 1/2 teaspoon sweet basil flakes
- salt and pepper to taste

Combine all ingredients in a saucepan, and simmer sauce for 5 minutes.

Herbed Eggplant Casserole with Ricotta & 5-Minute Tomato Sauce

This dish can be a complete meal, filled as it is with vegetables, eggs and cheese. The sauce is a wonderful accompaniment. It can be prepared in advance and heated before serving.

- 2 eggplants, (about 1 pound, each). Cut a thin slice from both ends and cut into fourths, lengthwise.
- 2 tablespoons oil

- 1 pint Ricotta cheese
- 4 ounces cream cheese
- 2 tablespoons dried onion flakes
- 1 teaspoon sweet basil flakes.
- 1/2 teaspoon Italian Herb Seasoning
- 1/4 cup grated Parmesan cheese
- 2 eggs
- salt and pepper to taste

Place eggplant in a 12x16-inch pan, drizzle with oil and cover tightly with foil. Bake in a 400° oven for about 30 minutes, or until eggplant is very soft. Allow to cool enough to handle.

Scrape eggplant off the shell and place in the large bowl of an electric mixer. Place skins (purple side down) in a greased, 9x13-inch porcelain baker, as a liner for the filling.

Add the remaining ingredients to the mixer bowl, and beat with the eggplant pulp until blended. Spread into prepared pan evenly. Bake in a 350° oven for 40 to 50 minutes or until filling is set and lightly browned. Cut into squares and serve with a spoonful of 5-Minute Tomato Sauce on top. Serves 8.

5-Minute Tomato Sauce

- 1 can (1 pound 12 ounces) crushed tomatoes in tomato puree
- 1 tablespoon oil
- 1 tablespoon sugar
- 1/2 teaspoon coarse-grind garlic powder
- 2 tablespoons dried onion flakes
- 2 teaspoons sweet basil flakes
- 1/2 teaspoon Italian Herb Seasoning
- 1 tablespoon dried parsley flakes
- 1/2 bay leaf
- 1/4 teaspoon red pepper flakes
- salt and pepper to taste

Combine all the ingredients in a Dutch oven casserole and simmer sauce, with cover slightly ajar, for 5 minutes.

Italian Green Beans
with Potatoes & Onions

This is an excellent dish to serve for a dinner buffet. It is an unusual way to serve Italian green beans, but it is very delicious, sparkled as it is with tomatoes, onions and broth. It is a casual dish and nice to serve when family and friends join for Sunday dinner.

    2 large potatoes, peeled and diced
    1 can (10 1/2 ounces) chicken broth
    1 small onion, minced
    1 can (1 pound) stewed tomatoes, chopped. Do not drain
    2 packages (10 ounces, each) frozen Italian green beans
    1 teaspoon oil (optional)
      salt and pepper to taste

    6 strips bacon, cooked crisp, drained and crumbled

In a Dutch oven casserole place first 7 ingredients and simmer mixture, covered, for about 30 minutes, or until potatoes are tender. Sprinkle top with crumbled bacon before serving. Serves 6 to 8.

Italian Green Beans with
Tomato, Onions & Cheese

    2 packages (10 ounces, each) frozen Italian green beans
    2 medium tomatoes, peeled, seeded and chopped
    1 small onion, minced
    1/2 cup rich chicken broth
    1/2 cup tomato sauce
      salt and pepper to taste

    2 tablespoons grated Parmesan cheese

In a saucepan, simmer together first 6 ingredients, until green beans are tender, about 15 minutes. Sprinkle top with grated cheese before serving. Serves 6.

Green Beans with Tomatoes, Onions, Chiles and Bacon

This is a delicious dish to serve with barbecued or roasted meats or poultry. Make certain that the vegetables stay crisp and tender, but not too raw. You can overdo "crisp" vegetables.

- **1 can (1 pound) stewed tomatoes, chopped. Do not drain.**
- **1 onion, chopped**
- **2 cloves garlic, minced**
- **1 teaspoon sugar**
- **1 teaspoon oil (optional)**

- **1 1/2 pounds fresh green beans. (Snap off the ends and remove any strings. Leave beans whole or cut in half.**
- **2 tablespoons canned diced green chiles (or more to taste)**

- **6 strips bacon, cooked crisp, drained and crumbled**

In a Dutch oven casserole, place first 5 ingredients and simmer sauce for 5 minutes. Lay the green beans as flat as possible in the sauce. Cover pan and simmer beans for about 15 to 20 minutes or until they are crisp tender. (Turn them every so often so as to cook in the sauce.) Stir in the diced chiles.

To serve, sprinkle crumbled bacon on top. Serves 6.

Note: — *Do not overcook, but don't undercook, either.*

    — *Dish can be prepared earlier in the day and heated at serving time.*

    — *The addition of the little bit of oil works wonders in "tightening" the sauce, but it can be omitted.*

Glazed Onions with Cinnamon & Raisins

1 pound frozen baby white onions, cooked in chicken
   broth for about 20 minutes or until tender and
   drained.

2 tablespoons sugar
1/4 teaspoon cinnamon
2 tablespoons butter

1/3 cup yellow raisins
   salt to taste

Prepare small white onions, and set aside. In a large skillet, heat together
sugar, cinnamon and butter. Add onions and cook, stirring, for about
5 minutes. Add the raisins and salt to taste and continue cooking for
about 5 minutes, or until onions are lightly browned and glazed. Watch
so that the raisins do not brown. They will plump up. Serves 8.

Honey Baked Onions in Butter & Broth

*Onions are a wonderful accompaniment to roasted or broiled meats. Somehow,
they are often neglected as a vegetable. These are delicious and very easy to
prepare. The honey will glaze them to a rich caramel color.*

8 onions, peeled, stemmed and cut into halves, crosswise

4 tablespoons butter, melted
4 tablespoons honey
2 tablespoons tomato sauce
1/4 cup chicken broth
1/4 teaspoon paprika
   salt to taste

In a 9x13-inch roasting pan, place onions, cut side down. Stir together
the remaining ingredients and pour over the onions. Cover pan tightly
with foil and bake in a 350° oven for 1 hour, or until onions are tender.
Serve with roasted or broiled meats. Serves 8.

Note: — *Onions can be prepared earlier in the day and heated before serving.
   Heat, uncovered, until onions are heated through. Baste with some
   of the caramel juices in pan.*

Vegetables

Peas in Mushroom & Onion Sauce

1/2 pound mushrooms, sliced
1 small onion, minced (1/2 cup)
1 clove garlic
2 tablespoons butter

1/2 cup cream
1 tablespoon lemon juice
1/8 teaspoon ground poultry seasoning
    salt and pepper to taste

2 packages (10 ounces, each) frozen peas

In a saucepan, saute together first 4 ingredients until onion is soft. Add the next 4 ingredients and simmer sauce for 2 minutes, stirring. Add the peas and simmer for 8 to 10 minutes or until peas are tender. Serves 8.

Peas with Parsley & Shallots

2 packages (10 ounces, each) frozen peas
1/2 cup concentrated chicken broth
2 shallots, finely chopped
2 tablespoons minced parsley
    salt and pepper to taste

Combine all the ingredients in a saucepan, and simmer mixture for about 8 to 10 minutes or until peas are tender, but firm. Serves 6.

Note: — *Both dishes can be prepared earlier in the day and stored in the refrigerator. Heat before serving.*

Italian-Style Stuffed Green Peppers with Beef & Rice in Tomato Sauce

6 green bell peppers, medium-sized. Cut in half, lengthwise (from top to bottom), remove seeds and membranes. You will have 12 half peppers.

Beef & Rice Filling:

    1 pound ground beef
1 1/2 cups cooked rice
    2 tomatoes, finely chopped and seeded
    1 teaspoon sweet basil flakes
1/8 teaspoon garlic powder
    1 tablespoon chopped parsley
1/2 onion, grated, (about 6 tablespoons)

Wash peppers and drain. Combine the filling ingredients and mix until nicely blended. Divide filling between the peppers and fill evenly. Place peppers in a 9x13-inch baking pan and pour Italian Tomato Sauce over all. Cover pan tightly with foil and bake in a 350° oven for 45 minutes. Remove foil and continue baking for about 20 minutes, or until peppers are tender. Serves 6.

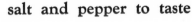

Italian Tomato Sauce

    1 can (1 pound) stewed tomatoes, chopped
    4 tablespoons tomato paste
    1 can (10 1/2 ounces) beef broth
1/2 onion, minced
    1 tablespoon sugar
    1 clove garlic, minced
    1 teaspoon sweet basil flakes
1/2 teaspoon Italian Herb Seasoning
    2 tablespoons minced parsley
    salt and pepper to taste

Stir together all the ingredients until blended.

Note: — **To Cook Rice:** *In a saucepan, stir together 2/3 cup rice, 1 can (10 1/2 ounces) chicken broth, 2 tablespoons butter, salt and pepper to taste. Cover pan and simmer mixture for about 25 minutes, or until rice is tender and liquid is absorbed. Yields 1 1/2 cups cooked rice.*

Spinach & Red Pepper Dumplings with Onions & Cheese

Vegetable dumplings are versatile, indeed. They can be served as a main course, small entree or hors d'oeurve. As an hors d'oeurve, they should be shaped into smaller patties.

>   1 package (10 ounces) frozen chopped spinach, defrosted
>   and thoroughly drained.
>   3 tablespoons roasted sweet red pepper strips or pimientos
>   2 eggs
>   2/3 cup fresh whole wheat bread crumbs
>   1/2 cup grated Parmesan cheese
>   3 tablespoons minced green onion
>   salt and pepper to taste (remember cheese is salty)

In a large bowl, stir together all the ingredients until mixture is blended. Shape spinach mixture into 2-inch patties and saute in an oiled teflon skillet until browned on both sides, adding a little oil as necessary. (These can also be baked in a 9x13-inch oiled teflon baking pan, about 10 minutes on each side.) Drain on paper towelling.

Before serving, heat in a 350° oven for about 10 minutes, or until heated through. Serve with a spoonful of Red Pepper Sauce. Yields 12 to 14 dumplings. Serves 4 to 6.

Red Pepper Sauce:
>   1/4 cup cream
>   1/4 cup sour cream
>   2 tablespoons red pepper strips
>   2 tablespoons chopped chives
>   1 teaspoon lemon juice
>   pinch of cayenne
>   salt to taste

Stir together all the ingredients and allow mixture to thicken for several hours at room temperature, and then refrigerate. Remove from the refrigerator about 30 minutes before serving and carefully heat through. Yields 1/2 cup sauce.

Potato & Onion Pancake
Made in a Casserole

This will decrease considerably preparation time in making potato pancakes. Making these in a casserole will also greatly diminish the amount of oil used. If you are serving this with a simple roast chicken, the Orange Applesauce is a grand accompaniment.

6 medium potatoes, peeled and grated
2 large onions, finely chopped

2 eggs, beaten
1/2 cup cracker meal
    salt and pepper to taste

2 tablespoons oil
1 tablespoon oil

In a bowl, combine potatoes, onions, eggs, cracker meal and seasonings, and stir to blend.

In a 9x13-inch baking pan, spread 2 tablespoons oil. Spread potato mixture evenly in pan and drizzle 1 tablespoon oil over the top.

Bake in a 350° oven for about 1 hour or until top is golden brown. To serve, cut into squares and spoon a little Orange Applesauce over the top. Serves 8.

Orange Applesauce

1 jar (1 pound) unsweetened applesauce
3 ounces (1/2 can) frozen orange juice concentrate, defrosted

Stir together the applesauce and orange juice until blended. Refrigerate until ready to serve.

Note: — *Potato casserole can be prepared earlier in the day and heated before serving.*

    — *Orange Applesauce can be prepared 1 day earlier and stored in the refrigerator.*

    — *If you serve this with a more complex dish, like Chicken with Red Cabbage, then omit the applesauce.*

Vegetables

Spinach with Tomatoes, Onions & Cici Peas

This is an old family recipe and I have hesitated to share it with you before. The combination seemed foreign with too many contrasts. Yet, I served it recently and everyone loved it, so here it is.

- **1** onion, chopped
- **1** shallot, minced
- **2** cloves garlic, minced
- **2** tablespoons butter

- **1/2** cup chicken broth
- **1** can (1 pound) cici peas (also known as garbanzo beans), drained
- **2** tomatoes, fresh or canned, peeled, seeded and chopped

- **2** packages (10 ounces, each) frozen chopped spinach, defrosted and drained
- salt and pepper to taste

In a Dutch oven casserole, saute onion, shallot and garlic in butter, until onion is tender, but not browned. Add the chicken broth, cici peas and tomatoes and simmer mixture for 15 minutes or until cici peas are a little softened. Add the spinach and seasonings and simmer for an additional 5 minutes, uncovered.

Serve with a slotted spoon. Serves 6 to 8.

Note: — This is a very attractive dish for a buffet, sparkled as it is with red and green.

— Entire dish can be prepared earlier in the day and stored in the refrigerator. Heat carefully before serving, to prevent spinach from scorching.

— Serve with roast chicken or veal. Rice made with chicken broth is also lovely with this dish.

Rice Cold Method: In a Dutch oven casserole, stir together 1 1/2 cups rice, 3 cups chicken broth, 2 tablespoons oil and salt and pepper to taste. Cover pan and simmer mixture for about 35 minutes, or until rice is tender and liquid is absorbed. Serves 6 to 8.

Molded Ramekins with Spinach, Noodles & Cheese

1 package (6 ounces) fine egg noodles, cooked until tender
   and drained
1 package (10 ounces) frozen chopped spinach, defrosted
   and drained
3 eggs
1 pint cottage cheese
1 cup cream
3/4 cup grated Parmesan cheese
1/4 cup chopped chives
   salt and pepper to taste

In a large bowl, stir together all the ingredients. Divide mixture between 8 buttered porcelain ramekins. Sprinkle tops with a little additional grated Parmesan cheese. Place ramekins in a pan with 1-inch hot water and bake in a 375° oven for about 25 minutes, or until a cake tester, inserted 1/2-inch off center, comes out clean. Serve directly from ramekins. Serves 8.

Note: — *These are best freshly baked, but they can be prepared earlier in the day and heated at serving time.*

   — *If you feel you must unmold the ramekins, then they must be heavily buttered and floured.*

Spiced Sweet Potatoes with Cinnamon, Honey & Walnuts

1 can (1 pound 12 ounces) sweet potatoes, drained and
   mashed
1/4 cup butter, softened
1/4 cup cream
1/3 cup maple syrup
1 teaspoon pumpkin pie spice
1/2 cup chopped walnuts
   salt to taste

Combine all the ingredients in a casserole and heat through, in a 325° oven. Sprinkle top with a few finely chopped walnuts. Serves 6.

Candied Sweet Potatoes with Glazed Walnuts

1 can (1 pound 12 ounces) sweet potatoes or yams, drained. Cut into 3/4-inch thick slices.

1/4 cup butter
1/2 cup dark brown sugar
1 teaspoon cinnamon
1/2 cup coarsely chopped walnuts

Place sweet potato slices in one layer in a shallow baker. Melt butter with brown sugar and cinnamon and cook for 1 minute. Stir in the walnuts until coated. Drizzle mixture evenly over the potatoes and bake in a 350° oven for about 25 minutes, or until top is candied and glazed. Serves 4 to 6.

Note: — *If you prefer to use fresh sweet potatoes, scrub 4 large sweet potatoes, place them in boiling water, and boil until tender. Remove from water, allow to cool a little, so they can be handled, and peel. Cut into 3/4-inch thick slices. Proceed as above.*

Stuffed Sweet Potatoes with Cinnamon Topping

8 medium sweet potatoes, scrubbed, baked in a 350° oven for about 40 to 45 minutes, or until tender. Slit the tops and scoop out the pulp, being careful not to tear the shells. Reserve shells.

1/2 cup butter
1/4 cup orange marmalade
1/4 cup brown sugar

4 teaspoons cinnamon sugar
1/2 cup chopped walnuts

Place potato pulp in a bowl. Heat together butter, marmalade and brown sugar until blended. Add to the potatoes in the bowl, and beat until blended. Divide mixture between the reserved shells, sprinkle tops with cinnamon sugar and chopped walnuts. (Pat nuts lightly into filling.) Place on a cookie sheet and bake in a 350° oven for 20 to 25 minutes or until heated through. Serves 8.

Old-Fashioned Tomatoes Stuffed with Rice, Tomatoes, Garlic & Herbs

12 medium tomatoes (about 3 pounds). Cut a 1/2-inch slice from the top. Scoop out the centers with a grapefruit knife and a teaspoon. Reserve tomato pulp.

Tomato & Rice Filling:
2 1/2 cups cooked rice
    Reserved tomato pulp, chopped, (discard seeds)
1 tablespoon oil
1 small onion, grated
1 teaspoon dried sweet basil flakes
3 tablespoons minced parsley
2 cloves garlic, minced
    salt and freshly ground pepper to taste

Combine all the filling ingredients and mix until blended. Stuff tomatoes with rice mixture and place any leftover rice mixture on the bottom of a 12-inch oval porcelain baker. Pour Tomato, Garlic & Herb Sauce over the top. Cover pan tightly with foil and bake in a 350° oven for about 40 minutes. Remove foil and continue baking for about 15 minutes, or until tomatoes are tender, but not mushy. (Cooking time will depend on the kind of tomato you are using. Thin-skinned tomatoes will cook more rapidly.) Serves 6.

Tomato, Garlic & Herb Sauce

1 tablespoon oil
1 can (1 pound) stewed tomatoes
4 tablespoons tomato paste
1 small onion, minced
1 tablespoon sugar
2 cloves garlic, minced
1 teaspoon sweet basil flakes
1 teaspoon Italian Herb Seasoning
1 tablespoon minced parsley
    salt and pepper to taste

Stir together all the ingredients until blended.

Note: — This dish can be prepared earlier in the day and heated before serving. Cover pan tightly with foil and heat in a 350° oven until hot.

Baked Tomatoes with Chiles & Cheese

This is a delicious accompaniment to roasted or barbecued meats or poultry. It is very attractive on a plate, flecked as it is with green and red.

  4 large tomatoes, cut into 1-inch thick slices, about 12 slices

  4 tablespoons finely chopped green onion
  4 tablespoons canned diced green chiles
1/2 cup sour cream
  1 jar (2 ounces) pimiento strips
1 1/2 cups grated Monterey Jack cheese

  2 tablespoons grated Parmesan cheese

Lay tomato slices in one layer on a lightly greased cookie sheet (with a rim). Stir together the green onions, chiles, sour cream, pimiento and cheese until blended. Spread cheese mixture over the tomatoes and sprinkle tops with grated Parmesan. (Can be held at this point.)

Before serving, broil tomatoes, about 6 inches from the heat, until cheese is melted and lightly browned. Serve at once. Serves 6.

Note: — Watch carefully while broiling so that tops don't burn.

Herbed Zucchini Mold with Cheese, Onions & Garlic

1 pound zucchini, sliced (not necessary to peel)
1 large onion, chopped
2 shallots, minced
2 cloves garlic, minced
4 tablespoons butter

3 cups cottage cheese
1 cup grated Parmesan cheese
1 cup fresh bread crumbs
1/2 teaspoon Italian Herb Seasoning flakes
    salt and pepper to taste

6 eggs, beaten

Saute together first 5 ingredients until onions are tender. In a large bowl, mix together zucchini mixture, cottage cheese, Parmesan, bread crumbs and seasonings. Stir in the beaten eggs.

Heavily grease a 2-quart ring mold and sprinkle generously with flour and lightly with paprika. Spoon zucchini mixture into mold and spread evenly.

Bake in a 350° oven for 1 hour or until top is golden brown and eggs are set. Allow to cool in pan for about 10 minutes and then loosen sides and invert onto a serving platter. Decorate with bouquets of parsley. Serve with a spoonful of Salsa Marinara on top. Serves 12.

Note: — Recipe can be halved, if you are serving 6.

   — If you prepare this earlier in the day, then loosen sides as described above, but leave in mold to store in the refrigerator. Reheat at 350° for about 20 minutes, or until heated through.

   — This can be baked in 9x13-inch pan and cut into squares to serve.

   — Individual ramekins are also nice. To make unmolding easier, be certain to grease and flour the pans.

   — Dusting the pan with paprika adds nice color to the outside of the zucchini mold.

Vegetables

Timbales of Zucchini, Tomatoes & Onions with Cheese

4 medium zucchini, grated. Do not peel.
1 medium onion, chopped
1 tomato (fresh or canned), peeled, seeded and chopped
2 shallots, minced
2 cloves garlic, minced
3 tablespoons butter

2 eggs
1/2 cup cream
1 cup grated Swiss cheese
1/4 cup grated Parmesan cheese
    salt and pepper to taste

In a skillet, saute together first 6 ingredients, until vegetables are soft, but not browned. Meanwhile, beat together the remaining ingredients until blended.

Divide vegetables between 6 individual buttered ramekins, and pour egg mixture evenly into each ramekin. Place ramekins on a cookie sheet and bake in a 350° oven until custard is set and top is browned, about 20 to 25 minutes. Serve at once. Serves 6.

Note: — *This is a lovely dish for lunch, much like a crustless quiche.*

    — *Assemble the casseroles earlier in the day, but best baked before serving.*

Zucchini & Onion Fritatta

6 medium zucchini, grated. Do not peel
2 large onions, finely chopped
1 clove garlic, minced
1/2 cup cracker crumbs
1/4 teaspoon baking powder
    salt and pepper to taste
2 eggs, beaten

Combine all the ingredients in a bowl until everything is nicely mixed. Oil a 9x13-inch baking pan. Spread zucchini mixture evenly in pan and drizzle 1 tablespoon oil on top. Bake casserole in a 350° oven for 40 to 45 minutes or until vegetables are tender and top is lightly browned. Serve as an accompaniment to roast chicken or veal. Serves 8.

Note: — *Entire dish can be prepared earlier in the day and heated before serving.*

Desserts

Desserts

Cakes & Tortes

Easiest & Best Apricot Nut Torte 248
Imperial Walnut Torte with Lemon Cream Cheese & Glazed Strawberries 249
Chocolate Torte Decadence with Chocolate Mousse Frosting 250
Viennese Chocolate Cake with Bittersweet Chocolate Glaze 251
Hungarian Walnut Torte with Apricot & Chocolate Buttercream 252
Pecan Torte with Raspberry & Lemon Glaze 253
Lemon Macaroon Torte with Strawberries & Walnuts 254
Chocolate & Mint Cloud Torte with Chocolate Mint Buttercream 255
Chocolate Mint Decadence with Chocolate Mousse Frosting 256
Macaroon Torte with Bananas, Walnuts & Chocolate Chips 257
Greek Honey Cake 258
Spicy Whole Wheat Apple Cake with Currants & Walnuts 259
Apricot & Almond Butter Cake with Almond Cream Glaze 260
Apricot Coffeecake with Cinnamon & Almond Streusel 261
Chocolate Apricot Cake with Walnuts & Bittersweet Chocolate Frosting 262
Double Chocolate Banana Cake with Chocolate Chips & Walnuts 263
Spiced Banana Cake with Cinnamon & Walnut Streusel Topping 264
Old-Fashioned Carrot Cake with Walnuts & Black Currants 265
Carrot & Apricot Cake with Cinnamon Walnut Topping 266
Thanksgiving Orange Pumpkin Apple Cake 267
Sour Cream Vanilla Cake with Chocolate Buttercream 268
Chocolate Fantasy Cake with Chocolate Buttercream 269
Springtime Lemon Cake with Fluffy Lemon Frosting 270
Bittersweet Chocolate Fudge Cake with Chocolate Cream 271
Mocha Roulade with Chocolate Kahlua Cream 272
Spiced Zucchini & Raisin Cake with Vanilla Cream Glaze 273
Royal Babka with Strawberry Jam & Walnuts 274
Cassata Romana with Chocolate & Raspberries 275

Cheesecakes

Light Lemon Cheesecake with Lemon Butter Cookie Crust 276
White Chocolate Cheesecake with Almond Macaroon Crust 277
No-Bake Chocolate Cheesecake with Chocolate & Almond Crust 278
The Ultimate Chocolate Cheesecake wtih Macaroon Crust 279
The Best Chocolate Ricotta Cheesecake 280
Imperial Chocolate Chestnut Cheesecake with Chestnut Cream 281
Easiest & Best Imperial Velvet Chocolate Cheesecake 282

Charlottes

Charlotte au Apricot with Glazed Brandied Apricots 283
Charlotte au Chocolate with Almonds & Amaretto Cream 284

Cookies

Biscocho di Almendra-Almond Biscuit 285
Velvet Brownies with Walnuts & Chocolate Buttercream 286
World's Best Double Chocolate Brownies 287
Bittersweet Saucepan Brownies with Dark Chocolate Frosting 288

Honey Cinnamon Chewies with Raisins & Pecans 289
Chocolate & Walnut Praline Bars 290
Hungarian Butter Cookies with Apricot Jam & Dark Chocolate 291
Lady Fingers-Biscuits a la Cuiller 292
Chunky Pecan & Raisin Spice Bar Cookies 293
Butter Pecan Cookies with Apricot Jam & Chocolate 294
Honey Butterscotch Oatmeal Chewies with Raisins & Pecans 295
Hungarian Butter Cookies—Pogacsas 296
Giant Granola Cookies with Raisins, Dates & Walnuts 297

Custard
Spiced Pumpkin Custard with Vanilla Caramel Sauce 298

Fruit
Spicy Orange Baked Apples with Pecan Streusel & Creme Vanilla 299
Honey Spiced Apples with Orange & Pecans 300

Iced Creams
Tartufo alla Tre Scalini Caffe 301
Iced Lemon Cream with Raspberry Sauce 302
Lemon Creme Glace with Lemon Almond Crust & Raspberry Sauce 303
Royal Orange Souffle Glace with Orange Cognac Cream 304

Mousses
Mousseline of Chocolate with Rum in Chocolate Couletes 305
Rum Mousse au Chocolat with Macaroons & White Chocolate Leaves 306
Imperial White Chocolate Mousse with Almond Crust & Raspberry Sauce 307
Chocolate Angel Mousse with Light Sauce Vanilla 308

Pies & Tarts
German Chocolate & Pecan Pie with Whipped Creme de Cacao 309
Apricot, Fig & Dried Fruit Winter Tart 310
Holiday Chocolate Pecan Pie with Vanilla Creme Fraiche 311
Sour Cream Apricot & Raisin Tart with Almond Macaroon Crust 312
Easiest & Best Butter Cookie Apple Pie with Raisins 313
Bourbon Apple Tart with Cinnamon on Butter Cookie Nut Crust 314
Deep Dish Apple Pie with Cognac Lemon Custard 315
Apricot Glazed French Apple Tart 316
Crustless Apple Pie with Lemon Meringue Topping 317
World's Best Old-Fashioned Apple Pie with Streusel 318
French Apple Lemon Tart with Cookie Crust & Apricot Glaze 319
Thanksgiving Spiced Honey Chestnut Pie with Praline Whipped Cream 320
Easiest & Best Apricot Tart with Lemon Cookie Crust 321
Sour Cream Peach Tart with Cinnamon Graham Crust 322
Fresh Peach & Almond Cream Pie 323
Fresh Pear Tart with Almond Cream & Almond Cookie Crust 324
Praline Pecan Tart with Flaky Butter Cookie Crust 325
Chocolate Chip Pecan Pie with Creme de Chocolat 326

Souffle
2-Minute Souffle au Grand Marnier with Raspberry Creme Fraiche 327

Strudel
Chocolate Chip Danish Pastry Rolls 328

Easiest & Best Apricot Nut Torte
with Whipped Creme Fraiche

Perhaps one of the easiest and most delicious tortes (if you love apricots and walnuts) is this marvelous chewy cake (or pie). It is tart and fruity, and the frosting is the perfect accompaniment. Hope you try it soon.

- 3 egg whites
- 1/2 cup sugar

- 3/4 cup dried apricots
- 1/2 cup sugar

- 1 cup soda cracker crumbs
- 3/4 cup chopped walnuts
- 1 teaspoon vanilla

Beat together whites and sugar until mixture is creamy. (Do not beat to stiff peaks.) In a food processor, chop apricots with sugar until apricots are finely chopped, but not pureed. Add apricots and remaining ingredients to beaten egg whites and stir to blend. Spread batter evenly into a greased 9-inch deep dish pie pan and bake in a 350° oven for 30 minutes, or until top is very lightly browned. Remove from oven and allow to cool in pan.

When cool, swirl top with Whipped Creme Fraiche. Decorate top with a sprinkling of finely grated walnuts. Serves 8.

Whipped Creme Fraiche:
- 1/2 cup cream
- 1 tablespoon sugar
- 1/2 teaspoon vanilla
- 1/4 cup sour cream

Beat cream with sugar and vanilla, until cream is stiff. Beat in sour cream until blended. (Can be prepared in advance and stored in the refrigerator until ready to frost torte.)

Note: — Pecans can be substituted for the walnuts.

Imperial Walnut Torte with Lemon Cream Cheese & Glazed Strawberries

There are few desserts you can make that are more impressive and delicious than this one. This is truly a poem of flavors. A chewy walnut torte is covered with a dense layer of cream cheese and decorated with plump, glazed strawberries . . . very new and very exciting.

Walnut Torte:

4	eggs
1 1/4	cups sugar
1 1/3	cups chopped walnuts
3/4	cup flour
1	teaspoon baking powder
2/3	cup vanilla-flavored yogurt
1 1/2	teaspoons vanilla

Place all the ingredients in a food processor and blend for 60 seconds, or until walnuts are very finely chopped. Place batter into a greased 10-inch springform pan and bake in a 350° oven for about 35 minutes, or until top is browned and a cake tester, inserted in center, comes out clean. Allow to cool in pan. When cool, frost top and sides with Lemon Cream Cheese. Decorate top with Glazed Strawberries a little while before serving. Serves 10.

Lemon Cream Cheese:

6	ounces cream cheese, at room temperature
1/2	cup cream, whipped
3	tablespoons sugar
2	tablespoons lemon juice
1/2	teaspoon vanilla

Beat cream cheese until light and fluffy. Beat cream until stiff and beat it into the cream cheese. Beat in sugar, lemon juice and vanilla until blended. Spread on top of cooled torte.

Glazed Strawberries:

2	pints strawberries, hulled, washed and patted dry
1/2	cup red currant jelly
1	teaspoon lemon juice

Place strawberries in a bowl. Heat together red currant jelly and lemon juice until jelly is melted. Allow to cool for 5 minutes, and then drizzle over the strawberries, turning to coat them evenly. (Strawberries could render some juice. Therefore, place strawberries on cake shortly before serving, so as not to discolor the beautiful cream cheese layer.)

Chocolate Torte Decadence
(Chocolate & Almond Cake with Chocolate Mousse Frosting)

Dark, dense, delicious are just a few words to describe this marvelous cake. The almond meal (finely grated almonds) can be purchased in health food stores. You can make your own, but you must use a nut grater. Almonds cannot be ground in the food processor for this torte.

- 4 eggs
- 1 cup sugar
- 1 teaspoon almond extract

- 4 tablespoons cocoa, sifted
- 1 cup almond meal or finely grated almonds
- 1/4 cup flour
- 1/2 teaspoon baking powder
- 1/2 cup butter, melted and cooled slightly

- 1/2 cup apricot jam, heated

Beat eggs with sugar and almond extract until mixture is light and tripled in volume, about 4 minutes, at high speed.

Combine cocoa, almond meal, flour and baking powder and beat into egg mixture at lowest speed, and only until blended. Beat in butter and only until blended. Pour batter into a greased 10-inch springform pan and bake in a 350° oven for about 30 to 35 minutes, or until a cake tester, inserted in center, comes out clean.

Allow to cool in pan and then remove from pan and place on a beautiful footed platter. Spread apricot jam on top and then swirl with Chocolate Mousse Frosting, allowing a little of the jam to show through. Serves 8 to 10.

Chocolate Mousse Frosting:
- 1/2 cup (3 ounces) semi-sweet chocolate chips
- 1/3 cup cream
- 1/2 teaspoon almond extract

Place chocolate chips in blender container. Heat cream to boiling point and pour into container. Carefully blend for 30 seconds or until chocolate is melted. Blend in almond extract.

Viennese Chocolate Cake
with Bittersweet Chocolate Glaze

While this cake is a bit more work, it is so delicious and chocolaty, I felt it must be included. It is a very light, moist cake, flavored with apricot jam and frosted with the shiniest chocolate glaze. Preparation is not difficult, but this recipe does require a little more attention.

 2/3 cup butter, softened
   1 cup sugar
 1/2 cup cocoa
 1/2 cup water
   1 teaspoon vanilla

 2/3 cup flour
 1 1/2 teaspoons baking powder
 1/2 teaspoon baking soda

   4 eggs
 3/4 cup apricot jam, heated

Beat together butter and sugar until very light and fluffy. Beat in cocoa, water and vanilla until totally incorporated, about 2 minutes, at high speed. At high speed, beat in flour, baking powder and soda. Beat in eggs, one at a time, until mixture is very light and fluffy, about 3 minutes.

Divide batter between 2 greased and parchment-lined springform pans and bake in a 350° oven for 25 minutes, or until a cake tester, inserted in center comes out clean. Allow to cool in pan. When cool, leave 1 layer in pan and spread the top with apricot jam. Remove parchment from second layer and place over first layer in pan. (Cake will be glazed in pan.) Pour Bittersweet Chocolate Glaze over the top and ease a little down the sides. Allow glaze to set. When set, remove from pan and place on a rimmed cake platter for serving. Decorate top with a glaceed cherry, no more. The shiny satin glaze is lovely alone. Serves 8 to 10.

Bittersweet Chocolate Glaze:
   1/2 cup cocoa
   1/2 cup cream
   1/2 cup sugar
   1/4 cup butter
   1/2 teaspoon vanilla

In a saucepan, over low heat, stir together all the ingredients, and continue cooking and stirring for about 5 minutes, or until glaze is very shiny and thickened. Allow to cool.

Hungarian Walnut Torte with Apricot & Chocolate Buttercream

This cake is light as air and with a moist and flavorful crumb. It is one of my favorites, because it is so delicious and so easy to prepare. The addition of the apricot jam layer and the swirl of Chocolate Buttercream is truly a poem of flavors.

      4 eggs
      1 cup sugar
      6 tablespoons flour
      1 teaspoon baking powder
      1 teaspoon vanilla
 1 1/2 cups walnuts, coarsely chopped

      1/2 cup apricot jam, heated

Place first 6 ingredients in the bowl of a food processor and blend until nuts are very finely chopped, about 1 minute. Pour batter into a greased 10-inch springform pan and bake in a 350° oven for about 25 to 30 minutes, or until a cake tester, inserted in center, comes out clean. Allow to cool for 20 minutes.

When cool, spread the heated apricot jam over the top and allow to cool thoroughly. Drizzle top with Chocolate Buttercream Frosting. Swirl it around in a decorative fashion, allowing some of the jam to show. Frost sides with a thin coating of Chocolate Buttercream. Serves 8.

To Make Chocolate Buttercream Frosting: Stir together 1/2 cup (3 ounces) semi-sweet chocolate chips (melted) with 1/4 cup butter (melted). Stir in 1 teaspoon vanilla.

Note: — Do not overbake, or cake will not be moist.

— Butter and chocolate can be melted together in a microwave oven, or in the top of a double boiler, over hot water.

Pecan Torte with Raspberry & Lemon Glaze

This is one of my very best nut cakes and one of the very best, too. Raspberry jam is wonderful with this and the Lemon Glaze adds just the right tartness.

      5 eggs
1 1/2 cups pecans
      1 cup sugar
      1 teaspoon vanilla
      4 tablespoons flour
      1 teaspoon baking powder

1/2 cup seedless red raspberry jam, heated

Place first 6 ingredients in a food processor and blend for 1 minute, or until pecans are very finely ground. Pour batter into a greased 10-inch springform pan and bake in a 350° oven for about 30 minutes, or until top is lightly browned, and a cake tester, inserted in center, comes out clean. Do not overbake.

Allow to cool in pan. When cool, spread top with raspberry jam (heating makes it easier to spread). Drizzle top with Lemon Glaze, in a lacy pattern, and allow some of the jam to show. Serves 8.

Lemon Glaze:
      1 tablespoon lemon juice
1/2 cup sifted powdered sugar

Stir together lemon juice and powdered sugar until blended. Add a little lemon juice or powdered sugar to make glaze a drizzling consistency.

Note: — Cake can be baked and glazed 1 day earlier. To store, place 4 or 5 toothpicks on cake and cover loosely with plastic wrap. Remove toothpicks and plastic wrap (of course) to serve.

Lemon Macaroon Torte with Strawberries & Walnuts & Lemon Creme

This is a variation of my macaroon torte. However, the character and taste are entirely different. Again, isn't it amazing how a few humble ingredients can produce such a fine tasting dessert.

        2 eggs
      3/4 cup sugar

      1 1/2 cups macaroon cookie crumbs
        2/3 cup fresh strawberries, thickly sliced and patted dry
          1 cup chopped walnuts
          1 tablespoon grated lemon peel
          1 teaspoon vanilla

In the large bowl of an electric mixer, beat eggs with sugar until well blended, about 1 minute, at high speed. Stir in the remaining ingredients until mixture is combined.

Scrape batter into a greased 10-inch pie pan and bake at 350° for about 30 to 35 minutes or until top is browned and a cake tester, inserted in center, comes out clean. Allow to cool in pan.

Decorate top with a layer of Lemon Creme Fraiche and fresh, plump strawberries. Cut into wedges to serve. Serves 8.

Lemon Creme Fraiche:
      1/3 cup cream
      1/3 cup sour cream
        1 tablespoon sugar
        1 tablespoon grated lemon

Stir together all the ingredients and refrigerate for 1 hour.

Note: — Make certain that the strawberries are dried, or batter will bake gummy.

— Macaroon cookies can easily be crumbed in food processor. Store unused crumbs in the freezer. You'll find these most useful to have on hand.

— Torte can be prepared earlier in the day and topped with Lemon Cream. Place strawberries on top before serving.

Chocolate & Mint Cloud Torte with Chocolate Mint Buttercream

For those who like a hint of mint with their chocolate, this is a nice cake to consider. It is very light and delicate. Eggs do not have to be separated, walnuts can be ground in the food processor, and total preparation time can he held to under 2 minutes, making this a good choice for a hurried time.

4 eggs
1 cup sugar
1 teaspoon vanilla
few drops peppermint extract
4 tablespoons flour
1 cup finely chopped walnuts
3 tablespoons cocoa
1 teaspoon baking powder

Place all the ingredients in the bowl of a food processor and blend mixture for 1 minute, or until walnuts are finely ground.

Pour batter into a greased 10-inch springform pan and bake in a 350° oven for about 25 minutes, or until a cake tester, inserted in center, comes out clean. Do not overbake. Allow to cool in pan.

When cool, swirl top and sides, in a decorative fashion, with Chocolate Mint Buttercream. Serves 8.

Chocolate Mint Buttercream:
1 cup butter (2 sticks) at room temperature
3/4 cup sifted powdered sugar
3 tablespoons sifted cocoa
1 teaspoon vanilla
few drops peppermint extract

Beat butter until light and creamy. Beat in the remaining ingredients until thoroughly blended.

Chocolate Mint Decadence with Chocolate Mint Mousse Frosting

Not quite a cake, not quite a mousse, but somewhere in-between, this very simple and elegant dessert will please the most refined chocolate palate. The faint hint of mint adds a refreshing touch.

- 1/2 cup (1 stick) butter
- 1/2 pound semi-sweet chocolate chips
- 4 tablespoons flour
- 1 teaspoon vanilla
- few drops peppermint extract

- 5 eggs
- 3/4 cup sugar

In the top of a double boiler, over hot, not simmering, water, melt the butter. Add the chocolate chips and stir until the chocolate is melted and mixture is smooth. Stir in the flour, vanilla and peppermint extract. Allow to cool for 10 minutes.

Beat eggs with sugar, at high speed, for about 5 minutes, or until eggs are very light and fluffy. Fold in the melted chocolate mixture until blended. (This can be done on lowest speed in a mixer.)

Grease and line the bottom of an 8-inch springform pan with parchment paper. Pour batter into prepared pan and bake in a 250° oven for 1 hour. Allow to cool in pan and then refrigerate for 4 to 6 hours or overnight. Remove from pan and frost top with Chocolate Mint Mousse Frosting. Keep the portions small and serve 10.

Chocolate Mint Mousse Frosting:
- 1/2 cup cream
- 1 package (6 ounces) semi-sweet chocolate chips
- 2 egg yolks
- 1/2 teaspoon vanilla
- few drops peppermint extract

In the top of a double boiler, heat cream. Add chocolate and stir until chocolate is melted. Stir in egg yolks, until blended. Stir in flavorings.

Macaroon Torte with Bananas, Walnuts & Chocolate Chips

This little recipe is so easy and so delicious, you will make it often on nights when you are running late. You will hardly believe that these few cupboard ingredients can produce such a fine tasting dessert. It serves beautifully with a dollup of unsweetened whipped cream.

> 2 eggs
> 3/4 cup sugar
>
> 1 1/2 cups macaroon cookie crumbs
> 1 cup chopped walnuts
> 3/4 cup semi-sweet chocolate chips
> 1 medium banana, coarsely chopped (do not mash)

In the large bowl of an electric mixer, beat eggs with sugar until well blended, about 1 minute, at high speed. Stir in the remaining ingredients until mixture is combined. Do not beat.

Scrape batter into a greased 10-inch pie pan and bake at 350° for about 30 to 35 minutes or until top is browned and a cake tester, inserted in center, comes out clean. Allow to cool in pan.

Decorate top with rosettes of whipped cream and a sprinkling of grated chocolate. Cut into wedges to serve. Serves 8.

Note: — *Be certain to stir in the banana. If you beat it in, batter will become too moist and become gummy when baked.*

— *Use about 1/2 cup cream, whipped, for decorating top.*

— *Can be prepared earlier in the day, decorated, and stored in the refrigerator.*

Greek Honey Cake

This is a very unusual and interesting cake that I made up especially for a dinner in a Greek theme. It is very different, but it does produce a marvelous dessert, that I am certain you will enjoy.

```
    3  eggs
  3/4  cup sugar

    2  cups Ritz cracker crumbs (about 42 crackers)
  3/4  cup sugar
    1  teaspoon baking powder
    1  teaspoon cinnamon
    1  teaspoon vanilla
    1  orange, grated (use fruit, juice and peel)
1 1/2  cups chopped walnuts
```

Beat eggs with 3/4 cup sugar until eggs are pale, about 3 minutes. On low speed, beat in the remaining ingredients until just blended.

Pour mixture into a lightly buttered 9-inch springform pan and bake at 350° for 30 minutes. Remove cake from oven and drizzle the cooled Honey Cinnamon Syrup on top. Cool cake in pan and cut into wedges to serve. Serves 8.

Honey Cinnamon Syrup:

```
  2/3  cup sugar
  2/3  cup water
  1/3  cup honey
    1  slice lemon (about 1/4-inch thick)
    1  cinnamon stick
```

Cook together all the ingredients, at a very low bubble, until mixture is syrupy, about 15 minutes. Remove lemon and cinnamon stick. Allow to cool. Pour syrup over cake.

Note: — Can be prepared 1 day earlier and stored in the refrigerator. Allow to come to room temperature before serving.

Spicy Whole Wheat Apple Cake
with Currants & Walnuts

This is a very dense and delicious apple cake, sparkled with spices and currants and walnuts. It is delicious served plain, but it can be dressed up with a lacy drizzle of Cream Glaze.

    1/2 cup butter
      1 cup sugar
      2 eggs
      1 large apple, peeled, cored and grated

      1 cup whole wheat flour
    1/2 cup flour
      1 teaspoon baking soda
      1 teaspoon baking powder
      2 teaspoons cinnamon
    1/2 teaspoon ground nutmeg
    1/4 teaspoon ground cloves
    3/4 cup dried currants
    3/4 cup chopped walnuts

Cream together butter and sugar until light and fluffy. Beat in eggs until thoroughly blended. Beat in apple. Add the remaining ingredients all at once and beat until blended.

Spread batter (it will be thick) into a greased 10-inch springform pan and bake in a 350° oven for about 35 minutes, or until a cake tester, inserted in center, comes out clean. Allow to cool in pan.

When cool, remove from pan and drizzle top with Cream Glaze (optional). Serves 10.

Cream Glaze: Stir together 1 tablespoon cream, 1/2 cup sifted powdered sugar and 1/2 teaspoon vanilla until blended. Add a little cream or powdered sugar to make glaze a drizzling consistency.

Apricot & Almond Butter Cake
with Almond Cream Glaze

The tart chewy apricots together with the almonds makes this cake a poem of flavors. It is dense and compact and truly delicious.

- **1 cup chopped dried apricots**
- **1 cup sugar**

- **1 cup butter, softened**
- **4 eggs**
- **1 teaspoon almond extract**

- **1 1/2 cups almond meal** (almonds grated to a floury consistency). This can be purchased in most supermarkets and health food stores.
- **3/4 cup flour**
- **1 1/2 teaspoons baking powder**

- **1/4 cup slivered almonds (for the top)**

In a food processor, chop apricots with sugar until apricots are finely chopped. In the large bowl of an electric mixer, beat butter, eggs, almond extract and apricot mixture until nicely blended, about 1 minute. Stir together almond meal, flour and baking powder and add, all at once, beating until blended.

Spread batter into a greased 10-inch springform pan and sprinkle top with slivered almonds. Press almonds gently into the batter. Bake in a 350° oven for about 40 minutes, or until a tester, inserted in center, comes out clean. Allow to cool in pan. When cool, drizzle top decoratively with Almond Cream Glaze. Serves 10.

Almond Cream Glaze: Stir together 2 tablespoons cream, 1/4 teaspoon almond extract and 1 cup sifted powdered sugar. Add a little cream or sugar to make glaze a drizzling consistency.

Note: — Check cake after 30 minutes baking, and if top is browning too quickly, place a piece of foil loosely on the top.

Apricot Coffeecake with Cinnamon & Almond Streusel

This is delicious coffeecake, not too sweet, very moist, simple, but by no means plain. Lovely to serve for a brunch or luncheon buffet.

- 1/2 cup butter, softened
- 1 cup sugar
- 3 eggs
- 1 cup sour cream
- 2 teaspoons vanilla

- 2 cups flour
- 1 teaspoon baking powder
- 1/2 teaspoon baking soda
- 1 cup chopped dried apricots

Cream butter with sugar. Beat in eggs, one at a time, until blended. Beat in sour cream and vanilla until blended. In a bowl, stir together the remaining ingredients, all at once, and beat until blended.

Place batter into a greased 10-inch springform pan and sprinkle top with Cinnamon & Almond Streusel. Bake in a 350° oven for about 40 to 45 minutes, or until a cake tester, inserted in center, comes out clean. Allow to cool in pan. When cool, remove from pan and place on a lovely footed platter. Serves 10.

Cinnamon & Almond Streusel:
- 1 tablespoon softened butter
- 1 tablespoon flour
- 1/4 cup sugar
- 1/2 teaspoon cinnamon
- 1/4 cup chopped almonds

Beat together first 4 ingredients until mixture is crumbly. Stir in almonds until blended.

Cakes & Tortes

Chocolate Apricot Cake with Walnuts & Bittersweet Chocolate Frosting

If you love chocolate with apricots, this is a spectacular dessert to consider. The fresh whole wheat bread crumbs can be prepared in seconds in a food processor. And chopping the apricots with the sugar is another time saver. This is a dense cake filled, as it is, with generous amounts of apricots and walnuts and a good choice around the holidays.

> 1 package (6 ounces) soft dried apricots
> 1 cup sugar
>
> 3/4 cup butter, softened
> 5 eggs
> 1 package (6 ounces) semi-sweet chocolate chips, melted
> 2 teaspoons vanilla
>
> 1 cup fresh whole wheat bread crumbs (about 3 slices)
> 1/2 cup flour
> 1 teaspoon baking powder
> 1 1/2 cups chopped walnuts
>
> 1/2 cup apricot jam, heated

In the bowl of a food processor, chop apricots with sugar, until apricots are finely chopped. Transfer to the large bowl of an electric mixer, and beat in butter, eggs, chocolate and vanilla, beating for 1 minute. Stir together bread crumbs, flour, baking powder and walnuts, and add all at once, beating until blended.

Spread batter evenly into a buttered 10-inch springform pan and bake in a 350° oven for 50 minutes, or until a cake tester, inserted in center, comes out clean. Allow to cool in pan. When cool, spread top with apricot jam. Remove from pan and swirl Bittersweet Chocolate Frosting on the top, allowing some of the jam to show. Serves 12.

Bittersweet Chocolate Frosting:
> 2/3 cup (4 ounces) semi-sweet chocolate chips
> 3/8 cup (3 ounces) butter
> 1/2 ounce unsweetened chocolate
> 1 teaspoon vanilla

In the top of a double boiler, over hot, not simmering water, place all the ingredients and stir until melted and blended.

Note: — After 30 minutes, I found it necessary to cover top loosely with a piece of foil, to prevent overbrowning top.

Double Chocolate Banana Cake
with Chocolate Chips & Walnuts

This is a dark and dense chocolate cake, very moist, and with a fine crumb. It can be cut into the thinnest slivers. It is delicious and full of flavor and needs no frosting or decoration.

- 1/2 cup butter, softened
- 1 1/4 cups sugar
- 2 eggs
- 1 1/4 cups sour cream
- 2 teaspoons vanilla

- 2 cups flour
- 4 tablespoons cocoa
- 1 teaspoon baking powder
- 1 teaspoon baking soda
  pinch of salt

- 2 bananas, coarsely mashed
- 1 cup semi-sweet chocolate chips

Beat together first 5 ingredients until blended. Stir together the next 5 ingredients and add, all at once, beating until blended. Stir in the bananas and chocolate chips.

Place batter into a greased 10-inch springform pan and bake in a 325° oven for about 65 minutes, or until a cake tester, inserted in center, comes out clean. Allow to cool in pan, and cut into wedges to serve. Serves 10.

Note: — Do not mash bananas to a pulp, or baking time will be slightly longer.
— ½ cup walnuts (optional) can be stirred into the batter.

Cakes & Tortes

Spiced Banana Cake with Cinnamon & Walnut Streusel Topping

There are few cakes you can make that are simpler or more delicious than this one. This is a lovely cake to serve at a buffet brunch or luncheon. Great to serve as dessert or with afternoon tea.

  1/3 cup butter, softened
1 1/3 cups sugar
     2 eggs
  1/4 cup water

     2 large ripe bananas, coarsely mashed and not pureed

1 2/3 cups flour
     1 teaspoon baking powder
     1 teaspoon baking soda
     2 teaspoons cinnamon

Beat together first 4 ingredients until mixture is blended. Beat in the bananas. Beat in the remaining ingredients until blended. Do not overbeat.

Spread batter into a greased 10-inch tube pan and sprinkle top evenly with Walnut Streusel Topping. Bake in a 325° oven for about 40 minutes, or until a cake tester, inserted in center, comes out clean. Allow to cool in pan. Serves 10.

Walnut Streusel Topping:
     2 tablespoons flour
     2 tablespoons melted butter
     3 tablespoons finely chopped walnuts
  1/2 teaspoon cinnamon

Stir together all the ingredients until mixture is blended and crumbly.

Old-Fashioned Carrot Cake with Walnuts & Black Currants

This is an adaptation of the old-fashioned carrot cake, with a few variations. Some people believe that the carrot cake has outlived its usefulness, as it was intensely popular some years ago. But I still think of it as an old friend and enjoy it every so often.

- 3 tablespoons grated orange (about 1/2 medium orange)
- 1 cup sugar
- 2 eggs
- 3/4 cup oil
- 1/4 pound cream cheese
- 1 1/2 cups grated carrots
- 1 1/2 teaspoons vanilla

- 1 cup flour
- 1 teaspoon baking powder
- 1/2 teaspoon baking soda
- 3/4 cup chopped walnuts
- 1/2 cup black currants
- 1/3 cup coconut flakes

Beat together first 7 ingredients until blended. Add the remaining ingredients and beat until blended. Do not overbeat.

Spread batter into a greased 10-inch tube pan and bake in a 350° oven for about 40 to 45 minutes, or until a cake tester, inserted in center, comes out clean.

Allow to cool in pan. When cool, remove pan and drizzle top with Orange Coconut Glaze. Serves 10.

Orange Coconut Glaze:
- 1 tablespoon orange juice
- 2 teaspoons grated orange peel
- 1 tablespoon coconut flakes
- 1/2 cup sifted powdered sugar

Stir together all the ingredients until blended. Add a little orange juice or sugar to make glaze a drizzling consistency.

Carrot & Apricot Cake with Cinnamon Walnut Topping

This is a dense, compact cake that is most delicious and satisfying. It does not contain cream, sour cream or cream cheese and it is moistened only with water. This is a good cake to choose for a buffet luncheon or afternoon tea. The cake is lovely, flecked as it is with apricots and walnuts.

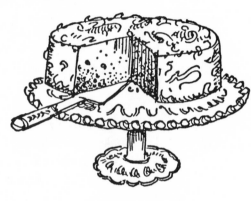

      1/4 cup butter
  1 1/2 cups sugar
      2 medium carrots, grated (about 1 1/2 cups)
  1 1/3 cups water
      2 teaspoons cinnamon
      1 cup chopped dried apricots

      1 egg, beaten

      2 cups flour
      2 teaspoons baking powder
      1 teaspoon vanilla

      1 tablespoon cinnamon sugar
  3/4 cup chopped walnuts

In a saucepan, heat together first 6 ingredients and bring mixture to a boil. Remove from heat and allow to come to room temperature. Beat in egg until blended. Beat in flour, baking powder and vanilla until blended.

Scrape batter into a greased 10-inch springform pan and sprinkle top with cinnamon sugar and walnuts. Press the walnuts gently into the batter. Bake at 350° for about 40 minutes, or until a cake tester, inserted in center, comes out clean. Allow to cool in pan and cut into wedges to serve. (This cake can be dressed up with a faint brushing of Orange Glaze, a delicious addition.) Serves 10.

Orange Glaze: Stir together 1/2 cup sifted powdered sugar and 1 tablespoon orange juice until blended. Brush onto cooled cake.

Thanksgiving Orange Pumpkin Apple Cake

This is a great cake to serve with hot spicy cider. It is moist, fruity and sparkled with spices. It is an especially fine choice as a gift from your kitchen during the holiday times. For gift giving, I would suggest you bake this in 4 mini-loaf foil pans, 6x3x2-inches, for about 40 minutes.

    1/2 **cup butter, softened**
1 1/4 **cups sugar**
     2 **eggs**
    1/2 **orange grated (3 tablespoons fruit, juice and peel)**
     2 **medium apples, peeled, cored and grated**
     1 **cup canned pumpkin puree**

     2 **cups flour**
     2 **teaspoons baking powder**
    1/2 **teaspoon baking soda**
     3 **teaspoons pumpkin pie spice**

    1/4 **cup chopped walnuts (for the top)**

Cream together butter and sugar. Beat in eggs until blended. Beat in orange, apples and pumpkin. Combine the next 4 ingredients and add, all at once, beating until blended. Spread batter into a greased 10-inch tube pan and sprinkle top with walnuts, pressing them lightly into the batter.

Bake in a 350° oven for about 40 to 45 minutes, or until a cake tester, inserted in center, comes out clean. Allow to cool in pan and cut into wedges to serve. Serves 10.

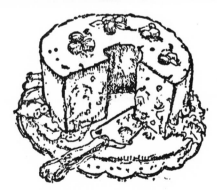

Cakes & Tortes

Sour Cream Vanilla Cake with Chocolate Chips & Chocolate Buttercream

Not only is this cake delicious, but it is rather easy to prepare. It naturally forms a second layer that is filled with a fudgy frosting. A thin layer of buttercream on top adds the perfect balance.

    1/2 cup butter, softened
      1 cup sugar
      2 eggs
      1 cup sour cream
      2 teaspoons vanilla

      2 cups flour
      1 teaspoon baking powder
      1 teaspoon baking soda

    1/2 cup semi-sweet mini-morsels
      3 tablespoons Nestle's Quik Chocolate Powder

Cream butter with sugar. Beat in eggs until blended. Beat in sour cream and vanilla until blended. Beat in flour, baking powder and baking soda until blended.

In a greased 10-inch springform pan, spread half the batter. (It will be thick.) Sprinkle with mini-morsels and chocolate powder. Spread remaining batter on top. Bake in a 350° oven for about 45 to 50 minutes, or until a cake tester, inserted in center, comes out clean. Allow to cool in pan. When cool, frost with Chocolate Buttercream on the top and sides. Serves 10.

Chocolate Buttercream:
    1/3 cup butter, softened
    1/3 cup semi-sweet chocolate chips, melted and cooled
    1/2 teaspoon vanilla

Beat butter until light and creamy. Beat in the melted chocolate and vanilla until blended. This will frost 1 layer.

Chocolate Fantasy Cake
with Chocolate Buttercream

I never tire of making new and different chocolate cakes, in my quest for the ultimate of ultimate cakes. This is a pretty good one ... very chocolaty, dense and quite delicious. Please note that it is made with oil and not butter, so do use a tasteless salad oil.

        3 eggs
        2 cups sugar
    3/4 cup oil
        1 cup sour cream
        2 teaspoons vanilla

        2 cups flour
    1/2 cup cocoa
  1 1/2 teaspoons baking powder
        1 teaspoon baking soda
            pinch of salt

        1 cup semi-sweet chocolate chips (6 ounces)

Beat together first 5 ingredients until nicely blended. Beat in the next 5 ingredients until blended. Stir in the chocolate chips.

Divide batter between 2 greased 10-inch springform pans and bake in a 350° oven for 35 minutes, or until a cake tester, inserted in center, comes out clean. When cool, remove from pans and fill and frost with Chocolate Buttercream. Serves 10 to 12.

Chocolate Buttercream:
    2/3 cup sifted powdered sugar
        1 egg

    3/4 cup semi-sweet chocolate chips, melted
    1/2 cup butter, at room temperature, cut into 4 pieces
        1 teaspoon vanilla

Beat together sugar and egg until mixture is thick and pale colored. Beat in the chocolate until blended. Beat in the butter, one piece at a time, until blended. Beat in the vanilla. Will fill and frost 1 10-inch cake.

Cakes & Tortes

Springtime Lemon Cake with Fluffy Lemon Frosting

Thin layers of pale lemon cake are filled with a tart and tangy Lemon Curd and frosted with Fluffy Lemon Frosting. This cake is attractive and rather "showy" and will serve well for a bridal or baby shower. The Lemon Curd has many uses... filling eclairs or pastry tarts. It is also delicious with toast and cream cheese.

    1/2 cup butter
    1/2 cup sugar
      2 eggs
    1/2 lemon, grated. Use fruit, juice and peel.

      1 cup water
  2 1/2 cups flour
      3 teaspoons baking powder

Cream butter with sugar until light and fluffy. Beat in eggs until thoroughly blended. Beat in lemon. Beat in water, alternately with flour and baking powder mixture, ending with the flour. Divide batter between 2 greased 10-inch springform pans and bake in a 350° oven for 25 minutes, or until tops are browned and a cake tester, inserted in center, comes out clean.

Allow to cool in pans. When cool, fill with Lemon Curd and frost with Fluffy Lemon Frosting. Serves 10 to 12.

Lemon Curd: In the top of a double boiler, over simmering water, stir constantly 2 egg yolks; 1/2 cup sugar; 2 tablespoons cornstarch; 1/2 cup water; 2 tablespoons grated lemon; and 1 tablespoon butter until mixture is thickened. Allow to cool. Reserve 1/4 cup curd for frosting.

Fluffy Lemon Frosting: In a saucepan, heat and stir together 1 cup sugar and 1/3 cup water until sugar is dissolved. Continue cooking, without stirring, until syrup registers 240° on a candy thermometer. Meanwhile, beat 2 egg whites until thickened. Drizzle in the hot syrup, beating at high speed, until frosting is fluffy and syrup is incorporated. Beat in the reserved 1/4 cup Lemon Curd until blended. Allow to cool.

Bittersweet Chocolate Fudge Cake
with Chocolate Cream Frosting

If you love chocolate cake, this is one of the best ... and I hope you try it soon. It is a poem of chocolate, very dark and delicious.

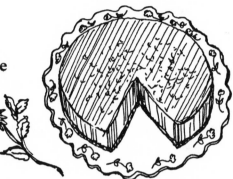

    1/2 cup butter softened
      1 cup sugar

      4 eggs
    1/2 cup water, at room temperature
      1 teaspoon vanilla

  1 1/4 cups flour
    1/2 cup cocoa
  1 1/2 teaspoons baking powder
      1 teaspoon baking soda
         pinch of salt

Cream butter with sugar until light and fluffy. Beat in eggs until blended. Beat in water and vanilla until blended. Combine the remaining ingredients and add, all at once. Beat until blended.

Place batter into a greased 10-inch springform pan and bake in a 350° oven for about 30 to 35 minutes, or until a cake tester, inserted in center, comes out clean. Do not overbake. Allow to cool in pan.

When cool, remove from pan and spread tops and sides with Chocolate Cream Frosting. (Frosting is very shiny when set. Do not refrigerate.) Serves 8.

Chocolate Cream Frosting:
    1/2 cup cream
      1 package (6 ounces) semi-sweet chocolate chips
    1/2 teaspoon vanilla

In a saucepan, bring cream to boiling point. Remove from heat and add chocolate chips. Stir until chocolate is melted and blended with cream. Stir in vanilla. (This produces a generous 1/4-inch layer of frosting.) Allow to cool for 10 minutes before spreading on cake.

Cakes & Tortes

Mocha Roulade with Chocolate Kahlua Cream

6 egg whites
1/2 cup sugar

6 egg yolks
1/2 cup sugar

2 cups finely grated walnuts (must use a nut grater)
2 teaspoons instant coffee
1 teaspoon baking powder
1 teaspoon vanilla

Preheat oven to 350°. Butter a 10x15-inch jelly roll pan. Line it with waxed paper extending 4-inches beyond the ends of the pan. Butter the waxed paper and set aside. Wet a towel and squeeze it until it is damp-dry.

In a large mixing bowl, beat egg whites until foamy. Continue beating, gradually adding 1/2 cup sugar, until whites are stiff and glossy. In another bowl, beat yolks with 1/2 cup sugar until mixture is very thick, about 5 minutes. Beat in nuts, coffee, baking powder and vanilla. Fold in beaten egg whites. Pour batter into prepared pan and spread evenly. Bake at 350° for about 25 minutes, or until top of cake is golden, and a cake tester, inserted in center, comes out clean. Immediately cover cake with dampened towel and allow cake to cool.

Turn cake out on 2 overlapping strips of waxed paper that have been sprinkled with a little sifted powdered sugar. Remove baking paper and trim edges of cake. Spread 2/3 Chocolate Kahlua Cream over cake. Using the waxed paper to help you, roll cake up and place on a long serving platter. Frost with remaining cream. Drizzle top with a few teaspoons of chocolate syrup in a lacy pattern. Serves 12 to 14.

Chocolate Kahlua Cream:

2 cups cream
3 teaspoons instant coffee powder
3/4 cup chocolate syrup
2 tablespoons Kahlua Liqueur

Beat cream with coffee powder until blended. Gradually add chocolate syrup and liqueur and continue beating until cream is stiff.

Note: — *Cake can be prepared 2 days earlier and stored in refrigerator.*

— *Cake can be frosted 1 day earlier and stored in the refrigerator.*

Spiced Zucchini & Raisin Cake with Vanilla Cream Glaze

This is an interesting variation of the traditional Zucchini Cake. Most zucchini cakes are prepared with 1 to 1 1/2 cups oil. This one is moistened with water and very little butter. Yet, it does produce a very delicious and satisfying cake.

    1/4 cup butter, softened
      1 egg, beaten
  1 1/2 cups sugar
      3 tablespoons grated orange (about 1/2 medium orange)
  1 1/2 cups peeled and grated zucchini
  1 1/3 cups warm tap water
      2 teaspoons cinnamon
      1 cup yellow raisins
      1 teaspoon vanilla

  2 1/3 cups flour
      2 teaspoons baking soda
      1 cup chopped walnuts

Beat together first set of ingredients until blended. Beat in the remaining ingredients until mixture is blended. Spread batter into a greased 9x13-inch baking pan and bake at 350° for 35 to 40 minutes, or until a cake tester, inserted in center, comes out clean. Allow to cool in pan. When cool, drizzle top, in a decorative fashion, with Vanilla Cream Glaze. Yields 12 servings.

Vanilla Cream Glaze:
    1/2 cup sifted powdered sugar
      1 tablespoon cream
    1/2 teaspoon vanilla

Stir together all the ingredients until blended. Add a little cream or sugar to make glaze a drizzling consistency.

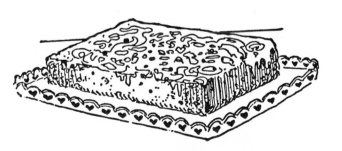

Cakes & Tortes

Royal Babka with
Strawberry Jam & Walnuts

This lovely coffee cake baking in your oven will bring the neighbors to your door. It is a delight to serve with hot coffee or chocolate. A glass of milk is good, too.

- 1/4 cup warm water (105°)
- 1 tablespoon sugar
- 1 package yeast
- 3/4 cup warm milk (105°)
- 1/2 cup butter, softened
- 1/2 cup sugar
- 2 eggs
- 3 cups flour, mixed with
- 1/4 teaspoon salt
- 1 cup flour

In a glass measuring cup, stir together water, sugar and yeast and allow to stand for 10 minutes or until yeast starts to foam. (If yeast does not foam, it is inactive and should be discarded.)

In the large bowl of an electric mixer, place yeast mixture, milk, butter, sugar and eggs. Beat for 15 seconds and start adding the flour and salt. After adding the 3 cups flour, beat mixture (with the paddle beater) for 5 minutes. (This takes place of kneading.)

Now add the remaining cup of flour slowly until a nice, soft dough forms. Place dough in an oiled bowl, cover and allow to rise in a warm place (85°) until doubled in bulk. Punch dough down and cut in half. Roll each half into a 12x15-inch rectangle. Spread with Strawberry Jam Walnut Filling. Roll up jelly-roll fashion, and place into a 10-inch, lightly greased, tube pan. Cover with plastic wrap and a towel and allow to rise again until doubled in volume. Repeat with second half of dough, in another pan.

Bake in a 350° oven for 30 to 35 minutes, or until top is browned and cake sounds hollow when thumped. Remove metal side and allow to cool in pan. Sift a little powdered sugar on top, and cut into wedges to serve. Serves 8 to 10, for each Babka. Yields 2 Babkas.

Strawberry Walnut Filling:

Stir together 1 cup strawberry jam, 1 cup chopped walnuts, 1/4 cup coconut flakes, 1/4 cup chopped raisins and 1/2 cup marshmallow cream. Will fill 2 Babkas.

Chocolate Filling:

Sprinkle on each Babka, 1/2 cup Nestle's Quik, 3/4 cup semi-sweet chocolate chips and 3/4 cup chopped walnuts. (This is a nice alternative filling for the Babkas.)

Cassata Romana with Chocolate & Raspberries

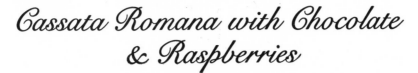

On a day when you are thinking of how to please or make some very special friends happy, you might like to prepare this grand dessert. It is light as air and marvelously flavored with chocolate and raspberries.

6 egg whites, at room temperature
1/2 cup sugar

6 egg yolks, at room temperature
1/2 cup sugar

1 3/4 cups finely grated walnuts
    (must use a nut grater)
2 tablespoons flour
1 teaspoon baking powder
1 teaspoon vanilla

Preheat oven to 350°. Butter a 10x15-inch jelly roll pan. Line it with waxed paper, extending 4-inches beyond the ends of the pan. Butter the waxed paper and set aside. Wet a dish towel and squeeze it until it is damp-dry.

Beat whites until foamy. Gradually add 1/2 cup sugar and continue beating until whites are stiff and glossy. In another bowl (can use the same beaters), beat yolks with 1/2 cup sugar until mixture is very thick. Beat in the nuts, flour, baking powder and vanilla. Fold in egg whites. Pour batter into prepared pan and bake at 350° for about 25 minutes, or until top is golden and a cake tester, inserted in center, comes out clean. Immediately cover cake with damp towel and allow to cool.

Turn cake out on 2 overlapping strips of waxed paper that have been sprinkled with sifted powdered sugar. Remove baking paper and trim edges of cake. Cut cake into thirds, yielding 3 strips measuring 14x3-inches. Fill and frost with Chocolate Chip Whipped Cream and Raspberries. Sprinkle top with a little shaved chocolate and decorate with whole raspberries. Serves 12 to 14.

Chocolate Chip Whipped Cream with Raspberries:

1 pint whipping cream
2 tablespoons sugar
2 tablespoons Grand Marnier Liqueur
1/2 cup semi-sweet chocolate chips, coarsely chopped
1 package (10 ounces) frozen raspberries in syrup, drained.
    (Reserve juice for another use.)

Beat cream with sugar and liqueur until stiff. Beat in the chopped chocolate. Stir in drained raspberries. Will fill and frost above cake.

Light Lemon Cheesecake
with Lemon Butter Cookie Crust

Cheesecake is always a welcomed dessert and everybody seems to love it. This is a lovely, light and very creamy one, just right for a spring dessert.

- 1 **pound cream cheese, softened**
- 4 **eggs**
- 2 **cups sour cream**
- 1 **cup sugar**
- 3 **tablespoons grated lemon (use fruit, juice and peel)**
- 2 **teaspoons vanilla**
- 1 **teaspoon almond extract**

Beat cream cheese until creamy. Beat in the remaining ingredients until blended. Do not overbeat. Pour mixture into Lemon Butter Cookie Crust and bake in a 350° oven for about 50 minutes, or until a cake tester, inserted in center, comes out clean, no longer. Do not overbake.

Allow to cool in pan for 30 minutes and then refrigerate for at least 4 to 6 hours. Overnight is good, too. Serve with a spoonful of Raspberry Lemon Sauce, as a lovely accompaniment. Serves 10.

Lemon Butter Cookie Crust:
- 2 **cups vanilla wafer crumbs**
- 1/3 **cup melted butter**
- 1 **tablespoon grated lemon peel**

Stir together all the ingredients until blended. Press mixture on the bottom and 1-inch up the sides of a 10-inch springform pan.

Raspberry Lemon Sauce:
- 1 **package (10 ounces) frozen raspberries in syrup, drained.**
  Reserve juice and place in a little saucepan.
- 1 **teaspoon cornstarch**
- 1 **tablespoon grated lemon**

Place raspberries in a bowl. In a saucepan, stir together raspberry juice and cornstarch, and cook over low heat, stirring until mixture is thickened and clear. Remove from heat and stir in the raspberries and lemon.

White Chocolate Cheesecake with Almond Macaroon Crust

When you prepare this glorious dessert, you will wonder how anything so extravagantly delicious could be so easy. A further bonus, this mousselike cheesecake does not have to be baked and can be assembled in very little time.

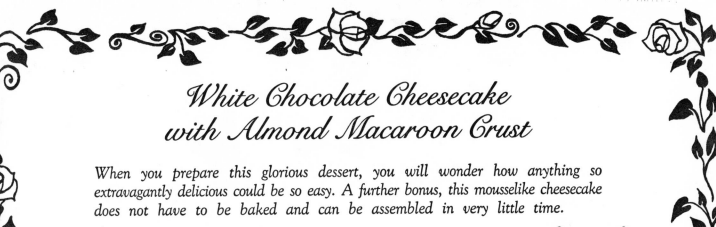

Almond Macaroon Crust:
- 1/3 cup butter, melted
- 3 tablespoons cinnamon sugar
- 1 1/2 cups macaroon cookie crumbs
- 1/2 cup chopped almonds

Stir together all the ingredients until blended. Pat mixture on the bottom of a 10-inch glass pie plate and bake in a 350° oven for 8 minutes. Allow to cool.

White Chocolate Cheesecake Filling:
- 1 package (8 ounces) cream cheese, at room temperature
- 3/4 cup sifted powdered sugar
- 6 ounces white chocolate, melted

- 1 1/2 cups cream
- 1 teaspoon vanilla
- 1 tablespoon rum

Beat cream cheese and sugar until cream cheese is light and fluffy. Beat in the melted white chocolate. (Place bowl into a larger bowl with warm water to keep chocolate from firming up too rapidly while you whip the cream.)

Beat cream with vanilla and rum until stiff. Remove bowl from water bath and beat in the whipped cream until blended. Pour mixture into prepared crust and refrigerate until firm.

Top can be decorated with grated semi-sweet chocolate and chocolate leaves. Or you may prefer to spoon a little raspberries in syrup, on the top, at serving time. Either are delicious accompaniments.

Note: — This dessert can be prepared a day ahead and stored in the refrigerator.

— White chocolate can be melted in the top of a double boiler over hot, not boiling water.

Cheesecakes

No-Bake Chocolate Cheesecake
with Chocolate and Almond Crust

This is a nice, easy dessert that serves quite glamorously and would be just grand for a formal dinner. Serve it informally any time. Who doesn't love chocolate cheesecake?

Chocolate & Almond Cookie Crust:
1 1/2 cups fudge cookie crumbs. (Use a brownie-like cookie, not the dark chocolate wafers. In absence of these, use chocolate chip cookies.)
1/3 cup melted butter
1/2 cup chopped almonds
1/4 cup grated semi-sweet chocolate

Stir together all the ingredients until blended. Pat mixture on the bottom of a 10-inch glass pie plate and bake in a 350° oven for 7 minutes. Allow to cool.

Chocolate Cheesecake Filling:
1 package (8 ounces) cream cheese, at room temperature
1/2 cup sifted powdered sugar

1 package (6 ounces) semi-sweet chocolate chips, melted
1 1/2 cups cream, whipped
2 tablespoons Creme de Kahlua liqueur

Beat cream cheese and sugar until mixture is light and fluffy. Beat in melted chocolate until blended. Beat in the whipped cream and liqueur. Pour mixture into prepared crust and refrigerate until firm.

Decorate top with dollups of whipped cream and finely grated chocolate. Serves 10.

Note: — Can be prepared a day ahead and stored in the refrigerator. Decorate with whipped cream on the day you are planning to serve this.

— Top can be decorated with chocolate leaves, dusted with sifted powdered sugar, to resemble snow.

The Ultimate Chocolate Cheesecake
with Macaroon Crust

This is one IMPRESSIVE dessert that is also immensely delicious. If you love cheesecake and are fond (like "mad") about chocolate, this is a little treasure you will use often. It is a dense filling, so please don't overbeat. You do not want too much air incorporated in the filling. Just beat until blended, no more.

    1 tablespoon butter
    1 cup macaroon cookie crumbs

 1 1/2 pounds cream cheese, at room temperature (3 8-ounce
          packages)
    1 cup sour cream, at room temperature
    3 eggs, at room temperature
  3/4 cup sugar
    2 teaspoons vanilla

    1 package (6 ounces) semi-sweet chocolate chips, melted

In a 10-inch springform pan, spread the butter on the bottom, and sprinkle crumbs evenly over all. Set pan aside.

In the large bowl of an electric mixer, beat together, cream cheese, sour cream, eggs, sugar and vanilla until blended. Do not overbeat. Beat in the melted chocolate until blended. Pour mixture into prepared pan and bake at 350° for 45 minutes. Allow to cool and then refrigerate. Decorate top with a generous sprinkling of grated chocolate.

To serve, cut into wedges and keep the portions small. Serves 12.

Note: — Can be prepared 1 day earlier and stored in the refrigerator.

  — 2 tablespoons of Creme de Cacao can be added to the cream cheese mixture, if you enjoy the subtle addition of liqueur.

The Best Chocolate Ricotta Cheese Cake

This is one of those glorious desserts that will linger long in the memory. Very smooth and velvety and richly flavored with chocolate.

Chocolate Walnut Crust:
- 1 1/2 cups chocolate wafer crumbs
- 1/3 cup melted butter
- 1/3 cup finely chopped walnuts

Mix together all the ingredients until blended. Press the mixture on the bottom of a 10-inch springform pan.

Filling:

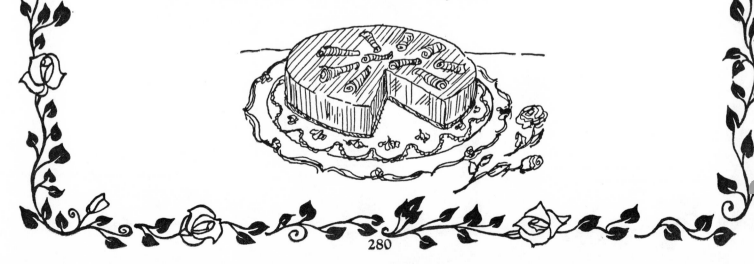

- 1/4 cup cream
- 8 ounces semi-sweet chocolate chips

- 1 pound (16 ounces) Ricotta cheese, at room temperature
- 1/2 pound cream cheese, at room temperature
- 1 cup sugar
- 3 eggs, at room temperature
- 1 cup sour cream
- 2 teaspoons vanilla

In a saucepan, heat the cream. Add the chocolate chips and stir until chocolate is melted. Do this over low heat so that chocolate does not scorch.

Beat together the remaining ingredients until blended. Beat in the melted chocolate. Pour into prepared crust and bake in a 350° oven for about 55 minutes, or until a cake tester, inserted 1-inch off center, comes out clean. Do not overbake. Allow to cool in pan and then refrigerate for 4 to 6 hours. Overnight is better.

Decorate top with chocolate curls. Remove from the refrigerator 20 minutes before serving. Serves 12.

Note: — To make Chocolate Curls: Run a vegetable peeler down the sides of a chocolate bar that is at room temperature.

Imperial Chocolate Chestnut Cheesecake with Vanilla Chestnut Cream

This is one of the grandest, most elegant desserts and a great finale to a fine Italian dinner. It is smooth as velvet, and the taste is truly glorious.

1/2 cup cream
8 ounces semi-sweet chocolate chips

2/3 cup sugar
1 pound Ricotta cheese, at room temperature
1 package (8 ounces) cream cheese, at room temperature
1 cup sour cream
4 eggs
1/2 cup canned sweetened chestnut puree
2 teaspoons vanilla

In a small saucepan, heat the cream. Add the chocolate chips and stir until chocolate is melted. Do this over low heat, stirring all the while, so that the chocolate does not scorch.

In the large bowl of an electric mixer, beat together the remaining ingredients until mixture is thoroughly blended. Beat in the melted chocolate. Pour mixture into Walnut & Chocolate Cookie Crust and bake in a 350° oven for 55 minutes, or until a cake tester, inserted in center, comes out clean, no longer. Do not overbake.

Allow to cool in pan for 20 minutes, and then refrigerate for 4 to 6 hours. Overnight is good, too. Decorate top with finely grated chocolate, and serve with a spoonful of Vanilla Chestnut Cream as a lovely accompaniment. Serves 10 to 12.

Walnut & Chocolate Cookie Crust:
2 cups chocolate wafer crumbs
1/3 cup melted butter
1/2 cup finely chopped walnuts

Stir together all the ingredients until blended. Press mixture on the bottom and 1-inch up the sides of a 10-inch springform pan.

Vanilla Chestnut Cream: Stir together 1/2 cup cream, 1/2 cup sour cream, 2 tablespoons sugar and 1 teaspoon vanilla until blended. Allow mixture to stand at room temperature for 4 hours and then stir in 3 tablespoons canned sweetened chestnut puree. Refrigerate until serving time.

Easiest & Best
Imperial Velvet Chocolate Cheesecake

The texture of this cheesecake is as smooth as velvet. And one bite into this chocolate velvet is sheer ecstacy. The Almond Macaroon Crust adds just the right crunch.

        1/2 **cup cream**
          8 **ounces semi-sweet chocolate chips**

          3 **packages (8 ounces, each) cream cheese, at room temperature**

          1 **cup sugar**
          3 **eggs**
          1 **cup sour cream**
          2 **teaspoons vanilla**

In a small saucepan heat the cream to boiling point. Remove the pan from the heat and add the chocolate chips, stirring until chocolate is melted. Set aside.

In the large bowl of an electric mixer, beat cream cheese until it is light (about 1 minute.) Beat in sugar, eggs, sour cream and vanilla until blended. Beat in the melted chocolate. Pour mixture into prepared crust and bake in a 325° oven for 55 minutes. (Top will appear soft in the middle, but it will firm up in the refrigerator.)

Allow to cool, and then refrigerate for 6 hours, or until thoroughly chilled. Overnight is good too. Decorate top with a thin layer of Vanilla Creme Fraiche and sprinkle top lightly with grated chocolate. Serves 10 to 12.

Vanilla Creme Fraiche: Stir together until blended, 1/3 cup cream, 1/3 cup sour cream, 1 tablespoon sugar and 1 teaspoon vanilla until blended. Allow mixture to stand at room temperature for about 3 hours, or until it is thickened. Refrigerate until ready to use.

Almond Macaroon Crust: Stir together 2 cups macaroon cookie crumbs, 1/3 cup melted butter and 1/3 cup finely chopped almonds, until blended. Pat mixture on the bottom of a 10-inch springform pan.

Charlotte au Apricot
with Glazed Brandied Apricots

24 ladyfingers, split (see Index, Cookies)

1 package (8 ounces) dried apricots
1 cup orange juice

2 packages unflavored gelatin
1/4 cup apricot brandy

5 eggs
2/3 cup sugar

2 cups cream, beaten until stiff

Line a 10-inch springform pan on the bottom and sides with ladyfingers.

Simmer apricots in orange juice until soft. Blend in a processor until pureed.

Soften gelatin in apricot brandy and place over hot water until gelatin is liquefied. (A metal measuring cup works well for this.)

Beat eggs with sugar until mixture is thick and lemon colored, about 5 minutes. Beat in the pureed apricots, gelatin mixture and whipped cream.

Pour apricot mixture into prepared pan and place remaining ladyfingers decoratively over the top in spoke fashion. Refrigerate until firm. Decorate top with Glazed Brandied Apricots. Cut into wedges to serve. Serves 12.

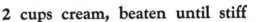

Glazed Brandied Apricots

1 package (8 ounces) dried apricots
1 cup orange juice
1/2 cup sugar
1/4 cup apricot brandy

Combine all the ingredients in a saucepan and simmer mixture for 20 minutes or until apricots are soft (but not mushy) and syrup is thickened. Place apricots on charlotte in a decorative fashion and brush entire top (including ladyfingers) with remaining glaze.

Note: — Can be prepared 1 day earlier and stored in the refrigerator. Decorate top early on day you are planning to serve this.

Charlotte au Chocolate with Almonds & Amaretto Cream

24 ladyfingers, split (see Index, Cookies)

1 cup butter, softened (2 sticks)
3/4 cup sugar
2 tablespoons Amaretto liqueur
1/2 teaspoon almond extract
1 cup finely grated toasted almonds

1 package (6 ounces) semi-sweet chocolate chips, melted

2 cups cream

Line the bottom and sides of an 8-inch springform pan with ladyfingers.

Beat butter and sugar until very light and fluffy. Beat in the liqueur, almond extract and toasted almonds until smooth. Beat in the melted chocolate. Whip cream until stiff and fold into chocolate mixture.

Pour chocolate cream into prepared pan and arrange remaining ladyfingers decoratively on top. Refrigerate for at least 6 hours or overnight. Decorate top with lots of grated chocolate and very finely chopped toasted almonds. Cut into wedges to serve. Serves 12.

Note: — This is exceedingly rich, so keep the portions small.

     — Can be served with a teaspoon of Amaretto on top. If this will be served after a formal dinner party, you might enjoy serving it with a delicate Amaretto Cream.

Amaretto Cream

6 egg yolks
3/4 cup sugar
2 teaspoons cornstarch

2 1/2 cups half and half (or milk)

2 tablespoons Amaretto liqueur
2 teaspoons vanilla

Beat yolks and sugar until light and fluffy, about 5 minutes. Beat in the cornstarch. Bring half and half or milk to a boil and beat it into the yolk mixture, a little at a time. Transfer to the top of a double boiler, and cook over hot water, stirring, until thick. DO NOT ALLOW TO BOIL. Stir in Amaretto and vanilla and refrigerate.

Biscocho di Almendra
(Almond Biscuit)

This is a variation of one of my biscuit recipes and is an interesting contrast served with a glass of dry red wine. Try it—it is a lovely combination. It has an interesting texture, on the dry side, and not as crisp as a Biscotti. Also good with coffee or tea or a glass of milk.

- 2 cups flour
- 2 teaspoons baking powder
- 1/2 cup sugar
- 1/3 cup butter

- 1/2 cup chopped toasted almonds

- 2 eggs
- 1/2 cup sour cream
- 1 teaspoon almond extract

- 1 tablespoon chopped almonds

Beat together first 4 ingredients until mixture resembles coarse meal. Beat in almonds. Beat together eggs, sour cream and almond extract until blended and add, all at once, to flour mixture. Beat until blended. Do not overbeat.

Spread batter (it will be very thick) into a greased 10-inch springform pan and sprinkle top with 1 tablespoon chopped almonds, pressing them gently into the dough. Bake in a 350° oven for 25 to 30 minutes, or until top is browned and a cake tester, inserted in center, comes out clean. Allow to cool in pan. When cool, remove from pan and cut into wedges to serve. Serves 8.

Note: — Can be stored in a heavy-duty plastic bag for several days.

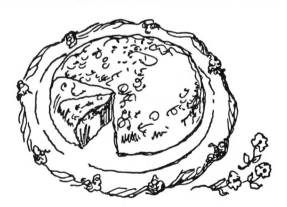

Velvet Brownies with Walnuts & Chocolate Buttercream

This is a super velvety brownie, that I know you will love. The only addition is chopped walnuts. Chocolate chips, dates, raisins, or even grated white chocolate can be added. The brownie base is truly delicious. Notice the large amount of vanilla.

     3/4 cup butter (1 1/2 sticks)
       4 ounces unsweetened chocolate
       1 teaspoon instant coffee

       4 eggs
       2 cups sugar
       1 tablespoon vanilla

       1 cup flour
     1/4 teaspoon salt

       1 cup chopped walnuts

In the top of a double boiler, over hot, not simmering water, stir together butter, chocolate and instant coffee until mixture is blended. Beat eggs with sugar and vanilla until mixture is creamy, about 5 minutes. Beat in the chocolate mixture until blended. Stir in the flour, salt and walnuts until blended.

Spread batter in a greased 9x13-inch baking pan and bake at 400° for 22 minutes, or until a cake tester, inserted in center, comes out clean and top looks dry. Allow to cool in pan. When cool, spread top with Chocolate Buttercream which is optional. Keep the portions small. Yields 48 brownies.

Chocolate Buttercream:
     2/3 cup melted semi-sweet chocolate chips
     1/3 cup melted butter
       1 teaspoon vanilla
         pinch of salt

Stir together all the ingredients until blended.

Note: — Do not overbake or brownies will be dry. On the other hand, do not underbake, or brownies will be pasty.

The World's Best Double Chocolate Brownies

I never tire of experimenting with brownies. Basically they are best made with lots of chocolate and little flour. These are by far my best, (for my taste)... exceedingly chocolaty and delicious beyond description. They appeal to all my senses, and are my favorites to date.

3 eggs
3/4 cup sugar

1 package (6 ounces) semi-sweet chocolate chips, melted
2 ounces unsweetened chocolate, melted
1/2 cup butter, melted
1 teaspoon vanilla

3/4 cup flour
1/2 teaspoon baking powder

1 cup chopped walnuts
1/2 cup semi-sweet chocolate chips (optional)

Beat together eggs and sugar until mixture is light and fluffy, about 5 minutes. Beat in melted chocolates and butter. Beat in flour and baking powder. Stir in walnuts and optional chocolate chips.

Spread mixture evenly into a greased 10-inch springform pan and bake in a 350° oven for 32 minutes. Do not overbake. Allow to cool in pan. Cut into small wedges to serve. Serves 10 to 12.

Note: — *Chocolates and butter can be melted together in the top of a double boiler, over hot, not simmering, water.*

— *Brownies are difficult to test. Top should appear dry and a cake tester, inserted 1 1/2-inches off center, should be almost clean. 32 minutes was the perfect time for my oven. However, as oven temperatures vary, watch carefully when you bake these for the first time.*

Cookies

Bittersweet Saucepan Brownies with Dark Chocolate Frosting

Even though the ingredients are simply stirred, this recipe produces a torte-like brownie, moist and velvety. Do not overbake or brownies will lose their moistness. Refrigerating the frosted brownies for several hours will make these easier to cut. The frosting is a good one for most chocolate cakes.

- 4 ounces unsweetened chocolate, broken up
- 2/3 cup vegetable shortening

- 2 cups sugar
- 4 eggs
- 1 tablespoon vanilla

- 1 1/4 cups flour
- 1 teaspoon baking powder
- 1/4 teaspoon salt

- 1 cup chopped walnuts
- 1 cup semi-sweet chocolate chips
  (optional, if you do not plan to frost)

In a saucepan, over low heat, melt together chocolate and shortening, stirring until blended. Stir in sugar, eggs and vanilla until blended. Stir in flour, baking powder and salt until blended. Stir in walnuts and optional chocolate chips.

Spread batter evenly into a greased 9x13-inch baking pan and bake at 350° for 28 minutes. (Top will appear dry.) Spread top with Dark Chocolate Frosting and allow to cool. Cut into 1 1/2-inch squares to serve. Yields 48 brownies.

Dark Chocolate Frosting:
- 3 ounces unsweetened chocolate, broken up
- 1/4 cup vegetable shortening
- 2 cups sifted powdered sugar
- 1/3 cup milk
- 2 teaspoons vanilla

In a saucepan, over low heat, melt together chocolate and shortening, stirring until blended. Stir in half the powdered sugar, milk, remaining powdered sugar and vanilla, stirring well after each addition. Yields enough frosting for 1 9x13-inch cake.

Honey Cinnamon Chewies with Raisins & Pecans

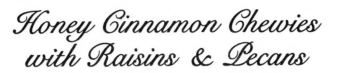

Let me say, right at the start, that this is one of my very favorites. They are very chewy, spicy and simply delicious with the raisins and pecans. I must also admit that my children thought they were quite ordinary, as these do not contain a trace of chocolate.

1/2 cup butter, softened
1 cup sugar
3/4 cup honey
2 eggs

1 1/2 cups flour
1 teaspoon baking powder
pinch of salt
1 teaspoon cinnamon
1 cup raisins
1 cup chopped pecans (or walnuts)

Beat together first 4 ingredients until blended. Stir together remaining ingredients and add, all at once, and beat until blended. (Do not overbeat. The whole process should not take more than 1 minute.)

Spread batter into a heavily greased 10x15x1-inch baking pan and sprinkle top with 1 tablespoon cinnamon sugar. Bake in a 350° oven for about 28 to 30 minutes or until top looks dry and takes on color. Allow to cool in pan.

When cool, cut into squares. Can be stored wrapped in waxed paper. Yields 4 dozen cookies.

Note: — *If you use a teflon-coated pan, please grease it generously, as well. These are very chewy and sticky.*

— *These cookies are not easy to test, so you must rely on color and appearance.*

Cookies

Chocolate & Walnut Praline Bars

A thin layer of Brown Sugar Cookie Crust, topped with a thin layer of praline with chocolate chips and walnuts, makes this one of the tastiest cookies ever. This is a very thin cookie, so don't think anything went wrong.

- 1/3 cup butter, softened
- 1/2 cup brown sugar
- 1 cup flour

- 2 eggs
- 1 1/4 cups brown sugar
- 2 tablespoons flour
- 1 teaspoon baking powder
- 1 teaspoon vanilla

- 1 cup chocolate chips
- 1 cup chopped walnuts

Beat together butter, sugar and flour until mixture is crumbly. Pat mixture on the bottom of a greased 9x13-inch baking pan and bake in a 350° oven for 10 minutes.

Meanwhile, beat together next 5 ingredients until blended. Stir in chocolate chips and walnuts until blended. Pour mixture over prepared crust and continue baking for 15 minutes, or until top is golden brown. Allow to cool in pan. When cool, cut into bars to serve. Decorate top with a faint sprinkle of sifted powdered sugar. Yields 36 bars.

Hungarian Butter Cookies with Apricot Jam & Dark Chocolate Topping

This is an interesting cookie, not too sweet, but quite tart and chocolaty and excellent with coffee. This recipe yields a generous 4 dozen cookies and they can be frozen.

Butter Cookie Crust:
- 1 cup butter (2 sticks), at room temperature
- 3/4 cup sugar
- 4 egg yolks
- 2 cups flour
- 1 teaspoon vanilla

- 1 cup apricot jam, heated

In an electric mixer, beat together first 5 ingredients, just until blended, and dough is soft. Do not overbeat. With a spatula or your fingers, spread dough on the bottom of a greased 10x15x1-inch baking pan and bake at 350° for 15 minutes or until dough is set. Spread apricot jam on top of cookie crust.

Spread Dark Chocolate Pecan Topping evenly over the apricot jam and continue baking in a 350° oven for about 35 minutes, or until topping is set and crust is browned. Allow to cool in pan and then cut into squares to serve. Yields 48 cookies.

Dark Chocolate Pecan Topping:
- 4 egg whites
- 2 tablespoons sugar

- 1 cup very finely chopped pecans
- 1 cup sifted powdered sugar
- 3/4 cup sifted cocoa

Beat whites with sugar until whites are stiff and glossy. Beat in the remaining ingredients until blended.

Note: — To check the color of the bottom of the crust, carefully lift up a corner of the crust with a long-handled knife. Crust should be baked through and lightly browned. (Careful with your fingers.)

Lady Fingers – Biscuits a la Cuiller

Ladyfingers are so easy to prepare (and inexpensive) that you may want to spend the little extra time. Homemade ladyfingers are also very delicious. Any extras can be sandwiched with a fruity preserve. Raspberry, strawberry or apricot jam is very lovely.

3	**egg whites**
1/4	**cup sugar**
3	**egg yolks**
1/4	**cup sugar**
1	**teaspoon vanilla**
1	**tablespoon very finely grated lemon peel (optional)**
10	**tablespoons flour**

sifted powdered sugar

Line 2 cookie sheets with parchment paper.* Preheat oven to 300°. Beat egg whites until foamy. Gradually add the sugar and continue beating until whites are very stiff.

In another bowl, beat egg yolks with 1/4 cup sugar and beat until very thick and pale. Beat in the vanilla, peel (optional) and flour until blended (Do this on low speed.) Gently fold in the beaten whites until blended.

Place batter in a pastry bag with a 1/2-inch straight tip. Pipe out the batter into 3-inch strips. Sift powdered sugar generously over the batter. Bake in a 300° oven for about 20 minutes or just until beginning to take on color. Remove from oven and lift parchment paper off pan and allow to cool. Yields 36 to 48 ladyfingers.

Note: — *If you do not have parchment paper available, then grease and flour the cookie sheets.

    — Grated orange peel is a nice substitute for the lemon peel. Peels add a good deal of flavor, but must harmonize with the flavor of the filling.

    — If you are lining a pan with ladyfingers and are planning to fill with chocolate mousse, then delete the peels.

Chunky Pecan & Raisin Spice Bar Cookies

These are highly spiced cookies that are filled with raisins and pecans. They are chunky and chewy and the essence of simplicity to prepare.

1 cup brown sugar
1/2 cup butter, softened
1/4 cup orange juice
1 egg
1 teaspoon vanilla

1 3/4 cups flour
1/2 teaspoon baking powder
1 teaspoon cinnamon
1/2 teaspoon ground nutmeg
pinch of salt

1 1/2 cups raisins
1 cup chopped pecans

Beat together the first 5 ingredients until blended. Beat in the next 5 ingredients until blended. Do not overbeat. Stir in the raisins and pecans. Spread batter into a greased 9x13-inch baking pan and bake in a 350° oven for about 17 minutes, or until top is lightly browned and a cake tester, inserted in center, comes out clean. Allow to cool in pan. When cool, cut into squares to serve. Yields 2 dozen cookies.

Note: — *These luscious cookies need only a faint sprinkling of powdered sugar for decoration. However, for a more dressy presentation, it would be lovely to drizzle a little Creamy Glaze on the top.*

Creamy Glaze: Stir together 1 tablespoon cream, 1/2 teaspoon vanilla and 1/2 cup of sifted powdered sugar until blended. Add a little sugar or cream to make glaze a drizzling consistency. Drizzle glaze on top of cooled cookies in a lacy, decorative pattern.

Butter Pecan Cookies with Apricot Jam & Chocolate

What a delicious cookie and so pretty and fancy for holiday serving and giving. It is a little bit more work, but worth every second of it, I promise you.

- **3/4 cup butter**
- **3/4 cup sugar**

- **1 egg**
- **1 teaspoon vanilla**

- **2 cups flour**
- **1/2 teaspoon baking powder**
- **1/3 cup finely chopped pecans**

- **1 cup apricot jam**
- **1/2 cup semi-sweet chocolate chips, melted**

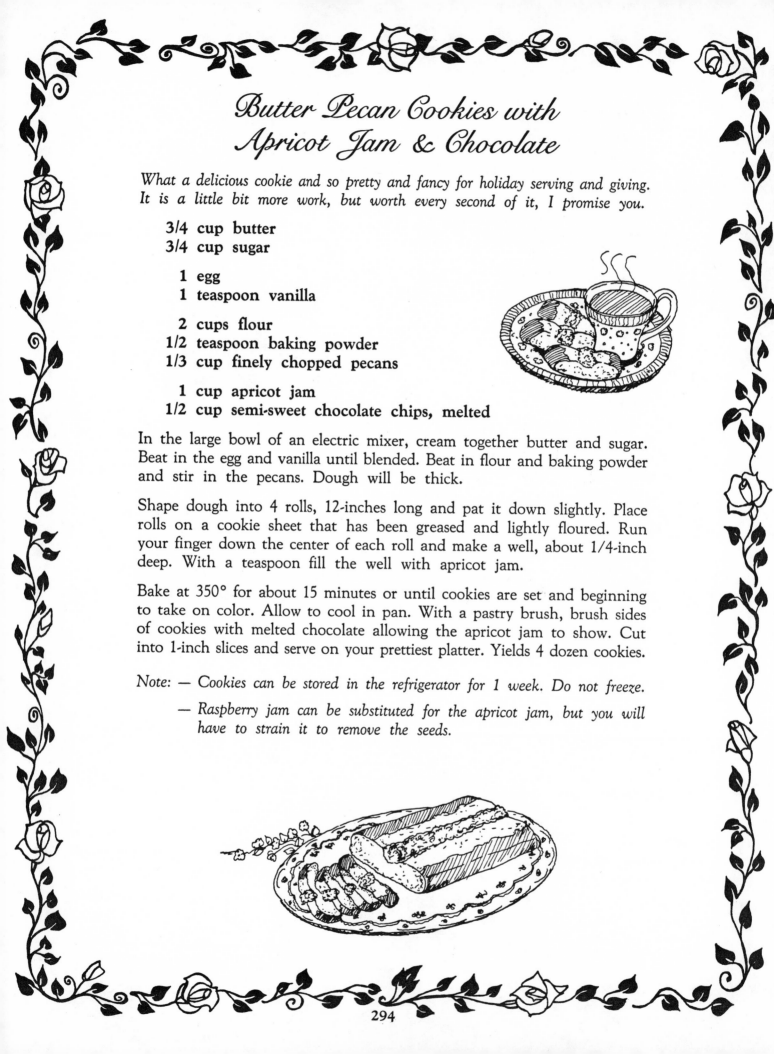

In the large bowl of an electric mixer, cream together butter and sugar. Beat in the egg and vanilla until blended. Beat in flour and baking powder and stir in the pecans. Dough will be thick.

Shape dough into 4 rolls, 12-inches long and pat it down slightly. Place rolls on a cookie sheet that has been greased and lightly floured. Run your finger down the center of each roll and make a well, about 1/4-inch deep. With a teaspoon fill the well with apricot jam.

Bake at 350° for about 15 minutes or until cookies are set and beginning to take on color. Allow to cool in pan. With a pastry brush, brush sides of cookies with melted chocolate allowing the apricot jam to show. Cut into 1-inch slices and serve on your prettiest platter. Yields 4 dozen cookies.

Note: — Cookies can be stored in the refrigerator for 1 week. Do not freeze.

— Raspberry jam can be substituted for the apricot jam, but you will have to strain it to remove the seeds.

Honey Butterscotch Oatmeal Chewies with Raisins & Pecans

Oh! what a cookie. I love oatmeal cookies that are chewy, chunky and filled with all manner of good things. This marvelous bar cookie is one of my favorites. It is truly delicious, and I hope you enjoy it as much as I do.

1 1/4 cups sugar
1/2 cup butter, softened
2 eggs
1/2 cup honey
1 teaspoon vanilla

1 3/4 cups flour
2 cups quick-cooking oats
1 teaspoon baking soda
pinch of salt

1 cup butterscotch chips
1 cup chopped pecans
1/2 cup raisins

Beat together first 5 ingredients until blended. Beat in the next 4 ingredients until blended. Stir in the remaining ingredients.

Spread batter evenly into a greased 10x15x1-inch jelly roll pan and bake in a 350° oven for 25 minutes or until top is browned and a cake tester, inserted in center, comes out clean. Allow to cool in pan and then cut into squares to serve. Yields 4 dozen cookies.

Note: — *Make certain that your jelly roll pan is at least 1-inch deep or batter will overflow while baking. Some jelly roll pans are 1/2 or 3/4-inch deep and are not deep enough for this recipe.*

— *Decorate with a faint sprinkling of sifted powdered sugar.*

Hungarian Butter Cookies — Pogacsas

These are the first cookies my mother-in-law served to me. They are very mild, buttery and not very sweet. They are habit-forming, though, so don't be innocently taken in. The original recipe was very difficult to acquire, because "measuring will spoil the cookies" and my mother-in-law always prepares a huge quantity "in case someone drops in." But here they are, tailored down to family size.

2 3/4 cups flour
1/2 cup sugar
1 cup butter

1/2 cup cream
2 egg yolks (reserve whites for browning tops)

In the large bowl of an electric mixer, beat flour, sugar and butter until mixture resembles coarse meal. Beat in the cream and egg yolks until blended.

Place dough on floured wax paper and shape into a 6-inch circle. Wrap dough in the wax paper and refrigerate for several hours or overnight.

Roll dough out to 3/4-inch thickness and cut into decorative shapes with cookie cutters. (Cutters should not measure larger than 1 1/4-inches, or cookies will be too big.) Place on a buttered cookie sheet and baste tops with beaten egg white.

Bake in a 350° oven for 15 minutes or until top is lightly browned. (Bake in the middle rack of the oven.) Remove from pan and cool on brown paper. Yields 2 to 3 dozen cookies, depending on the size of the cutters used.

Note: — These cookies freeze beautifully.

Giant Granola Cookies with Raisins, Dates & Walnuts

This is a delicious cookie, filled with all manner of good things. The kids will run home from school, if they knew these awaited them. Not to mention the neighbors who will happen to drop by, when the aroma, of these heavenly cookies, drifts down the street.

- 1 1/2 cups flour
- 1 1/3 cups prepared granola
- 1 teaspoon baking powder
- 1/2 teaspoon baking soda
- 1/2 teaspoon salt

- 1 cup butter, at room temperature
- 1 cup sugar
- 1 cup brown sugar
- 2 teaspoons vanilla
- 2 eggs
- 1 cup yellow raisins
- 1/2 cup chopped dates
- 1 cup chopped walnuts

In a bowl, combine first 5 ingredients and stir to blend. In the large bowl of an electric mixer, cream together butter, sugars and vanilla. Beat in eggs, one at a time, beating well after each addition. Beat in flour mixture until blended. Stir in fruits and nuts.

Drop batter, by the heaping tablespoonful on a greased cookie sheet, making about 12 cookies at one time. Bake in a 375° oven for about 12 minutes or until cookies are just set and beginning to take on a little color along the edges. (Do not overbake or cookies will be too crisp and lose their chewy quality.)

Allow to cool on brown paper bags. Yields about 3 dozen cookies.

Note: — These cookies freeze beautifully. However, they rarely make it to the freezer, so don't count on these for stocking up.

Spiced Pumpkin Custard
with Vanilla Caramel Sauce

After an indulgent Thanksgiving dinner, you might consider this light and very refreshing dessert, as an alternative to either the cookies, cakes or pies. I would not choose this as the only dessert. It has a good deal of character, but not enough substance. On any other night, it stands alone quite well. The Caramel Topping is really delicious.

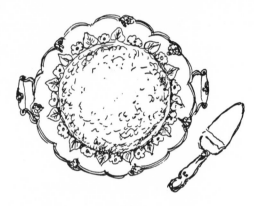

    1/2 cup prepared Caramel Topping
      1 teaspoon vanilla

      4 eggs
      1 cup cream
      1 cup milk
      1 cup canned pumpkin puree
    1/2 cup sugar
      1 teaspoon cinnamon
    1/4 teaspoon nutmeg
    1/4 teaspoon ground cloves
      1 teaspoon vanilla

Stir together Caramel Topping and vanilla and spread evenly on the bottom of a 10-inch porcelain quiche baker. Beat together the remaining ingredients until blended, and gently pour mixture over the caramel. Now, place baker in a 12x16-inch baking pan, place pan in a 350° oven, and pour boiling water into the pan to come 1/2 up the side. Bake for about 1 hour, or until a cake tester, inserted 1-inch off center, comes out clean. Remove quiche baker from hot water bath and allow to cool.

When cool, invert onto a rimmed serving platter, cover with plastic wrap and refrigerate. Cut into wedges to serve and spoon a little sauce on top. Serves 8.

Note: — *When you invert the custard onto a serving platter, sauce will be loose, but it will thicken up in the refrigerator.*

   — *It is easier to place the quiche baker in the larger pan and then pour boiling water into the pan.*

Spicy Orange Baked Apples with Pecan Streusel Topping & Creme Vanilla

This is a lovely dessert filled, as it is, with sugar and spice and everything nice.

- 6 medium apples, peeled, cored and sliced
- 2 tablespoons grated orange peel
- 1/2 cup apricot jam
- 1/2 cup sugar (or to taste)
- 1 teaspoon cinnamon
- 1/4 teaspoon nutmeg
- 1/4 teaspoon ground cloves

Streusel Topping:
- 1/3 cup butter
- 1/2 cup brown sugar
- 1/3 cup flour
- 3/4 cup chopped pecans

In a large bowl, combine first 7 ingredients and stir until well mixed. Place mixture into a buttered 12-inch oval porcelain baker.

Beat butter with brown sugar and flour until mixture resembles coarse crumbs. Stir in the pecans and sprinkle mixture over the apples. Bake in a 350° oven for about 50 minutes or until apples are tender and streusel is browned.

To serve, spoon into serving dishes and top with a tablespoon of vanilla flavored whipped cream or Creme Vanilla. Serves 6.

Creme Vanilla:
- 3 ounces cream
- 3 ounces sour cream
- 1 tablespoon sugar
- 1 teaspoon vanilla

Stir together all the ingredients and store in the refrigerator for several hours or overnight. Yields 12 tablespoons sauce.

Note: — Apples and topping can be baked earlier in the day and heated at time of serving.

— Creme Vanilla can be prepared several days earlier and stored in the refrigerator.

Honey Spiced Apples with Orange & Pecans

Apples poached in an orange-flavored syrup with spices and nuts are always the biggest hit at our home. Everybody spoons up the last drops of syrup with pecans. Serve with a little Creme Fraiche for dessert. These are also wonderful as an accompaniment to roast chicken. And for lunch, with quiche or calzones... delicious!

4 apples, peeled, cored and cut into 1/2-inch thick slices, about 1 1/2 pounds fruit

2 tablespoons grated orange
1 tablespoon grated lemon
1/2 cup orange juice
1/2 cup honey
1/4 cup butter
3/4 teaspoon cinnamon
1/4 teaspoon ground cloves
1/4 teaspoon ground nutmeg
1/2 teaspoon vanilla
1/2 cup coarsely chopped pecans

In a 12-inch skillet, lay apple slices evenly. Stir together the remaining ingredients until blended and pour over the apples. Cook over low heat, stirring now and again, until apples are tender and juice is syrupy. Do not overcook, but apples should not be too firm, either.

Serve with a little whipped cream, ice cream or creme fraiche for dessert. Can be served as an accompaniment to a savory dish as well. Serves 4 to 5.

Note: — Peaches or apricots can be substituted.

— When the fruit is being poached in the syrup, it sometimes renders a large amount of juice. If that occurs, then raise the heat and allow most of it to bubble away.

— Can be prepared 1 day earlier and stored in the refrigerator. Heat before serving.

Tartufo alla Tre Scalini Caffe

This delightful chocolate ice cream dessert is the famous specialty of the Caffe Tre Scalini in Rome. Their chocolate ice cream is a zealously guarded secret, but using an excellent quality chocolate ice cream is a good substitute.

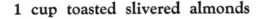

- **16 glaceed cherries**
- **2 tablespoons rum**

- **8 large scoops of chocolate ice cream**

- **1 package (12 ounces) semi-sweet chocolate chips**
- **1/2 cup butter (1 stick)**

- **1 cup toasted slivered almonds**

Soak cherries in rum. With a large ice cream scooper, scoop out 8 balls of ice cream on a wax paper-lined cookie sheet. Press 2 cherries into each center, working quickly. Place ice cream balls in freezer and freeze until very firm.

In the top of a double boiler, over hot, not boiling, water, melt together chocolate and butter, stirring until blended. Allow to cool for 20 minutes. Spear each ice cream ball with a fork and quickly dip and roll it into the melted chocolate. Return it to the wax paper, sprinkle it with almonds and return it to the freezer immediately. Proceed with the remaining balls in the same manner.

At Tre Scallini, they are served with additional rum-soaked cherries and in glass dessert dishes. Serves 8.

Note: — *After the ice cream balls are frozen firm, they must be covered securely with plastic wrap.*

— *Entire dessert can be prepared 2 or 3 days earlier and stored in the freezer.*

— *Remove from the freezer 5 minutes before serving.*

Iced Lemon Cream with Raspberry Sauce

There is no iced dessert that is easier or more beautiful than this one. It is a variation of a recipe I shared with you in "The Joy of Eating" except this one is made a little lighter with half and half. This is a great dessert to serve after a hefty meal.

    2 packages (12 count, each) lady fingers, split in half*

    1 cup whipping cream
    1 cup half and half
    4 tablespoons lemon juice
    1/2 lemon, finely grated. Remove any large pieces
           of membrane.
    1 cup sugar

Line an 8-inch springform pan by criss-crossing 2 strips of plastic wrap, extending 4-inches beyond the edge of the pan. (Don't worry if it is a little wrinkled for it will not show.) Now, line the bottom and sides of the pan with lady fingers, attaching with a smidge of butter. (See note.)

In a bowl, place the remaining ingredients and stir until sugar is dissolved, about 1 minute. Pour this into the prepared pan, cover with plastic wrap and freeze until firm. Remove from the freezer about 10 minutes before serving, peel off the plastic wrap and place on a lovely platter. To serve, cut into thin wedges and spoon a little Raspberry Sauce on top. Serves 10 to 12.

Raspberry Sauce:
    1 package (10 ounces) frozen raspberries in syrup, defrosted
    1 tablespoon lemon juice

Simply stir ingredients together until blended. Store in the refrigerator until ready to serve.

Note: — *Lemon cream can be divided between 12 paper-lined muffin cups and frozen until firm. To serve, remove the paper liners and place in a lovely stemmed glass. Spoon a little Raspberry Sauce on top.*

    — **The lady fingers used to line the **sides** of the pan should be cut in half again. This is a low dessert.*

Lemon Creme Glace with Lemon Vanilla Almond Crust & Raspberry Sauce

What a lovely dessert for a hot sultry evening. It is tart and cool, and a grand finale for a summer evening. It can be prepared in advance, properly stored in your freezer, and is grand to have on hand.

> 6 egg whites
> 1/2 cup sugar
>
> 2 cups cream
> 1/4 cup sugar
> 6 tablespoons grated lemon. (About 1 1/2 lemons, grated. Use fruit, juice and peel. Remove any large pieces of membrane.)
>
> 1 package (10 ounces) raspberries in syrup, defrosted

Beat whites until foamy. Continue beating, adding sugar slowly, until whites form a stiff meringue. Set aside.

In another bowl, whip cream and sugar until stiff. Beat in grated lemon until blended. Fold in beaten whites until blended. Spread creamed mixture into prepared crust and freeze until firm.

To serve, cut into wedges and spoon 1 tablespoon of raspberries with syrup over the top. Serves 8.

Vanilla Almond Crust:
> 1 1/2 cups vanilla wafer crumbs
> 1/2 cup chopped almonds
> 1/3 cup melted butter
> 1 tablespoon grated lemon

Stir together all the ingredients until blended. Pat them on the bottom and 1-inch up the sides of a 10-inch springform pan. Bake in a 350° oven for 7 minutes or until top is just beginning to take on color. Allow to cool.

Note: — 2 tablespoons of frozen orange juice concentrate can be added to the raspberries in syrup for a delicious fillip to the sauce.

— If fresh raspberries are in season, add these to the sauce.

Royal Orange Souffle Glace with Macaroon Crust & Orange Cognac Cream

What a beautiful, refreshing dessert, exciting, glamorous and fit for a king. It can be prepared up to 1 week in advance, properly wrapped, in your freezer.

Macaroon Crust:
- 1 1/4 cups macaroon cookie crumbs
- 2 tablespoons butter

Spread butter on the bottom of a 10-inch springform pan. Sprinkle macaroon crumbs evenly on top and set aside.

Orange Souffle Glace:
- 6 egg whites
- 1/2 cup sugar
- 2 cups cream
- 3 tablespoons orange liqueur
- 2 tablespoons sugar
- 3 ounces frozen orange juice concentrate, defrosted
- 2/3 cup macaroon cookie crumbs (fine crumbs)
- 1/2 cup finely chopped toasted hazelnuts

In the large bowl of an electric mixer, beat egg whites until foamy. Add sugar slowly and continue beating until whites are stiff.

In another bowl, beat cream with liqueur and sugar until stiff. Beat in orange juice, crumbs and hazelnuts. Fold egg whites into cream mixture. (This can be done carefully, on the lowest speed of your mixer, but be careful not to overbeat.)

Pour mixture into prepared pan and spread evenly. Freeze until firm, and wrap securely with double thickness of plastic wrap and then foil. Remove from the freezer about 10 minutes before serving. Decorate top with mandarin sections and finely chopped hazelnuts. To serve, cut into wedges and spoon 1 tablespoon Orange Cognac Cream on top. Serves 12.

Orange Cognac Cream:
- 1/2 cup orange juice
- 1 tablespoon grated orange peel
- 2 tablespoons lemon juice
- 1 teaspoon grated lemon peel
- 1/2 cup orange marmalade
- 4 tablespoons sugar
- 2 tablespoons Cognac
- 3 tablespoons cream

Place all the ingredients in a saucepan and simmer until mixture is syrupy, stirring often, about 4 minutes.

Mousseline of Chocolate with Rum in Chocolate Couletes

An *incredible chocolate mousse, served in chocolate cups and decorated with a sprinkling of white chocolate is truly fit for a king. The mousse can be flavored with rum or cognac, whichever is your pleasure. All ingredients should be at room temperature, to avoid chocolate stiffening up when mixing.*

    8 ounces semi-sweet chocolate chips
    3 egg yolks
1/2 cup (1 stick) butter, cut into 8 pieces
    2 teaspoons vanilla
    2 tablespoons rum

    3 egg whites
    2 tablespoons sugar

Melt chocolate in the top of a double boiler, over hot, not boiling water. Remove chocolate to the large bowl of an electric mixer. Beat in the egg yolks until blended. Beat in the softened butter, piece by piece, until blended. Beat in the vanilla and rum.

In another bowl, with clean beaters, beat egg whites until foamy. Gradually add the sugar and continue beating until whites are a stiff meringue.

Stir 1/3 of the whites into the chocolate to loosen. Fold in the remaining whites until blended. Spoon mousseline into the chocolate cups and refrigerate until firm. Decorate top with finely grated white chocolate or a dollup of whipped cream flavored with rum, or a spoonful of sweetened Creme Fraiche flavored with rum. (Mousse can be served in stemmed glasses if you prefer to omit the chocolate cups.) Serves 8.

Chocolate Couletes:
    4 ounces (2/3 cup) semi-sweet chocolate chips, melted
    8 muffin paper liners (use a waxy liner)

Spoon about 1 1/2 tablespoons melted chocolate into muffin paper liner and with the back of a spoon, spread chocolate on the bottom and up the sides, until liner is completely coated. Place liners in muffin pan and refrigerate until firm. After thoroughly firmed, peel off paper and you will have a lovely fluted cup, to serve mousses, ice creams, ices or custards. Yields 8 cups.

Rum Mousse au Chocolat with Macaroons & Almonds & White Chocolate Leaves

Oh what a mousse, and perfectly fool proof, with the addition of gelatin. Flavor the chocolate with 1 teaspoon powdered coffee, if you like, for a slight mocha flavor. Keep the liqueur soaked crumbs on the bottom as a surprise.

1 tablespoon unflavored gelatin (1 packet)
1/3 cup rum

4 eggs, at room temperature
1/2 cup sugar

1 package (12 ounces) semi-sweet chocolate, melted and
    slightly cooled
1 cup cream, beaten until stiff

In a metal measuring cup, soften gelatin in rum. Place in a pan with simmering water until gelatin is dissolved. Set aside.

Beat eggs with sugar until eggs are lemon colored, about 5 minutes at high speed. Beat in the melted chocolate. Beat in the whipped cream. (This can be done on the lowest speed of an electric mixer.)

Spoon mixture into 8 lovely stemmed glasses that have been prepared with Chocolate Macaroon Crumbs, and refrigerate until firm. Decorate top with white chocolate leaves, a sprinkling of grated chocolate, and a drizzle of chocolate liqueur. Serve with majesty and pride. Serves 8.

Chocolate Macaroon Crumbs:
8 tablespoons macaroon cookie crumbs
8 teaspoons finely chopped toasted almonds
8 teaspoons finely grated chocolate
8 teaspoons Creme de Cacao, chocolate liqueur

Into each of 8 lovely stemmed glasses (balloon glasses are especially nice for this dessert) place 1 tablespoon crumbs, 1 teaspoon almonds, 1 teaspoon grated chocolate and 1 teaspoon chocolate liqueur. Allow to rest until crumbs are moistened. Proceed to fill as described above.

Note: — This recipe can be stretched to serve 10.

— To make white chocolate leaves, melt 1/4 cup (2 ounces) white chocolate. With a spoon, spread white chocolate on the backs of scrubbed and dried camellia leaves. Place on wax paper and refrigerate. When firm, peel off the camellia leaves and Voila! pretty white leaves to decorate this grand dish.

Imperial White Chocolate Mousse
with Almond Crust & Raspberry Sauce

Now, if you are looking for a dessert to really impress, this is a great one to consider. While the preparation of this mousse is very unorthodox, it does produce a magnificent dessert. It is a dense mousse with a good deal of character. It is a bit more work to prepare, but truly worth every minute of it.

    1   envelope unflavored gelatin (1 tablespoon)
    1/4 cup rum

    1/2 cup cream
    1/4 cup butter (1/2 stick)
    1/2 pound white chocolate, coarsely chopped
    1   teaspoon almond extract

    2   egg yolks
    1   cup sifted powdered sugar

  1 1/2 cups cream, whipped stiff

In a metal measuring cup, soften gelatin in rum. Place it in a pan of simmering water until dissolved.

In the top of a double boiler, over hot water, heat cream with butter until butter is melted. Add the white chocolate and almond extract and stir until chocolate is melted. Place mixture into the large bowl of an electric mixer, and beat in the egg yolks and powdered sugar. Beat in the whipped cream until blended. Beat in the dissolved gelatin until blended.

Place mixture in prepared crust and refrigerate until firm, overnight is good, too. Decorate top with finely grated chocolate, or chocolate leaves. To serve, cut into wedges and spoon a little Raspberry Sauce on top. Memorable! Keep the portions small and serve 12.

Almond Crust: Stir together 1 1/2 cups macaroon crumbs; 1/4 cup butter, melted; 1/4 cup finely chopped almonds until blended. Press mixture on the bottom of a 10-inch glass pie plate and bake in a 350° oven for 7 minutes. Allow to cool.

Raspberry Sauce: Stir together 1 package (10 ounces) raspberries in syrup; and 3 ounces frozen orange juice concentrate until blended. Refrigerate until serving time.

Chocolate Angel Mousse with Light Sauce Vanilla

This is a heavenly mousse with the marvelous dense texture so characteristic of French mousses. The Light Sauce Vanilla is traditionally made with egg yolks, but using the egg whites produces a very light and delicate sauce. The Chocolate Sauce is a lovely variation and can be used over numerous desserts. Mousse and sauce can be prepared earlier in the day and stored in the refrigerator.

1/4 cup water
8 ounces semi-sweet chocolate chips
4 egg yolks, beaten
1/2 cup butter, at room temperature, cut into 8 pieces

4 egg whites
2 tablespoons sugar
2 teaspoons vanilla or 1 tablespoon rum

In a saucepan, over very low heat, stir together water and chocolate, until chocolate is melted. Slowly stir in the egg yolks until blended. Add 1 piece of butter at a time, stirring until blended. Chocolate will become shiny and satiny. Remove from heat and allow to cool for 5 minutes.

Beat whites until foamy. Slowly add the sugar and continue beating until whites are stiff. On low speed, beat in chocolate and vanilla until blended. Place mousse into a footed glass server and refrigerate until firm. To serve, place a little Light Sauce Vanilla on a dessert plate and a scoop of mousse on top. Serves 6.

Light Sauce Vanilla:
2 eggs
1/2 cup sugar
1 teaspoon cornstarch
1 cup half and half or light cream
1 teaspoon vanilla or 1 teaspoon rum

Beat together eggs and sugar until mixture is light and fluffy, about 5 minutes. Meanwhile, in a saucepan, bring cream to a boil. Slowly beat cream into egg mixture. Return this to the saucepan and cook, over low heat, stirring all the while, until sauce coats a spoon. Do not allow to boil or sauce will curdle. Stir in vanilla. Place sauce in a jar with a tight-fitting lid, and refrigerate until ready to serve.

To make Chocolate Sauce: When sauce is finished cooking, quickly stir in 4 ounces semi-sweet chocolate chips until melted. Excellent over ice cream or sponge cakes.

German Chocolate Chip & Pecan Chocolate Pie with Whipped Creme de Cacao

This is a quick and easy dessert that you can prepare some evening when you are running late. It is not the traditional pecan pie, so don't think anything went wrong. It is very delicious and I know you will use it often.

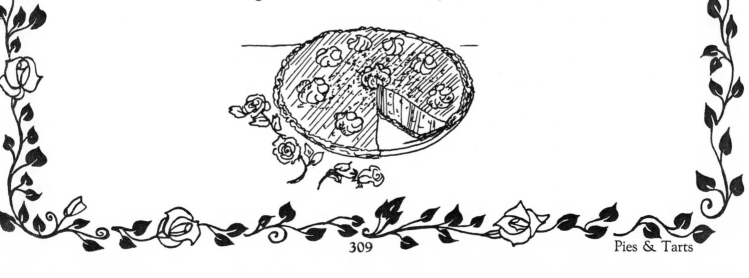

      2 tablespoons butter
      1 cup coconut macaroon crumbs

      2 eggs
    3/4 cup sugar
    1/2 cup butter, (1 stick), softened
    1/2 cup flour
      3 tablespoons cocoa

      1 cup (6 ounces) semi-sweet chocolate chips
      1 cup chopped pecans
    1/2 cup coconut flakes
      2 teaspoons vanilla

Spread the 2 tablespoons butter on the bottom and sides of a 10-inch pie pan. Press macaroon crumbs evenly on the bottom and sides. Set aside.

Beat eggs, sugar, butter, flour and cocoa until blended. Stir in the remaining ingredients until blended. Spread mixture evenly into prepared pan and bake at 350° for 30 minutes, or until a cake tester, inserted in center, comes out clean. Allow to cool.

When cool, pipe rosettes of Whipped Creme de Cacao on top and decorate with a sprinkle of sifted cocoa and finely chopped toasted pecans. Serves 8.

Whipped Creme de Cacao:
    3/4 cup cream
      1 tablespoon sugar
      1 tablespoon Creme de Cacao Liqueur

Beat cream with sugar until stiff. Beat in liqueur until blended.

Apricot, Fig & Dried Fruit Winter Tart

This sturdy pie is a good choice to serve after a day on the slopes or a trudge in the snow. The crust is filled with almonds and spice and is a delicious base for the dried fruit filling.

Filling:
- 1 pound mixed dried fruit (or a combination of apricots, figs, peaches, pitted prunes, pears, to taste)
- 1 cup orange juice
- 1/2 cup water
- 3/4 cup sugar
- 1 teaspoon cinnamon
- 2 tablespoons lemon juice

Almond Custard:
- 1/2 cup cream
- 1 egg
- 3 tablespoons sugar
- 1/4 cup finely grated almonds (almond meal)
- 1/2 teaspoon almond extract

Cook together all the filling ingredients until fruit is soft, about 30 minutes, and drain. Beat together custard ingredients until blended. Place custard into prepared crust and place fruit decoratively on top. Bake in a 350° oven for 30 minutes, or until custard is set. Allow to cool in pan. Serve with hot cider. Serves 8.

Spicy Butter Crust:
- 1 1/2 cups flour
- 1 cup finely grated almonds (almond meal)
- 1/2 cup sugar
- 1 teaspoon pumpkin pie spice
- 1/2 cup butter, cut into 8 pieces

- 1 egg
- 2 tablespoons water
- 1/2 teaspoon almond extract

Beat together first 5 ingredients until mixture resembles coarse meal. Beat together egg, water and almond extract until blended, and add, beating until dough clumps together. Pat dough on the bottom and 1-inch up the sides of a greased 10-inch springform pan and bake in a 350° oven for 20 to 25 minutes, or until dough appears dry and is just beginning to take on color.

Holiday Chocolate Pecan Pie with Vanilla Creme Fraiche

This is sinfully rich and extravagant, but when it is around holiday times, we do tend to splurge a little. Keep the portions small. The Vanilla Creme Fraiche is a grand accompaniment, but optional.

- 1 1/4 cups light corn syrup
- 1/2 cup brown sugar
- 3 tablespoons cocoa
- 1 tablespoon flour
- 1/4 cup butter, melted
- 3 eggs
- 2 teaspoons vanilla

- 1 1/2 cups chopped pecans
- 1/2 cup semi-sweet chocolate chips

- 1 9-inch frozen deep dish pie shell, defrosted for 10 minutes

Beat together first 7 ingredients until blended. Stir in pecans and chocolate chips. Pour mixture into pie shell. Place pan on a cookie sheet and bake in a 350° oven for about 55 minutes to 1 hour, or until filling is set in center. (After 30 minutes, tent pie loosely with foil to avoid overbrowning.)

Allow to cool in pan. Cut into wedges and serve with a spoonful of Vanilla Creme Fraiche. Serves 10.

Vanilla Creme Fraiche:
- 1/4 cup sour cream
- 1/4 cup cream
- 2 tablespoons brown sugar
- 1/2 teaspoon vanilla

Stir together all the ingredients until blended. Allow mixture to stand at room temperature for 2 to 3 hours, or until thickened. Cover and refrigerate until ready to use.

Note: — Pie can be prepared 1 day earlier and stored at room temperature.

— Vanilla Creme Fraiche can be prepared 3 days before serving.

Pies & Tarts

Sour Cream Apricot & Raisin Tart with Almond Macaroon Crust

What a delicious and unusual tart that is just bursting with flavor. It is the essence of simplicity to prepare and is a cool and refreshing dessert for a sultry evening.

Almond Macaroon Crust:
- 1 3/4 cups macaroon crumbs
- 1/2 cup chopped almonds
- 1/3 cup butter, melted

Stir together all the ingredients and press mixture on the bottom and 1/2-inch up the sides of a 10-inch springform pan. Bake in a 350° oven for 8 minutes. Seal crust with a thin layer of apricot jam that has been sieved and heated. (Heating the jam will allow it to spread easily.)

Pour Sour Cream Apricot & Raisin Filling into prepared crust and spread fruit evenly. Bake in a 350° oven for 45 minutes, or until custard is set. Allow to cool and then refrigerate for several hours. Overnight is good, too. Serves 8 to 10.

Sour Cream Apricot & Raisin Filling:
- 1 package (6 ounces) dried apricots
- 1 cup yellow raisins
- 1 cup orange juice
- 2/3 cup sugar

- 2 eggs
- 1 cup sour cream
- 2 tablespoons flour
- 1 teaspoon vanilla
- 1/2 teaspoon almond extract

In a saucepan, simmer together apricots, raisins, orange juice and sugar for about 10 minutes, or until apricots are tender. Allow to cool.

Meanwhile, beat together the remaining ingredients until blended. Stir in apricot mixture (with syrup) until blended. Yields enough filling for 1 10-inch tart.

Easiest & Best Butter Cookie Apple Pie with Raisins & Cinnamon

This is one of the most delicious crusts, flaky and light, and marvelous as a base for apple, peach, or apricot pies. Preparation is especially easy, as it is made in a mixer. Do not overbeat. The whole process should not take more than 1 minute.

Butter Cookie Crust:
- 1 cup cold butter (2 sticks), cut into 8 pieces
- 2 cups flour
- 4 tablespoons sugar

- 3 to 4 tablespoons water

Apple Filling:
- 4 large apples, peeled, cored and very thinly sliced, about 2 1/2 pounds
- 1/2 cup sugar
- 1/2 cup yellow raisins
- 2 tablespoons apricot jam
- 1 teaspoon cinnamon
- 1/4 teaspoon nutmeg

In the large bowl of an electric mixer, beat together butter, flour and sugar until mixture resembles coarse meal. Add the water, a little at a time, and only enough to form a soft dough. (As soon as the dough clumps together, it is ready.)

Knead it once or twice until it is smooth, wrap with wax paper and refrigerate for 20 minutes. Cut dough in half and roll one half out to measure a 12-inch circle. Place in a greased deep-dish 9-inch pie plate.

Toss together the filling ingredients and place into prepared pie crust. Roll out the second half of dough to measure 11-inches and place over the apples. Pinch edges together to seal, cut a few slits on the top, brush top with a little milk and sprinkle with 1 teaspoon sugar. Place pie on a cookie sheet and bake in a 375° oven for about 45 minutes, or until top is browned. Delicious served fresh and warm. Serves 8.

Bourbon Apple Tart with Cinnamon & Cloves on Butter Cookie Nut Crust

The crust on this pie is so delicious, it hardly needs a topping at all. It is exceedingly simple to prepare and handle, so I know you will use it often. The fruit topping is traditional, but I added ground cloves which adds a little new dimension.

Butter Cookie Nut Crust:
1 1/2 cups flour
 6 tablespoons butter (3/4 stick)
 2 tablespoons sugar

1/4 cup chopped walnuts

1/2 cup cream

In the large bowl of an electric mixer, beat together flour, butter and sugar until mixture resembles coarse meal. Do not overbeat. Mix in the walnuts until blended. Now, beat in the cream until a dough forms, no longer. Pat mixture on the bottom and 3/4-inch up the sides of a buttered 10-inch springform pan and bake in a 350° oven for 15 minutes or until dough is set and just beginning to take on color. Remove from oven. Crust is ready for filling.

Apple Filling with Cinnamon & Cloves:
 4 large apples, peeled, cored and thinly sliced
 3 tablespoons bourbon
1/4 cup sugar, or more to taste
 1 teaspoon cinnamon
1/4 teaspoon ground cloves
 2 tablespoons grated lemon
 2 tablespoons butter
1/2 cup apricot jam

In a covered skillet, cook together first 7 ingredients until apples are softened.* Stir in the apricot jam. Arrange apple mixture onto prepared crust. Bake in a 350° oven for 35 to 45 minutes or until apples are soft. Allow to cool in pan. Cut into wedges to serve. A little ice cream on top? Why not? Serves 8.

Note: — *If the apples have rendered too much juice, uncover pan and cook until juices have evaporated.*

   — Can be prepared a day before serving. Crust will not become soggy.

Deep Dish Apple Pie with Raisins & Cognac Lemon Custard

Good Heavens! this pie is delicious. It has deep and solid character with the addition of Cognac and a hint of lemon.

> 1 9-inch deep dish frozen pie shell. Bake in a 400° oven for 6 minutes, or just until set.

Apple Filling:
> 3 medium apples, peeled, cored and cut lengthwise into 1/4-inch slices
> 1/2 cup apricot jam
> 1/2 cup yellow raisins
> 1/4 cup sugar
> 1/2 teaspoon cinnamon

In a bowl, stir together all the ingredients and place evenly into prepared pie shell. Place pan on a cookie sheet, and bake in a 350° oven for 30 minutes.

Meanwhile, prepare Cognac Lemon Custard and pour evenly over the apples. Return to oven and continue baking for about 20 minutes or until top is golden brown. This can be served warm or at room temperature. Serves 8.

Cognac Lemon Custard:
> 1 egg
> 1/3 cup sugar
>
> 1/4 cup flour
> 1/2 cup cream
> 2 tablespoons Cognac
> 2 teaspoons finely grated lemon peel

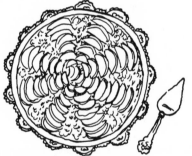

Beat eggs with sugar until light and fluffy. Beat in the remaining ingredients until blended.

Note: — *Using the frozen pie shells, makes this exceedingly easy. However, if you find you have a little extra time, you might enjoy making the following pie shell, which does add a lovely touch.*

Brown Sugar Butter Crust:
> 1 cup flour
> 1/2 cup brown sugar
> 1/2 cup butter, softened

Beat all the ingredients together until mixture is blended. Pat mixture on the bottom and sides of a greased 9-inch deep dish pie pan. Bake in a 400° oven for 7 minutes or just until set.

Apricot Glazed French Apple Tart

This is a very thin, crispy apple tart, that serves well for a brunch or luncheon buffet. It is not complex, just a delicious pastry topped with glazed apples, and just right for brunch.

Crust:
- 1 cup butter (2 sticks)
- 1/2 pound cream cheese
- 2 cups flour
- 5 heaping tablespoons sifted powdered sugar

Beat together butter and cream cheese until blended. Beat in flour and sugar until blended. Pat dough into an 8-inch circle, and refrigerate for 1 hour. Butter a 9x13-inch baking pan and pat dough on the bottom of the pan. Bake in a 350° oven for 12 minutes.

Topping:
- 3/4 cup apricot jam, warmed
- 4 or 5 apples, peeled, cored and cut in half, vertically. Place cut ends down and cut into very thin slices (about 1/8-inch thick).
- 4 tablespoons cinnamon sugar

Paint crust with a thin coating of apricot jam. Line dough with rows of apple slices (fan the apples out in rows) and sprinkle top with cinnamon sugar. Bake in a 350° oven for 40 minutes. Baste top with remaining apricot jam, increase oven temperature to 400°, and bake for another 10 minutes to set apricot glaze. Serves 12.

Note: — Can be prepared earlier in the day or 1 day earlier.

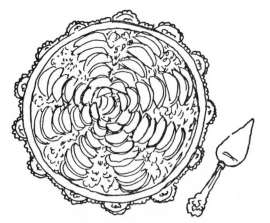

Crustless Apple Pie with Lemon Meringue Topping

This is a delicious little dessert that is somewhat lower in calories than its crusty cousin. It is a light dessert and nice to serve after a hardy meal.

3 medium apples, peeled, cored and sliced

1/2 cup sugar
3 tablespoons flour
3 tablespoons butter, softened
2 egg yolks
1/2 cup cream
1 teaspoon apple pie spice (or 1 teaspoon cinnamon)

Place apples in a food processor, and blend for about 5 seconds, or until apples are coarsely chopped. Add the remaining ingredients and blend until apples are finely chopped, but not pureed. Place apple mixture in a buttered 9-inch pie plate and bake in a 350° oven for 35 minutes or until pie is almost set.

Spread top with Lemon Meringue Topping, return to oven and continue baking for about 20 minutes or until top is golden brown. Allow to cool and cut into wedges to serve. Serves 8.

Note: — The only thing to watch is that the apples don't get pureed in blending. If you blend too long, apples will turn into a soupy sauce and pie will not bake properly.

Lemon Meringue Topping:
2 egg whites
1/4 cup sugar

1 tablespoon grated lemon peel

Beat egg whites until foamy. Gradually add sugar and beat until meringue is stiff. (This is not a light meringue, but a denser version.) Beat in the lemon peel.

World's Best Old-Fashioned Apple Pie with Spicy Streusel Topping

1 frozen 9-inch deep dish pie shell

6 apples, peeled, cored and cut into 1/4-inch slices
1 cup sugar
1/4 cup apricot jam
1/4 cup brown sugar
1/2 cup yellow raisins
2 tablespoons grated lemon, use fruit, juice and peel
1 tablespoon melted butter
1 tablespoon flour
1 teaspoon cinnamon
1/4 teaspoon nutmeg
1/4 teaspoon ground cloves

Place pie shell on a cookie sheet. In a bowl, toss together the remaining ingredients until nicely mixed. Place apple mixture evenly into crust. Sprinkle Spicy Streusel Topping over the apples. Bake in a 350° oven for about 1 hour or until crust is cooked through and apples are tender. Allow to cool in pan.

When pie has cooled, drizzle top with Creamy Lemon Glaze. Serves 8.

Spicy Streusel Topping:
1/2 cup flour
1/3 cup butter
1/4 cup sugar
1/4 cup brown sugar
1/2 teaspoon cinnamon
1/8 teaspoon nutmeg
1/8 teaspoon ground cloves

Cut butter into flour until mixture resembles coarse meal. Toss in the remaining ingredients until blended.

Creamy Lemon Glaze:
1 tablespoon sour cream
1 tablespoon cream
1 teaspoon lemon juice
sifted powdered sugar

Stir together sour cream, cream and lemon juice. Add enough powdered sugar to make glaze a drizzling consistency.

French Apple Lemon Tart with Butter Cookie Crust & Apricot Glaze

This is a rather sophisticated tart with a delicate combination of apples, lemon and apricot. The cookie dough base is delicious and can be used for numerous pies and pastries. Making the dough in the mixer and patting it into the pan is especially easy and I know you will love the taste and texture.

Butter Cookie Crust:
- 1 1/3 cups flour
- 1/2 cup butter (1 stick), cold
- 1/3 cup sugar

- 1 egg beaten
- 1/2 lemon, grated, about 2 tablespoons
- 1 teaspoon vanilla

In the large bowl of an electric mixer, beat together flour, butter and sugar until mixture resembles coarse meal. Combine beaten egg, lemon and vanilla and beat into flour mixture until blended. (Do not overbeat. Beat only until a dough forms.) Pat mixture on the bottom and 1/2-inch up the sides of a greased 10-inch springform pan and bake in a 350° oven for 15 minutes. Allow to cool for 10 minutes.

Apple Filling:
- 2 apples, peeled, cored and quartered. Cut each quarter into thin slices.
- 1 cup sugar
- 1/4 cup flour
- 3 eggs
- 1/2 cup butter, heated until sizzling hot
- 2 tablespoons grated lemon (about 1/2 lemon)

- 1/2 cup apricot jam, heated

In a spoke fashion, place apples in 8 rows on prepared cookie crust. Beat sugar, flour and eggs until blended. Beat in butter and lemon until blended. Pour mixture over the apples and bake in a 350° oven for about 40 to 45 minutes, or until top is golden brown. Remove from oven and baste top with heated apricot jam. Allow to cool in pan.

To serve, cut into wedges. A dollup of whipped cream is festive and lovely, but optional. Serves 8.

Note: — Dough can be prepared in a food processor, with excellent results. Follow the procedure described above.

Thanksgiving Spiced Honey Chestnut Pie on Pecan Crust with Praline Whipped Cream

This beautiful pie can easily become a tradition around the holidays. It is new and exciting, spicy and delicious, and an excellent choice for Thanksgiving.

Pecan Crust:
- 3/4 cup grated pecans (must use a nut grater)
- 3/4 cup flour
- 1/3 cup sugar
- 1/3 cup butter, cut into 4 pieces

In the large bowl of an electric mixer, beat together all the ingredients until mixture resembles coarse meal. Pat mixture on the bottom and sides of a 9-inch deep-dish pie plate. Bake in a 350° oven for 7 minutes.

Chestnut Filling:
- 1 can (15 1/2 ounces) unsweetened chestnut puree
- 3/4 cup sugar
- 3 eggs
- 1 cup cream
- 3 teaspoons pumpkin pie spice
- 1 teaspoon vanilla
- pinch of salt

Beat together filling ingredients until blended and pour into prepared crust. Bake in a 350° oven for about 1 hour, or until a cake tester, inserted 1-inch off center, comes out clean. Allow to cool and then refrigerate. Remove from the refrigerator about 20 minutes before serving. Serve with a dollup of Praline Whipped Cream. Serves 8.

Praline Whipped Cream: Beat together 1 cup cream, 2 tablespoons sifted brown sugar and 1/2 teaspoon vanilla until cream is stiff.

Easiest & Best Apricot Tart
with Lemon Butter Cookie Crust

The crust on this tart is so delicious, you will enjoy using it for fruit tarts or as a base for apple cakes. This recipe is similar to a Linzer Tart, but the petals on the top gives it a loveliness and character all its own. Dough is soft, but easily handled.

1 3/4 cups flour
    1 teaspoon baking powder
3/4 cup sugar
3/4 cup butter (1 1/2 sticks), cut into 12 pieces

    3 tablespoons grated lemon (use the fruit, juice and peel)
    1 cup chopped pecans
    1 egg, beaten

    1 cup apricot jam

In the large bowl of an electric mixer, beat together the first 4 ingredients until the mixture resembles coarse meal. Beat in the next 3 ingredients, until a dough forms. Do not overbeat.

Reserve 3/4 cup dough. Spread the remaining dough on the bottom and 1/2-inch up the sides of a 10-inch springform pan. Spread apricot jam over the dough. Divide the remaining dough into 8 pieces. With floured hands, shape each piece into a 2-inch petal. Place petals over the jam to resemble a flower.

Bake tart in a 350° oven for about 35 to 40 minutes or until top is browned. Allow to cool in pan. Sprinkle faintly with powdered sugar to decorate, and cut into wedges to serve. Serves 8.

Note: — *When spreading dough on the bottom of the 10-inch pan, either use a spatula to spread or pat down with floured hands. Dough is soft, but sprinkled with flour, is easily handled.*

    — *Tart can be frozen in doubled thicknesses of plastic wrap and then foil. Remove wrappers to defrost. Serve at room temperature.*

Pies & Tarts

Sour Cream Peach Tart with Cinnamon Graham Crust

Fresh peaches on a Cinnamon Graham Crust, painted with apricot jam and topped with sour cream . what a wonderful union of flavors and textures.

- 2 cups graham cracker crumbs
- 1/2 cup (1 stick) butter, melted
- 1/2 cup chopped walnuts
- 3 tablespoons cinnamon sugar

- 6 tablespoons apricot jam, heated
- 4 peaches, thinly sliced (remove stone but do not peel)

- 1 cup sour cream
- 1 egg
- 3 tablespoons sugar
- 1/2 teaspoon vanilla

Stir together crumbs, butter, walnuts and sugar until blended, and pat mixture evenly on the bottom and 1-inch up the sides of a greased 10-inch springform pan. Bake crust at 350° for 8 minutes.

Carefully (not to burn your fingers) spread apricot jam evenly over the crust. Place peach slices decoratively on top. Beat together sour cream, egg, sugar and vanilla until blended and pour mixture over the peaches. Return to oven and continue baking at 350° for about 35 minutes, or until top is lightly browned. Serve 8 to 10.

Note: — Apple tart can be prepared earlier in the day and stored in the refrigerator

— This tart is delicious served warm or at room temperature.

Fresh Peach & Almond Cream Pie

The tender and flaky crust is filled with a delicious almond layer and fresh juicy peaches. It is a lovely balance of flavors.

Filling:
- 1/2 cup butter, softened
- 1/2 cup sugar
- 2 eggs
- 1 cup finely grated almonds (almond meal)
- 1/2 teaspoon almond extract

- 1 1/2 pounds peaches, peeled, stoned and sliced
- 3 tablespoons apricot jam, heated

Beat together first 5 ingredients until blended, and pour into prepared crust. Lay peaches over the almond layer in a decorative circular fashion. Bake in a 350° oven for 45 to 50 minutes, or until top is browned. Remove from the oven and brush top with heated apricot jam. Allow to cool in pan. Serves 8.

Butter Cookie Crust:
- 1 1/2 cups flour
- 1/2 cup butter, cut into 8 pieces
- 1/4 cup sugar
- 1/4 cup water

In a food processor, blend together flour, butter and sugar until mixture resembles coarse meal, about 10 on/off turns. Slowly blend in the water until dough clumps together, about 5 on/off turns. Do not overmix. Pat dough on the bottom and 1-inch up the sides of a 10-inch springform pan and bake in a 350° oven for 20 to 25 minutes, or until dough appears dry and is beginning to take on color.

Note: — If peaches are out of season, frozen peaches can be substituted, but they must be defrosted and patted dry with paper towelling.

Fresh Pear Tart with Almond Cream & Almond Cookie Crust

This lovely tart, made with fresh pears and ground almonds has the character of fresh fruit with a marzipan cream. The crust is a butter almond shell, filled with fresh pears, delicately surrounded by an almond cream filling. It is not very sweet, but rather, strongly flavored with butter and almonds.

- 1 10-inch Almond Cookie Crust
- 2 fresh Bartlett pears, peeled, cored and very thinly sliced
- 2 eggs
- 1/3 cup cream
- 1/3 cup sour cream
- 1/3 cup sugar
- 1/3 cup almond meal (finely grated almonds that can be purchased in a health food store)
- 1/2 teaspoon almond extract

Place pears into prepared crust in a decorative fashion. Beat together the remaining ingredients until blended. Do not overbeat. Pour cream filling over the pears evenly. Place pan on a cookie sheet and bake in a 350° oven for 40 minutes or until custard is set and top is lightly browned. Allow to cool in pan.

When cool, remove metal ring and place on a lovely footed platter. Decorate top with the faintest sprinkle of very finely chopped almonds. Serves 8.

Almond Cookie Crust:
- 1 1/2 cups flour
- 1/4 cup sugar
- 1/4 cup almond meal
- 1/2 cup butter, cut into 8 pieces
- 1 egg
- 1 tablespoon water
- 1 teaspoon almond extract

In the large bowl of an electric mixer, beat together first 4 ingredients until mixture is like coarse meal. Beat together egg, water and almond extract, and beat it into the butter mixture until a dough forms. Do not overbeat. Pat mixture on the bottom and sides of a 10-inch fluted tart pan with a removeable bottom, and bake in a 350° oven for 20 minutes or until dough is set.

Praline Pecan Tart with Flaky Butter Cookie Crust

This is an adaptation of an incredible pecan tart I recently enjoyed in one of the restaurants in town. The pastry chef would not share the recipe, but, not to worry, this tastes exactly like the original. I think you will enjoy making it around the holiday time as it is a grand finale for the holiday feast. Basically, it is a low tart, with a flaky cookie crust, covered with a layer of pralined pecans. Delicious!

Flaky Butter Cookie Crust:
    1/2 cup (1 stick) butter
    1/3 cup sugar
      2 egg yolks
 1 1/4 cups flour

In the large bowl of an electric mixer, beat together butter and sugar until mixture resembles coarse meal. Beat in the egg yolks until combined. Beat in the flour until dough is just formed. Do not overbeat.

Collect dough into a ball, and with your fingers, pat it on the bottom and sides of a greased 10-inch tart pan with a removable bottom. Place pan on a cookie sheet, and bake in a 375° oven for about 15 minutes or until crust is cooked through and lightly browned. Set aside to cool.

Praline Pecan Filling:
    2 heaping cups coarsely broken pecans

    3/4 cup light brown sugar
    1/3 cup butter
    1/3 cup dark corn syrup
      3 tablespoons cream

Sprinkle pecans evenly on the bottom of prepared shell. Combine the remaining ingredients in a saucepan and bring mixture to a boil. Lower heat and keep mixture at a slow bubble for 2 minutes. Pour syrup evenly over pecans and bake tart (leave it on the cookie sheet to catch any drippings) in a 375° oven for about 12 to 15 minutes or until mixture is bubbling briskly. Remove from oven and allow to cool a little. Remove the fluted edge and continue cooling on a rack.

To serve, cut into small wedges and serve 12.

Note: — Tart can be prepared 1 day earlier and stored at room temperature, loosely covered with wax paper.

— Tart can be frozen.

Pies & Tarts

Chocolate Chip Pecan Pie
with Creme de Chocolat

This "easy as pie" dessert is one of the simplest and best-tasting. It needs a few hours in the refrigerator to allow flavors to blend, so it is a good choice to prepare earlier in the day or even 1 day earlier.

- 3 eggs
- 1/2 cup sugar

- 2 cups vanilla wafer crumbs
- 1/2 cup sugar
- 1 teaspoon baking powder
- 1 teaspoon vanilla

- 3/4 cup coarsely chopped pecans
- 3/4 cup semi-sweet chocolate chips

Beat eggs with sugar until nicely blended, about 2 minutes. Stir in the remaining ingredients until blended.

Pour batter into a lightly buttered 10-inch pie plate and bake at 350° for 30 minutes, or until top is lightly browned. Allow to cool in pan. When cool, frost with Creme de Chocolat and refrigerate for 6 hours or overnight. Serves 6.

Creme de Chocolat:
- 3/4 cup cream
- 1 tablespoon sugar
- 1 tablespoon Creme de Cacao liqueur (or other chocolate liqueur)
- 2 tablespoons chopped semi-sweet chocolate chips

Beat cream with sugar and liqueur until cream is stiff. Beat in chocolate chips.

Note: — Pie can be frozen with or without frosting. Wrap in double thicknesses of plastic wrap and then foil. Allow to thaw in the refrigerator if frozen with the frosting.

2-Minute Souffle au Grand Marnier with Raspberry Creme Fraiche

When you consider that this majestic souffle takes 2-minutes to assemble, and that it can also be assembled in advance, you will keep this little treasure handy. I don't have to remind you that as souffles require a good deal of preparation (separating eggs, making a white sauce, beating whites separately, folding at the last minute) they are not often considered for company. This little gem can be assembled earlier in the day and baked before serving.

    5 **eggs**
    1 **package (8 ounces) cream cheese, cut into 8 pieces**
  3/4 **cup cream**
  1/4 **cup Grand Marnier liqueur**
  1/2 **cup sugar**

In a food processor, place all the ingredients and blend for 2 minutes. Pour mixture into a 1-quart souffle dish that has been buttered and dusted lightly with sugar. (Can be held in the refrigerator at this point.)

Bake in a 375° oven for about 50 minutes to 1 hour or until top is crowned and golden. Serve immediately with a spoonful of Raspberry Creme Fraiche or lightly whipped cream. Serves 6.

Note: — *Remove from the refrigerator 10 minutes before baking.*

     — *Serve at once, or souffle will fall.*

Raspberry Creme Fraiche:
  1/3 **cup cream**
  1/3 **cup sour cream**
   1 **tablespoon Grand Marnier liqueur**
   2 **teaspoons sugar**
  1/4 **cup fresh or frozen raspberries**

Earlier in the day, stir together all the ingredients until blended. Store in the refrigerator until serving time. Yields about 3/4 cup sauce.

Chocolate Chip Danish Pastry Rolls

These are always such a hit when served. Everybody loves them. They are great to serve for a brunch or luncheon buffet.

Cream Cheese Pastry:
- 1/2 pound cream cheese
- 1 cup butter (2 sticks)
- 1 egg yolk
- 2 cups flour

In the large bowl of an electric mixer, beat together the butter and cream cheese until the mixture is blended. Beat in the egg yolk. Add the flour and beat until blended. Do not overbeat. Turn dough out on floured wax paper, form dough into a circle, wrap it in wax paper and refrigerate for several hours or overnight.

Divide dough into fourths. Roll out one part at a time to measure a 10-inch square. Spread 1/4 of the filling over the dough. Roll it up, jelly-roll fashion to measure a 10x3-inch roll. Place, seam-side down, on a 12x16-inch teflon-coated baking pan. Repeat with the remaining 3 parts of dough.

Bake in a 350° oven for 30 minutes or until the top is lightly browned. Cool in pan. Cut into slices and sprinkle tops generously with sifted powdered sugar. Yields 24 to 28 slices.

Chocolate Filling:
- 16 tablespoons Nestle's Chocolate Quik
- 8 ounces semi-sweet chocolate chips
- 1 cup chopped walnuts

Use 1/4 of the above amounts on each of the strudels.

Note: — These can be prepared 1 day earlier and wrapped securely with plastic wrap.

— These can be frozen after they are baked. Sprinkle with sifted powdered sugar before serving.

Potpourri

Potpourri

Tart Cranberry Relish with Apple & Orange 331
Cranberry Relish with Apricots 331
Cranberry Relish with Raisins 331
Cranberry Relish with Currants 331
Cranberry Relish with Walnuts 331
Cranberry Relish with Cinnamon 331
Cranberry Marmalade Relish 331
Cranberry Pineapple Relish 331
Orange Cranberry Sauce with Raisins 332
Cranberry Sauce with Pears & Almonds 332
Spiced Pumpkin Pudding with Raisins & Walnuts 333
Spiced Carrot Pudding with Raisins & Walnuts 334
Hot Spiced Cider with Cinnamon & Cloves 334
Mimosa Champagne Orange Punch 335
Greek Coffee Demi-Tasse 335
Hot Spiced Apple Cider with Orange & Lemon 336
Hot Spiced Peach or Apricot Nectar 336
Hot Spiced Wine 336
Cappuccino Supremo 337
Mulled Spiced Wine with Orange, Apricots & Raisins 338
Hot Spiced Apple Tea with Lemon & Cinnamon 338

Tart Cranberry Relish with Apple & Orange

1 pound fresh cranberries, washed and picked over
1 medium orange, grated. Use fruit, juice and peel.
1 large apple, peeled, cored and grated
1 cup orange juice
1 cup sugar
2 thin slices of lemon (about 1/4-inch thick, each)

In a saucepan, combine all the ingredients and simmer mixture for about 20 minutes, or until apple is tender and cranberries are almost all popped. Allow to cool and then store in the refrigerator. Remove lemon slices when serving. Yields about 3 cups relish.

Note: — *To the above recipe, you can sparkle the relish with the following variations:*

Cranberry Relish with Apricots — Substitute apple with 1 cup chopped, dried apricots.

Cranberry Relish with Raisins — To the basic recipe, add 1/2 cup yellow raisins.

Cranberry Relish with Currants — To the basic recipe, add 1/2 cup dried black currants.

Cranberry Relish with Walnuts — To the basic recipe, add 3/4 cup coarsely chopped, toasted walnuts. This can be added to any of the variations, as well.

Cranberry Relish with Cinnamon — To the basic recipe add 1/4 teaspoon cinnamon and delete the lemon slices.

Cranberry Marmalade Relish — To the basic recipe, add 1/2 cup orange marmalade and delete 1 medium grated orange.

Cranberry Pineapple Relish — To the basic recipe, add 3/4 cup crushed pineapple, drained and delete 1 grated apple.

Orange Cranberry Sauce with Raisins & Walnuts

Here's another cranberry recipe to add to the many I have given you in the past. This is an exceedingly thick relish. Don't reserve using this only at holiday time. Store a few bags of cranberries in your freezer, and enjoy this any time of year.

- 1 bag (1 pound) fresh or frozen cranberries
- 1 cup sugar
- 1/2 cup currant jelly
- 1 cup orange juice
- 2 tablespoons grated orange peel
- 1 slice lemon (about 1/8-inch thick)

- 1/2 cup coarsely chopped walnuts, toasted

In a saucepan, simmer together first 6 ingredients for about 20 minutes or until cranberries are tender and popped. Stir in the chopped walnuts and discard lemon slice. Refrigerate until ready to serve. Serve with chicken or turkey. Serves 6.

Cranberry Sauce with Pears & Almonds

- 1 bag (1 pound) fresh or frozen cranberries
- 1 cup sugar
- 1 cup orange juice
- 3 medium Bartlett pears, peeled, cored and chopped
- 2 tablespoons grated orange peel
- 1 slice lemon

- 1/2 cup coarsely chopped toasted almonds

In a saucepan, simmer together first 6 ingredients for about 20 minutes or until cranberries are tender and popped. Stir in the chopped almonds. Discard the lemon slice. Place in a lovely crystal bowl and refrigerate until serving time. Serve with chicken or turkey. Serves 6 to 8.

Note: — These relishes can be prepared 1 or 2 days earlier. Store in the refrigerator until serving time.

Spiced Pumpkin Pudding with Raisins and Walnuts

1/3 cup butter, at room temperature
1/2 cup brown sugar
1/4 cup sugar
 2 eggs
 1 cup pumpkin puree
 2 teaspoons pumpkin pie spice

 1 cup flour
 1 teaspoon baking powder
   pinch of salt

1/2 cup yellow raisins
1/2 cup chopped walnuts
1/2 teaspoon vanilla

In the large bowl of an electric mixer, beat together first 6 ingredients until blended. Beat in the flour, baking powder and salt until blended. Stir in the raisins, walnuts and vanilla. Pour mixture into a 10-inch pie pan and bake in a 350° oven for 30 to 35 minutes, or until a cake tester, inserted in center, comes out clean. Serve warm with hot cider. Serves 8.

Spiced Carrot Pudding with Raisins & Walnuts

3 egg yolks
1/4 cup cream
1/4 cup sour cream
1 cup vanilla wafer crumbs
3/4 cup brown sugar
1 cup cooked, mashed carrots
2 teaspoons pumpkin pie spice

1/2 cup yellow raisins
1/2 cup chopped walnuts

3 egg whites
2 tablespoons brown sugar

In the large bowl of an electric mixer, beat together first 7 ingredients until blended. Stir in the raisins and walnuts. In a clean bowl, beat egg whites until foamy. Add the brown sugar, 1 tablespoon at a time, while you continue beating until whites are stiff. Fold whites into carrot mixture.

Pour mixture into a 10-inch greased pie pan and bake in a 350° oven for 35 to 40 minutes, or until a cake tester, inserted in center, comes out clean. Serve warm. Serves 8.

Hot Spiced Cider with Cinnamon & Cloves

4 cups apple cider
1 teaspoon whole cloves
1 stick cinnamon
4 teaspoons sugar, or to taste
1/2-inch slice orange
1/4-inch slice lemon

Combine all the ingredients in an enamel pan and simmer mixture for 10 minutes. Do not boil. Strain to serve. Serves 4 to 6.

Mimosa Champagne Orange Punch

2 quarts orange juice
1/4 cup lemon juice
1/4 cup sugar, or to taste
    orange slices, lemon slices, strawberries
2 bottles (25 ounces each), chilled Champagne

In a large bowl, combine orange juice, lemon juice, sugar and fruit and refrigerate. (If your punch bowl fits in the refrigerator, it should be used.) Just before serving, add the chilled champagne and Fruited Ice Mold and Fruited Orange Cubes. Serve in lovely stemmed glasses with a strawberry and orange slice for garnish. Yields about 1 gallon punch and about 24 5-ounce servings.

To make Fruited Ice Mold: Fill a ring mold with strawberries, lemon slices, orange slices and camellia leaves. Fill with water, cover with foil (to hold fruit down) and freeze until firm. To unmold, dip into water for a few seconds and it will easily slip out. If fruit tends to pop up, press back into mold when partially frozen.

To make Fruited Orange Cubes: Place 1 strawberry or maraschino cherry in each compartment of an ice cube tray, fill with orange juice and freeze. These cubes will not dilute the punch.

Note: — Ice molds can be prepared 1 week earlier.

Greek Coffee Demi-Tasse

2 cups water
6 cubes sugar
6 teaspoons pulverized ground coffee

In a saucepan or brass Greek coffee brewer, stir together all the ingredients and bring mixture to a boil. Stir briskly and remove from heat. Wait for a few seconds to allow coffee grounds to settle and pour coffee into demi-tasse cups. Yields 6 cups.

Hot Spiced Apple Cider with Orange & Lemon

It is so much fun to serve spicy hot cider, as an alternative to coffee, during the holidays. A spicy cake or bread is a good accompaniment. Tie the spices and peels in a cheesecloth for easy removal . . . or else, cider must be strained.

Spice Base:
- 4 sticks cinnamon, broken into 1-inch pieces
- 2 teaspoons whole cloves
- 1 whole nutmeg or 1/2 teaspoon ground nutmeg
  peel from 1/2 orange, cut into 1/2-inch pieces
  peel from 1/2 lemon, cut into 1/2-inch pieces

Spiced Apple Cider:
- 2 quarts apple cider
- 1 cup orange juice
- 1/4 cup lemon juice
- 1/4 cup sugar (or to taste)

In a large enamel pot (do not use a metal pot) heat together spices and juices. Keep mixture hot, just below the boiling point for 15 minutes. Do not allow to bubble and boil. Remove spice bag or strain to serve. Serve with a dollup of whipped cream and a sprinkle of cinnamon. Yields 12 (6 ounce) servings.

Variations:
Hot Spiced Peach or Apricot Nectar:
- 2 quarts peach or apricot nectar
- 1 recipe Spice Base

In a large enamel pot, heat together spices and nectar for about 15 minutes. Do not allow to bubble or boil. Serve with a dollup of whipped cream and a sprinkling of nutmeg.

Hot Spiced Wine:
- 2 quarts Burgundy wine
- 1 quart apple juice or cider
- 1 cup orange juice
- 1 medium orange, sliced
- 1/4 cup sugar (or to taste)
- 1 recipe Spice Base

In a large enamel pot, heat together all the ingredients and mull mixture for 5 minutes. Do not allow to bubble and boil. Serve with a thin slice of fresh orange. Do not use the orange that is in the wine. Yields about 16 (6 ounce) servings.

Cappuccino Supremo

Traditionally, Cappuccino is made with equal amounts of expresso coffee and hot milk. Served with a dollup of whipped cream and a sprinkling of cinnamon or nutmeg, it is truly delicious. The addition of liqueurs and cream adds a good deal of excitement and "spirit" to the occasion.

Cappuccino Mix:
- 4 tablespoons instant expresso coffee
- 2 tablespoons cocoa
- 2 tablespoons sugar

Liqueurs:
- 5 ounces coffee liqueur
- 5 ounces Creme de Cacao liqueur
- 2 ounces Cognac or brandy

Milk Mixture:
- 4 1/2 cups boiling water
- 1 1/2 cups milk
- 1 1/2 cups cream

Combine Cappuccino Mix in a jar with a tight-fitting lid and shake to blend. In another jar, combine the liqueurs and brandy.

When you are ready to serve, boil together water, milk and cream.

To serve, place 1 teaspoon coffee mixture into each cup. Stir in about 5 ounces boiling Milk Mixture. Stir in 1 ounce of Liqueur Mixture. Top with a dollup of whipped cream and a sprinkle of cinnamon or nutmeg or shaved chocolate. Yields 12 servings.

Note: — *Cappuccino Mix can be stored for weeks in the refrigerator and is nice to keep on hand. Use as you would instant coffee.*

— *Liqueurs can be stored indefinitely and are also nice to keep on hand.*

— *If you are feeling adventuresome, try different combinations of your favorite liqueurs; Galliano (herb liqueur) or Amaretto (almond liqueur) or Frangelico (hazelnut liqueur) are especially good.*

Beverages

Mulled Spiced Wine with Orange, Apricots & Raisins

1 bottle red wine (Cabernet or Burgundy)
1 bottle port wine
1 cup Brandy or Cognac

1 orange, cut into thin slices
1/2 cup yellow raisins
10 dried apricots, chopped
1/2 cup water
sugar to taste (I use 3 tablespoons)
2 teaspoons whole cloves
2 sticks cinnamon

Combine all the ingredients in an enamel pan and simmer mixture (do not allow to boil) for 10 minutes. Ladle into glasses, with a few apricots and raisins in each. Yields 10 5-ounce servings.

Hot Spiced Apple Tea with Lemon & Cinnamon

2 cups boiling water
2 cups apple juice
1 teaspoon whole cloves
1 stick cinnamon
4 teaspoons sugar, or to taste

2 tea bags
1/4 cup lemon juice
2 slices lemon, (1/4-inch thick, each)

Combine first 5 ingredients in an enamel pan, and simmer mixture for 5 minutes. Add the remaining ingredients and steep tea for 2 or 3 minutes, covered. Ladle into glasses to serve hot, or allow to cool and serve over ice. Serves 4 to 6.

The Index

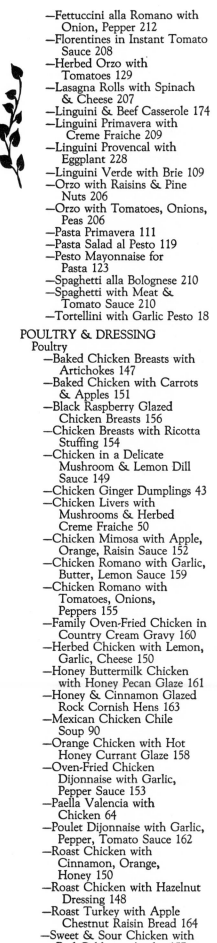

Asparagus- 216 - great
White
Choc. Cheesecake great